D0401904

UNDERSTANDING DREAMS

Mary Ann Mattoon

SPRING PUBLICATIONS, INC.
DALLAS, TEXAS

© 1978 by Mary Ann Mattoon. "Preface to Softcover Edition" © 1984 by Mary Ann Mattoon. All rights reserved
Third Printing 1988

Revised edition first published 1984 by Spring Publications, Inc.; P.O. Box 222069; Dallas, Texas 75222. Printed in the United States of America

Cover design and production by Patricia Mora and Maribeth Lipscomb. Color selection by Catherine Meehan Doehner.

Published originally in 1978 as *Applied Dream Analysis: A Jungian Approach*, LC catalog card number 78-8959, ISBN 0-470-26418-7.

International Distributors:
Spring; Postfach; 8803 Ruschlikon; Switzerland.
Japan Spring Sha, Inc.; 12-10, 2-Chome, Nigawa Takamaru;
  Takarazuka 665, Japan.
Element Books Ltd; Longmead Shaftesbury;
  Dorset SP7 8PL; England.
Astam Books Pty. Ltd.; 27B Llewellyn St.; Balmain, Sydney,
  N.S.W. 2041; Australia.

Library of Congress Cataloging in Publication Data

Mattoon, Mary Ann.
    Understanding dreams.

    Rev. ed. of: Applied dream analysis. 1978.
    Bibliography: p.
    Includes index.
    1. Dreams. 2. Jung, Carl Gustav, 1875-1961.
I. Mattoon, Mary Ann. Applied dream analysis.
II. Title.
BF1078.M36 1984   154.6'34   84-5523
ISBN 0-88214-326-3

DEDICATED TO

LILIANE FREY-ROHN

ACKNOWLEDGMENTS

Grateful acknowledgment is made to:

Auke Tellegen, for encouragement and help in researching and writing the dissertation on which this book is based.

Joseph B. Wheelwright and Jean Charnley, for careful reading of the manuscript and many valuable suggestions for improving it.

Many other colleagues and friends who read the manuscript and shared their thoughts and responses.

My analysands, especially those whose dreams appear in the book, with the dreamers' willing, even enthusiastic permission.

Sylvia W. Rosen, for skillful editing of the manuscript.

Lynda Cowan, for typing and retyping many drafts of the manuscript.

Diane Elms, Richard Solly, Ruth Hurwicz, Jean Fess, and Harriet Crosby, for checking references and helping with final preparation of the manuscript.

The C. G. Jung Institute in Zurich, Switzerland, for advice and support.

The C. G. Jung Heirs, and by arrangement with Princeton University Press, for permission to quote from students' notes from seminars of C. G. Jung: *Dream Analysis*, Vol. 1; *Modern Psychology*, Vols. I–II; *Psychological Interpretation of Children's Dreams*, 1938–39; *Psychological Analysis of Nietzsche's Zarathustra*, Vol. 8.

Pantheon Books, for permission to quote from *Memories, Dreams, Reflections* by C. G. Jung, recorded and edited by Aniela Jaffé, translated by Richard and Clara Winston © 1962 by Random House, Inc. © 1963 by Random House, Inc., reprinted by permission of Pantheon Books, a division of Random House, Inc.

William Collins Sons and Company, Ltd., for permission to quote from *Memories, Dreams, Reflections*.

Excerpts from the following are reprinted by permission of Princeton University Press and Routledge & Kegan Paul, Ltd.:

The Collected Works of C. G. Jung, Bollingen Series XX

Vol. 4: *Freud and Psychoanalysis,* trans. R. F. C. Hull, copyright © 1961 by Princeton University Press.

Vol. 5: *Symbols of Transformation,* trans. R. F. C. Hull, copyright © 1956 by Princeton University Press.

Vol. 6: *Psychological Types,* trans. R. F. C. Hull and H. G. Baynes, copyright © 1971 by Princeton University Press.

Vol. 7: *Two Essays on Analytical Psychology,* trans. R. F. C. Hull, copyright 1953, © 1966 by Princeton University Press.

Vol. 8: *The Structure and Dynamics of the Psyche,* trans. R. F. C. Hull, copyright © 1960, 1969 by Princeton University Press.

Vol. 9,I: *The Archetypes and the Collective Unconscious,* trans. R. F. C. Hull, copyright © 1959, 1969 by Princeton University Press.

Vol. 9,II: *Aion: Researches into the Phenomenology of the Self,* trans. R. F. C. Hull, copyright © 1959 by Princeton University Press.

Vol. 10: *Civilization in Transition,* trans. R. F. C. Hull, copyright © 1964, 1970 by Princeton University Press.

Vol. 11: *Psychology and Religion: West and East,* trans. R. F. C. Hull, copyright © 1958, 1969 by Princeton University Press.

Vol. 12: *Psychology and Alchemy,* trans. R. F. C. Hull, copyright 1953, © 1968 by Princeton University Press.

Vol. 13: *Alchemical Studies,* trans. R. F. C. Hull, copyright © 1967 by Princeton University Press.

Vol. 14: *Mysterium Coniunctionis,* trans. R. F. C. Hull, copyright © 1965, 1970 by Princeton University Press.

Vol. 16: *The Practice of Psychotherapy,* trans. R. F. C. Hull, copyright 1954, © 1966 by Princeton University Press.

Vol. 17: *The Development of Personality,* trans. R. F. C. Hull, copyright 1954 by Princeton University Press.

Vol. 18: *The Symbolic Life,* trans. R. F. C. Hull, copyright 1950, 1953, copyright © 1955, 1958, 1959, 1963, 1968, 1969, 1970, 1973, 1976 by Princeton University Press.

C. G. Jung, *Letters,* ed. Gerhard Adler and Aniela Jaffé, trans. R. F. C. Hull, Bollingen Series XCV. Vol. 1: *1906-1950,* copyright © 1971, 1973 by Princeton University Press. Vol. 2: *1951-1961,* copyright © 1953, 1955, 1961, 1963, 1968, 1971, 1972, 1974, 1975 by Princeton University Press.

CONTENTS

FOREWORD

This is a book that is long overdue.

Jung considered dreams of central importance in the analytic process, and had a great deal to say about them. But he never pulled his thoughts together; they are scattered through the 20 volumes of his work, published by Pantheon Press and Princeton University Press—the Bollingen Series. To say that this state of affairs has been awkward is putting it mildly. Not only have I become frantic when trying to read up on his ideas about dreams, but it has been literally impossible to give references to students and interested persons. It seems incredible that in all these years no one has gone through his letters, speeches, and writings and brought them together systematically in one book. This essential service has at long last been performed by Dr. Mattoon, and a sigh of relief from Jungian analysts will be heard around the world. Dr. Mattoon has collected from every nook and cranny virtually everything that Jung ever said about dreams. She has done this with consummate scholarliness, and yet managed to make her work lively and vivid. There are many Jung quotes, impeccably accurate; also quotes of quite a few others who have different ideas about dreams and their interpretations. The author also presents some of her ideas that differ from or modify Jung's, carefully distinguishing them as her own.

Many readers will have some familiarity with Jung's typology. He speaks of sensation types, meaning people with a sharp eye for facts, and intuitives [See p. 16 for other types.] who are more concerned with possibilities. Jung belonged to the latter group, and not surprisingly so do some 80% of his followers. Sensation types have not had an easy time in the Jungian world. However, were it not for her highly developed sensation function, Dr. Mattoon could never have accomplished this herculean task.

A relatively small number of Jungian analysts are extraverted, among them myself. For many of us, the reality-based interaction with our analysands tends to be more important than dream analysis, so it is amusing and flattering that Dr. Mattoon should have asked me to write this introduction. I can say that after two careful readings of her manuscript, I find myself in much better relation to my own dream world and that of my patients.

I consider this book indispensable for qualified and aspiring Jungian psychotherapists. However, Dr. Mattoon has so successfully eschewed jargon that her book could not fail to be clear to any psychotherapist or student in the field. In her restricted use of technical words, she provides easily understood definitions. Thanks to her labors, a collection of Jung's invaluable insights into dreams and their uses and meanings are at last available to the profession and other readers. This is an eagerly awaited and most important book.

Joseph B. Wheelwright
San Francisco

PREFACE
TO SOFTCOVER EDITION

Since the initial publication of this book in hardcover (1978), other works on dreams and their interpretation have continued to appear. None, however, has approached the accomplishment of this book—to systematize Jung's theory of dream interpretation, give examples of each major point, suggest desirable supplementation and modifications (each illustrated), and present reports of or suggestions for relevant empirical research. Thus, this volume's contribution to the literature remains unique.

Jung's approach to dream interpretation, moreover, is still the most comprehensive and generally applicable. Because it imposes no theory of personality on the dreamer, and no preconceived interpretation on the dream, this approach provides a framework of dream interpretation that can be applied to any dream of any dreamer.

The books on dreams that have been published since 1978 include several by students of Jungian psychology, but with different emphases and themes from this volume. For example, James Hillman in *The Dream and the Underworld* (Harper & Row, 1979) used his thorough and profound knowledge of Jungian psychology in questioning some of Jung's major hypotheses. Hillman advocates a departure from dream interpretation in favor of an "attempt to re-vision the dream in the light of myth." James Hall's book, *Jungian Dream Interpretation: A Handbook of Theory and Practice* (Inner City Books, 1983), in effect complements mine. After a brief overview of Jung's approach to dreams, Hall focuses on its applications in terms of specific Jungian topics such as synchronicity and alchemical motifs. Both books can be read profitably in conjunction with the present book.

An additional resource is the Bollingen edition (Vol. XCIX : I) of the first volume of Jung's seminars on Dream Analysis (cited in this volume as DA1); the ideas set forth in those seminars are included here. (An earlier Bollingen volume by Jung, *Dreams*, is a compilation of essays from the *Collected Works*; these essays were resources for my exposition of Jung's dream theory.)

The major alternative to the Jungian approach to dreams continues to be the psychoanalytic (Freudian) model, although psychoanalytic theorists increasingly embrace ideas that were propounded by Jung decades ago. Indeed, recent commentaries on Freud's own work by his students document additional Jungian ideas that Freud rejected explicitly but came to accept implicitly. An example is the importance of personal associations. In 1913 Freud wrote that psychoanalysts were "able to some extent to translate the content of dreams independently of the dreamer's associations." By 1925, however, he had come to the conclusion that "dream interpretation . . . without reference to the dreamer's associations would . . . remain a piece of unscientific virtuosity of the most doubtful value." Thus Freud acknowledged the view already held by Jung that knowledge of the dreamer's individual context is essential to valid dream interpretation.

During the few years since I completed this book, burgeoning information on human brain function has expanded our understanding of the process of dreaming. There is considerable evidence now that dreams arise in the part of the brain that is used less by most people when they are awake. This part is the right hemisphere, which is the source of images—the stuff of dreams. (The left side is the source of words and concepts—the language of ego-consciousness—and functions more in the waking state.) These findings tend to support Jung's major hypothesis that dreams are composed of contents which compensate those that are readily available to the ego.

There are still skeptics (e.g., the British geneticist Francis Crick) who regard dreams as essentially meaningless. Most psychologists, however, accept dreams as important manifestations of unconscious contents. Even B. F. Skinner, a leader of the behaviorist school of psychology, recognized in his *Notebooks* that analysis of dreams "may illuminate aspects of one's behavior." He even observed that common themes can be found in many persons' dreams: "The archetypal patterns are borrowed dreams."

The present edition of this book is identical with the first except for the addition of this Preface, correction of typographical errors, revision of the index, and elimination of the generic pronoun "he."

March 1984   Mary Ann Mattoon

PREFACE
TO FIRST EDITION

For my doctoral dissertation at the University of Minnesota in the late 1960s, I elected initially to test a hypothesis derived from Jung's concept of the compensatory function of dreams, perhaps the most important concept in his theory of dream interpretation. When the careful empirical study I conducted produced insignificant results, I concluded that the theory was imprecise and insufficiently defined. Indeed, it was evident that before any further empirical study of Jung's method of dream interpretation could be undertaken, his rich body of writings on the theory of dream interpretation would have to be systematized and clarified. Thus, I undertook the task for my doctoral dissertation (Mattoon, 1970) and it was accepted by the faculty of the Department of Psychology, which has been renowned for its "dust-bowl empiricism." For the dissertation, I searched Jung's works and students' notes* from his seminars for all his theoretical statements on dreams and their interpretation, and I amassed 972 separate entries ranging from a few words to passages of several hundred words.

This book is a much revised version of that dissertation. It retains the accurate recording of the available ideas and examples of dreams from Jung's

*The notes were not edited by Jung or his heirs. Their accuracy is attested in each volume.

work and supplements them with (a) conclusions drawn from my clinical work and that of other Jungian analysts, (b) examples of dreams from my clinical practice, (c) reports of research testing Jung's hypotheses, and (d) suggestions for further explorations.

Like many psychotherapists, Jungian and non-Jungian, I spend a considerable amount of my time working with dreams. For over 20 years, I have recorded all my own remembered dreams and attempted to understand them, with or without the assistance of another interpreter. Yet, until I undertook the dissertation, there was no single source for the procedures leading to interpretation of dreams according to Jung's method. This book, I hope, will provide such a source for psychotherapists now in training or in practice.

Each reader will find some chapters of greater interest than others, depending upon background in Jungian and other psychologies and in dream interpretation. The systematic presentation gives the novice enough of a background to follow the step-by-step study of dream interpretation and, at the same time, permits the experienced interpreter to study the specific steps that most interest him or her.

The book answers a number of questions:

Chapter 1: Why is dream interpretation important?
            What are the major theories of dream interpretation?
            Why is Jung's theory of dream interpretation the most advantageous to use?
Chapter 2: What is the theory of archetypes, and how does it affect dream interpretation?
            How does Jung's theory of personality depend on dreams and their interpretation?
Chapter 3: What are the sources of dream images?
            How do we know that dreams are meaningful?
Chapter 4: How is a Jungian analyst trained to interpret dreams?
            What are the procedures for interpreting dreams?
Chapters 5-14: How does one apply the procedures to dreams in practice?
Chapter 15: How does one hypothesize an interpretation?
Chapter 16: How does one verify the hypothesis of an interpretation?
Chapter 17: How is a complete dream interpretation accomplished?
Chapter 18: What is valuable and what is questionable in Jung's theory?

Throughout the book, each dream text, whether a direct quotation or a summary, is italicized. Dreams for which additional material is available in the Appendix are designated, D1, D2, ... D19. Notes appear at the end of each chapter.

Italicized terms in Chapter 4, in what is essentially an outline of dream interpretation, are defined in subsequent chapters. Indeed, every term that has a technical significance in the interpretation of dreams is defined clearly in the most suitable context.

A number of abbreviations are used throughout the book to indicate the written sources of quotations and dreams. These abbreviations and the works for which they stand are ordered at the beginning of the list of references.

The test of any theory is whether it can be applied by other practitioners in different times and places and with a large number of different persons. Jung's theory has met this test successfully. It has surmounted translation into many languages, withstood application to dreams of many cultures, and survived two world wars and six decades of changes in a rapidly changing world. The theory is timeless, in that it relates dreamers to their origins, and time oriented in that it relates the interpretation of dreams to the here and now.

Minneapolis, Minnesota   **Mary Ann Mattoon**
December 1977

UNDERSTANDING DREAMS

Chapter 1

INTRODUCTION

> A dream that is not understood remains a mere occurrence; understood, it becomes a living experience.
>
> C.G. Jung

Jungian analysts, more than any other group of psychotherapists, probably, are occupied with dreams, our own and those of our analysands. For interpreting dreams we make use of the comprehensive, flexible theory developed by C. G. Jung. Yet, until now, many years after Jung's death, no one source has provided a thorough, systematic conception of the Jungian approach to interpreting dreams.

This book is designed to fill that gap for psychotherapists and, also, for the increasing number of people who are interested in their dreams. Among these interested people are many who seek an intellectually satisfactory method of interpreting dreams and, therefore, need to know about Jung's theory. Jung wrote that he had no "theory" of dreams (Let-2, p. 293), but he seemed to mean that he had no preconceived idea of what the interpretation of a dream should be, as opposed to Freud who interpreted all dreams as wish fulfillment. For Jung's ideas on dream interpretation do constitute a theory, in the sense of an organized body of concepts, based on clinical experience, by which dreams can be interpreted.

1

Jung developed his theory of dream interpretation over a lifetime. He was constantly testing, modifying, elaborating, and illustrating it, so that relevant statements are found in nearly all the volumes of his *Collected Works*,[1] other publications,[2] and privately printed materials.[3] He never felt compelled to organize formally his body of concepts because he never considered his formulations final.[4] Nevertheless, the sum total of his work on dreams comprises a highly developed and clinically well-tested theory. To make the theory accessible to Jungian and non-Jungian psychotherapists and other persons, both for application to the analysis of specific dreams and for comparison with other theories of dream interpretation, this book presents a documented systematization of all of Jung's published and unpublished works on his theory of dream interpretation.

Dreaming and Dreams

All of us dream, several times a night and for increasing periods. It may be that we sleep in order to dream. The psychophysiological data accumulated since 1952 demonstrate that if we are deprived of rapid eye movement (REM) sleep, which is associated with dreaming more than is non-REM sleep, our REM sleep increases on subsequent nights (e.g., Witkin & Lewis, 1967). Further, if we are prevented from completing our dreams during sleep, we engage in dream-like thinking during our waking states (Fiss, Klein, & Bokert, 1966).

But dreaming must be distinguished from dreams (Jones, 1970), the act from the content, the process from the product. The act is physiological, the content—images, anecdotes, activities, emotions, and thoughts—psychological. The focus of this book is on dreams, the product of dreaming. Jung did not discuss the distinction. He assumed that his readers were familiar with Freud's distinction between dreams, that is, their interpretation (Freud, SE4, Chs. 1-6), and dreaming (Freud, SE5, Ch. 7).

The dictionary definition of "dream" is, "A series of images, ideas, and emotions occurring in certain stages of sleep" (*American Heritage Dictionary of the English Language*, 1969). This definition holds good for Jung's theory if the images, ideas, and emotions are assumed to be unconsciously determined. In dream interpretation, the dream images are accepted as facts presented by the dreamer's unconscious psyche; the interpreter seeks the meaning of the facts to make a psychological statement that is relevant to the dreamer.

Although the support for the importance of dreams and their interpretation is as yet mainly clinical, the empirical evidence is mounting in quantity and acceptability. Calvin Hall, a leader in the experimental research on dream content who is not identified with the Jungian school, stated, "We study dreams in order to enlarge our understanding of man" (1951, p. 63). A person's dreams yield information on the dreamer's self-concept, information that is often not available from other sources, and information on the relation between self-concept and behavior.

Why Interpret Dreams?

Dreams sometimes have a salutary effect, according to Jung, even when they are not interpreted. The benefit of uninterpreted dreams, however, is usually weak and transitory; if the message contained in a dream is not taken into consciousness it "fades back to chaos . . . but then it starts once more" (VS1, p. 180),[5] that is, it recurs in subsequent dreams until the dreamer "listens" to it.

In exceptional cases, life or death may hinge on attention to a dream. Jung cited repeatedly the example of an acquaintance, a mountain-climbing enthusiast, who made fun of dream interpretation and whose death was hastened because he did not take seriously his dream *of feeling ecstasy as he climbed higher and higher on a mountain until he stepped into empty air* (D1).[6] Although Jung had implored the dreamer always to take two guides on his expeditions and to follow their lead implicitly, the advice had been met with laughter. Later, the mountain climber acted out the dream and both he and a companion fell to their deaths.

The life-and-death importance of attention to dreams is not original with Jung; in *Julius Caesar*, Shakespeare attributed to Caesar's wife, Calpurnia, a dream warning of Caesar's assassination:

> *Caesar:* Nor heaven nor earth have been at peace tonight, Thrice hath Calpurnia in her sleep cried out, 'Help, ho! They murder Caesar!' . . . . (Act II, Scene II)

Although the popular conception of dream interpretation tends to focus on the dramatic impact of dreams that predict death, misfortune, or unexpected success, in fact such dreams are rare in life if not in literature. In psychotherapy, a somewhat more common type of dream carrying life-or-death significance is one that reveals a patient's suicidal thoughts which have been concealed from the therapist. Such a revelation may help to guide the conduct of the therapy.

Dreams, such as those revealing suicidal thoughts, and others carrying less dramatic information, which may be consciously withheld by the patient, demonstrate that dreams are sources of specific information for the therapist. Dreams provide access to the various levels of the psyche (see Ch. 2 for Jung's concept of the structure of the psyche) and to the nature and causes of individual problems.

Accordingly, dreams were central to the psychotherapeutic process, for Jung, so much so that he characterized the analysis of dreams as a therapist's "professional duty" (CW16, par. 295). He valued dream analysis as a diagnostic tool, especially to discover the aetiology of a patient's neurosis. Dream interpretation also facilitates healing by supplementing the dreamer's conscious experiences, thus releasing repressed energies and opening the conscious mind to unconscious mental contents. Jung hypothesized that psychological problems are due to a psychic split that separates the unconscious from the conscious mind. For psychotherapy to be effective, therefore, the treatment must heal that split; the patient needs to know what is occurring in the unconscious, and to assimilate unconscious contents. "The dreams fetch up the essential points, bit by bit and with the nicest choice" (CW7, par. 218).

A person suffering from a neurosis or a severe complex[7] lives too much in one side of the personality. Jung advised such a person to seek to recognize this one-sidedness and the unworkable attitudes that result from it. Learning to understand one's dreams permits the person to enrich the conscious mind. Although the material added to consciousness may be unpleasant, it leads, usually, to deeper self-knowledge and greater mental stability. By making an integral connection between the conscious and the unconscious, the individual may achieve a wider mental horizon, a new orientation toward life, and an ordering of a world that has been bewildering. Dormant qualities in the individual begin to awaken and the personality may develop more completely than would have been possible if the neurosis never had occurred. Dreams are essential to the developmental process as a major source of unconscious contents.

Although Jung deemed dream interpretation to be essential to psychotherapy, he considered it also to be a valuable education for persons who do not undergo psychotherapy. For such persons, the widening of consciousness resulting from the incorporation of unconscious contents through dream analysis enhances development of their personalities. Some evidence for this statement is found in the "phenomenal emotional maturity" (Noone & Holman, 1972, p. 23) of the Temiar, a tribe of the Senoi people of Malaya, known for their attention to dreams in everyday life.

Thus the understanding of dreams can help a person to understand human behavior, including one's own, and to live more productively. Frequently, one finds more of a sense of meaning in life by incorporating a dimension that has been ignored by many people, the "sphere of irrational experience" (CW16, par. 96).

Major Theories of Dream Interpretation

Most current theories of dream interpretation are historically rooted in or in general accord with one of three schools: Freudian, Jungian, or

Existentialist. Although anthropological, historical, and Biblical sources suggest that humankind always has been concerned with the significance of dreams, Freud was the first person to undertake the development of a scientific method for dream interpretation. Despite the mockery of many of his early colleagues, he courageously opened the way to a psychological understanding of dreams. His theory is better known than Jung's, probably because it appears easier to understand and because Jung's writings on dreams are dispersed among his many works with little systematization. Furthermore, Jung was a poetic writer and, consequently, obscured some of his ideas in the language he used.

To Freud, everything in the unconscious was once conscious and then repressed. To Jung, the unconscious contains several kinds of content: that which was once conscious and then repressed; subliminal perceptions; memories too unimportant to be remembered (Freud's pre-conscious); and contents arising independently from the collective unconscious, a stratum common to all human beings that provides the creative and healing forces which are so important to meaningful human life (see Ch. 2).

Freud and Jung differed also over which "content" of the dream should be interpreted, the "manifest" (the dream images as they appear to the dreamer) or the "latent" (the dream thoughts underlying the images). Freud insisted that the meaning of a dream lies in the latent dream thoughts, which can be discovered only by the process of free association to the images (see Ch. 5). Jung, on the other hand, adhered to the interpretation of the manifest content—the images themselves—because, he insisted, the dream is not a disguise. Consequently, the two men differed in their view of dream symbolism (see Ch. 9).

Freud called the interpretation of dreams "the royal road to a knowledge of the unconscious activities of the mind" (SE5, p. 608). Jung accepted the statement at first (CW7, par. 25), but then modified it to hypothesize that the complex is the royal road to the unconscious and "the architect of dreams and of symptoms" (CW8, par. 210). Thus Jung attempted to state briefly his view that the aim of dream interpretation is to discover both the complexes and what the unconscious says about the complexes.

Alfred Adler was, with Freud and Jung, one of the original "big three" figures of psychoanalysis,[8] but his contribution to dream theory was minor. Most important, probably, is his idea that "The purpose of dreams must be in the feelings they arouse [and leave] behind" (Adler, 1958, p. 98). Accordingly, the dream helps the dreamer to self-deception in order to maintain a customary life style.

Other depth psychologists have shared many concepts with both Freud and Jung. Examples are Erich Fromm (1951) with his "forgotten language" of dreams, and the "focal conflict" theory of Thomas French and Erika Fromm (1964).

Followers of the existential-phenomenological approach to psychotherapy are distinguished from both Freud and Jung in that they do not hypothesize unconscious mental contents. They seem closer to Jung than to Freud, however, inasmuch as their dream interpretations are based on the manifest content of dreams. The major dream theorist of this school of psychotherapy is Medard Boss (1957); others who are well known are Leopold Caligor and Rollo May (1968) and Fritz Perls (1969). Although Boss rejected the idea of subjective and objective interpretations (see Ch. 10), his dream analyses seem to me to fulfill Jung's specifications for subjective interpretations: Boss considered dream images to refer to various parts of the dreamer's psyche.

The Advantages of Jung's Theory

Admittedly, little empirical evidence is at hand to verify specific dream interpretations, and even less to support a theoretical system for interpreting dreams. Consequently, one cannot demonstrate unequivocally that any theory is preferable to other theories. Jung himself advocated exhaustive research to approach the truth and he contributed to the research in his clinical work by analyzing some 2,000 dreams[9] a year for many years. More systematic research is needed, however, including the testing of specific Jungian hypotheses.

The breadth of Jung's theory makes it an unusually rich source of dream interpretations. This breadth is created by Jung's view of the dream as nearly always compensating the dreamer's conscious situation and, thus, subject to as wide a range of interpretive possibilities as marks human experience. This view contrasts with the restrictions imposed by such theories as Freud's, in which dreams are wish fulfillment, and other theories that share with Freud's an attempt to find a formula by which to interpret all dreams: for example, French and Fromm's (1964) theory, in which dreams are said to arise out of "focal" and "subfocal" conflicts. Like Freud, Jung was interested in what dreams reveal of the aetiology, prognosis, and possible cure of a patient's neurosis. However, Jung saw dreams also as normal phenomena experienced by "normal" people. In this view, he anticipated the recent research findings on the universal and nightly occurrence of dreaming in sleep.

Although few non-Jungian theorists explicitly recognize Jung's contributions to dream interpretation, many implicitly accept his work by rejecting Freud's concept that the manifest dream is a disguise for the latent dream content and adopting an approach that is closer to Jung's idea that the dream says what it means. In addition, many psychotherapists have emulated Jung in finding it more useful to extract from a patient's dreams comments on the meaning of the complexes than merely to focus, like Freud, on what the complexes are. Moreover, when dreams are interpreted as constructive as well as causal, as in the Jungian theory, the dreamer can be helped to see possibilities for growth rather than just to examine the past, whence the problems came.

The breadth of Jung's approach is demonstrated further in that in his acceptance of the subjective analysis of dreams he did not reject the objective interpretation advocated by Freud—that dream images refer to actual persons and things (see Ch. 10). The probable validity of this combined approach tends to be confirmed by its increasing adoption by other theorists.

Perhaps the most distinctive element in Jung's dream theory is his hypothesis that some dream images derive from collective or archetypal contents rather than from the dreamer's personal experiences. Considerable debate still centers on Jung's original conception of the collective component of the unconscious; nevertheless, the concept is considered virtually self-evident to persons who make extensive use of it (see Chs. 2 & 6).

The Scope of This Work

Against the background presented thus far—brief discussions of the importance of dream interpretation and the major theories of interpretation—succeeding chapters present additional background material on Jung's life and psychological theories (without critical comment on these theories), a discussion of the nature of dreams, a description of how a prospective Jungian analyst is trained in dream interpretation, and an overview of Jungian dream analysis. Subsequent chapters present a step-by-step description and application of the principles of Jungian dream interpretation, a consideration of the relation of dreams to the psychotherapeutic process, and a discussion of methods of verifying dream interpretations. To illustrate how the principles are applied, there is included also a detailed dream interpretation. The final chapter presents an appraisal of Jung's theory of the interpretation of dreams.

Jung's work on dreams was in process throughout his life. Frequently, he introduced new ideas in answer to questions that arose in his seminars or in the development of a particular theme, such as his psychological theory relating to alchemy.[10] Although his essay, "Symbols and the Interpretation of Dreams" (CW18, pars. 416-607), written shortly before his death, consolidated many of his ideas, Jung never attempted a comprehensive review, probably because he was continually modifying his ideas and because he was always generating the next "big idea." In this book, I add to the usefulness of Jung's theories by making available here in systematic form all of his ideas relating to dream interpretation and by suggesting minor additions where the theory is not complete.

To illustrate the various aspects of his theory, I use many of Jung's dream examples, and some from my analysands and other persons. In illustrating each theoretical point, I include in the text only as much of a dream and its interpretation as is necessary to clarify that point. Supplementing each example from Jung's work for which additional information (text, context, interpretation, and comments by Jung) is available, the entire dream and all of the relevant information are presented in the Appendix. (Because Jung offered dreams as illustrations of theoretical points that are not necessarily related to dreams, he almost never presented a complete interpretation of a dream.) The portions given in the text are, in my judgment, true to the totality of the interpretation. This manner of presentation tends to make the theory clearer and more readily applicable than would fewer full interpretations presented, of necessity, less systematically.

In many instances in this book, I apply Jung's dream theories more completely than he did. Such elaboration is possible because I have access to the complete historical development of his work. He was a creative theorist who tried ideas successively but not always cumulatively. Those he rejected ultimately are omitted from this book; others were given decreasing emphasis by him but are included because they form parts of his total theory. The complete historical development of each point in Jung's dream theory can be found in Mattoon (1970). Here I discuss only those changes in his thought that relate to his apparent contradictions. Others of Jung's statements that seem erroneous are treated by modifying some of his generalizations to relative statements. For example, he sometimes used "never" or "always" when "seldom" or "generally" would designate the frequency of a phenomenon more accurately.

There are, however, points where my experiences, or other data, lead me to depart from Jung's view. Since Jung presented his ideas as hypotheses to be tested, not as dogma to be believed, I consider my challenges to enhance Jung's contribution to dream theory, not to cast doubt on it. To this end, each disputed point is discussed with relevant data, including examples of dreams and their interpretations.

In this book I avoid mentioning specific dream symbols, except in examples of interpretive hypotheses, because specific symbols do not contribute to the theory. Moreover, the interpretations of most symbols apply only to particular situations and should not be generalized. Jung warned, in fact, against the use of "dream books" or "dictionaries" of dream symbols.

Terms

Some of the terms which are used frequently in this book require explanation or definition. Strictly speaking, the term "the unconscious" should not be used because there is no such entity; nevertheless, Jung used the term repeatedly (and defined it as "the totality of all psychic phenomena that lack the quality of consciousness" [CW8, par. 270]). In this book, "the unconscious" is used to denote in brief what more accurately, but more ponderously, would be termed "unconscious contents" or "unconscious mental contents."

Jung's terms for the principals in the psychotherapeutic process varied. He used the term "patient" essentially interchangeably with "analysand," and "doctor" with "analyst" or "psychotherapist." (Jung was a physician and sometimes seemed to think of an analyst as also a medical doctor. He insisted, however, that analysts need not be medical doctors and, therefore, accepted for training persons with other professional backgrounds. This training practice continues in all Jungian training centers.)

I use the terms "analyst," "psychotherapist" or "therapist," and "analysand" or "patient" when the focus is on the analysis or psychotherapy. (All fully trained Jungian psychotherapists are analysts, and no clear distinction is made–among Jungians–between psychotherapy and analysis.) When the focus is on dream interpretation, whether or not in the context of psychotherapy, I follow Jung's lead in using the term "dreamer" but depart from his practice by using quite consistently "dream interpreter" or "interpreter" for the therapist. (Jung used the term "interpreter" only on rare occasions.) It is important to bear in mind, however, that *both* therapist and patient participate in the interpretation of a dream.

Like Jung, I use "dream analysis" more or less synonymously with "dream interpretation," despite the fact that even in a therapeutic setting not all dream analysis, that is, consideration of a dream, leads to an interpretation.[11] Frequently, the therapist and patient discuss dream images and their content without arriving at an actual interpretation. Other terms that need explanation are defined in the contexts in which they arise.

A few references to Freud's ideas on dreams and personality theory are included when they clarify Jung's comments, many of which were written in response to Freudian ideas. The various theories of dream interpretation are not compared otherwise; such a comparison is beyond the scope of this work.

Notes

[1] Jung's major essays specifically on dream interpretation are gathered in *Dreams* (1974). Additional chapters giving major emphasis to dreams and their interpretation are, "Morton Prince, 'Mechanism and Interpretation of Dreams': A Critical Review," in CW4; "The Personal and the Collective (or Transpersonal) Unconscious," "The Synthetic or Constructive Method," and "The Archetypes of the Collective Unconscious," in CW7;" "The Meaning of Psychology for Modern Man," in CW10; "The Autonomy of the Unconscious," in CW11; "The Significance of the Unconscious in Individual Education," in CW17;

"Sigmund Freud: 'On Dreams,' " pars. 129-262 of "The Tavistock Lectures"; and "Symbols and the Interpretation of Dreams," in CW18.

[2]MDR, Let–1 & 2, FJ.

[3]AP; CD36, 38, 40; DA1, 2; KY; MPI-II, III-IV, V-VI; SW; VS1 & 2; and Z1-10.

[4]Jung's interpreters have limited their presentations of his theory of dream interpretation to summaries, rather than complete explications, and to case material in which dream interpretations illustrate various Jungian theories. See, for example, Baynes (1950), Bennet (1962, 1967), Fordham (1953), Frey-Rohn (1974), Goldbrunner (1964), Hall & Nordby (1973), Hochheimer (1969), Jacobi (1942), Marjasch (1966b), Meier (1969), Nell (1968), and Singer (1972). Other interpreters, such as Kelsey (1968), Mahoney (1966), Meier (1972), Rossi (1972), and Sanford (1968), have dealt almost exclusively with dreams from a practical, historical, or philosophical point of view, but without a systematic presentation of Jung's complete theory of dream interpretation.

[5]Jung's seemingly contradictory statement, "Only when a dream is very impressive, or repeats itself often, do interpretation and conscious understanding become desirable" (CW18, par. 476), was made in the context of arguing that symbols need not be understood consciously in order to be effective. As we shall see, Jung considered the interpretation of dreams to be essential to the psychotherapeutic process.

[6]Each dream text, whether a direct quotation or summary, complete or incomplete, is italicized. Dreams for which additional material is available are designated D1, D2, etc. The additional material is in the Appendix.

[7]In Jung's usage, a neurosis is a combination of complexes (see Ch. 2) or symptoms: physical, behavioral, or affective. A complex (or emotionally toned complex) is a content of the unconscious which is incompatible with the habitual attitude of consciousness. The complex is surrounded by strong emotion and functions autonomously to produce disturbances of memory and to influence speech and action. It may appear in dreams in personified form. (This definition is derived from two sources: CW8, pars. 201-211, and MDR, pp. 381-382.)

[8]"Psychoanalysis" later came to mean the Freudian school of psychotherapy but in the early days it designated the entire movement, in which Jung and Adler participated.

[9]Jung wrote, "I investigate yearly some fifteen hundred to two thousand dreams" (CW8, par. 474); "I have analyzed about 2,000 dreams or more every year" (DA1, p. 18); and "At that time [1907] I analyzed at least four thousand dreams a year" (CW3, par. 557).

[10]Jung saw the work of the medieval alchemists as a projection of their own psychic individuation processes into the matter which they were trying to transform—from a lesser substance, the "prima materia" (e.g., lead, earth, water, or dung) into a more valuable substance (e.g., gold). There were a few alchemists who seemed to be conscious of the meaning of their work, in that their "laboratory work was primarily a matter of symbols and their psychic effect" (CW12, par. 40).

[11]Indeed, there is rarely time in a therapy session for a complete dream interpretation. For the complete interpretation in Chapter 17, for example, I spent five hours with the dreamer establishing the context and discussing the interpretive hypothesis.

Chapter 2

DREAMS IN THE DEVELOPMENT OF JUNG'S PSYCHOLOGICAL THEORIES

Jung's Life

Carl Gustav Jung[1] was born on July 26, 1875, in Kesswil (on Lake Constance), Switzerland, and died in Küsnacht, near Zurich, on June 6, 1961. His family, although limited in means, was deeply concerned with medicine and religion. Carl was named for his paternal grandfather, a German-born physician and professor of surgery at the University of Basel. Carl's father, Johann, was a pastor and an Oriental and classical scholar.

His father began to instruct Carl in Latin when he reached the age of six. He continued his study of the language as he grew older and learned to read old texts with ease. The skill facilitated his lifelong study of the classics, history, anthropology, and religion. His interest in these studies seems to have started with an illustrated children's book of exotic religions which his mother, Emilie (Preiswerk), read to him during his childhood. He never tired of studying the pictures of Hindu gods in the book.

In 1879, the family moved to the environs of Basel where, in 1884, the Jungs' daughter, Gertrud, was born. Carl entered school in Basel and

11

completed his formal education there. Upon receiving his medical degree in 1900, he was appointed an Assistant Physician (equivalent to a psychiatric resident in the United States) at the Burghölzli Hospital (a public psychiatric institution in Zurich), of which Eugen Bleuler was then director. Five years later, Jung was appointed Senior Physician at the hospital and Lecturer in Psychiatry at the University of Zurich. In 1903, he married Emma Rauschenbach; four daughters and a son were born to them. Until her death in 1955, Emma collaborated closely with her husband in his work. Like his hospital and university colleagues, Jung carried on a private practice. By 1909 it had become sufficiently remunerative to enable him to resign his hospital post; four years later he resigned from the University also. From then on, he spent considerable time writing and traveling.

Throughout his life, Jung was interested in dreams. In *Memories, Dreams, Reflections*, he recounted some of his dreams and fantasies from early childhood. Beginning then, according to these memoirs, he considered his inner life to be more "eventful" than his outer one. This interest in dreams increased with his psychological studies and practice.

As a young man, Jung had thought of making a career in archeology; lacking the funds to attend a university offering such a course of study, he relinquished the idea. He decided on a career in science partly because of two dreams he had had a few weeks before he entered the University of Basel (MDR),[2] and he chose medicine because it was the scientific field in which he could make an adequate living. The required studies in psychiatry did not interest him until his last year. Introduced then to Krafft-Ebing's *Lehrbuch der Psychiatrie* (*Textbook of Psychiatry*), he saw the specialty as a way of combining his philosophical interests with his commitment to the natural sciences.

Another lifelong interest was aroused during Jung's last year in medical school. Two experiences brought to the fore his fascination with the occult, the seeds of which probably had been planted during his childhood by superstitious peasants of the Lake Constance area. While he was studying at home one day, Jung heard a loud noise like a pistol shot coming from the dining room, which was next to his room. Running into the dining room, he found that a 70-year-old, solid walnut, round table had split from the rim to beyond the center. No explanation could be found for the occurrence. The second experience came two weeks later. He returned home one evening to find the household in great distress. His mother, sister, and the maid had heard a deafening crack in the dining room but they had not found anything broken. Jung searched the room. In a cupboard, he discovered the breadknife in pieces, each piece lying in a different corner of the breadbasket. The improbability of a natural explanation for the break and the distribution of pieces impressed him deeply, and he kept the pieces of the knife all his life as evidence of the event.

His concern with the occult was intensified a few weeks after the knife incident when Jung observed a 15-year-old girl of little education who, while in a trance, spoke stilted High German instead of her accustomed Swiss dialect. She also saw visions and was an excellent medium. His notes on the girl and the seances in which she participated formed an important part of his thesis for the degree of Doctor of Medicine. The paper was published in 1902 under the title, "Zur Psychologie und Pathologie sogenannter occulter Phänomene" (On the Psychology and Pathology of So-called Occult Phenomena; CW1).

At the Burghölzli Hospital, Jung sought to discover the causes of mental illness by examining brain tissue, and to cure such illnesses by hypnosis; both attempts failed. With some colleagues, he developed a Word Association Test and made a "major contribution in standardizing the methods of administration and interpretation" (Bell, 1948, p. 16).[3] He used several diagnostic indicators: the type of response (e.g., a synonym of the stimulus word), incorrect reproduction of the response word, reaction-time, and other test behavior.[4] A combination of two or more indicators was considered by Jung to support his diagnostic impression.[5]

Since 1950, interest in the word association method has undergone a revival, but for purposes different from Jung's in his early professional life. His interest was in clinical diagnosis and his theory of what he called initially "emotionally toned complexes" but later shortened to "complexes." Now, the focus is on the study of verbal behavior and cognitive processes.

Jung's test was the forerunner of later projective techniques. In Bell's (1948) opinion,

> no over-all picture of projective devices could be considered complete without this aged parent of so many other tests. . . . Whatever its place in the future, no one will challenge the position of the word-association test as the progenitor of the majority of our modern non-questionnaire-type of personality tests. (p. 15)

Jung's work on the Word Association Test and the theory of complexes contributed to his study of unconscious mental contents. Later, his observations of the content of patients' dreams, hallucinations, and delusions provided some of the data for his hypothesis of the existence of collective (archetypal) material in the unconscious psyche (discussed later in this chapter).

At Bleuler's suggestion, Jung read Freud's *Interpretation of Dreams* in 1900, the year of its publication. The book had little impact on him until three years later when he realized that it provided a helpful explanation of the mechanism of repression, which he had noted in his word association experiments. In 1906 Jung sent Freud a copy of *Diagnostische Assoziations-*

studien: Beiträge zur experimentellen Psychopathologie (Diagnostic Association Studies: Contributions to Experimental Psychopathology; see (CW2). Freud's letter of thanks (FJ, 1F), admitting that in his impatience he had acquired the book already, began a correspondence that continued for some seven years. The two men met for the first time on March 3, 1907, in Vienna, and they talked for 13 consecutive hours. During subsequent private meetings—including the journey, in 1909, to Clark University, Worcester, Massachusetts, where both men were awarded honorary degrees—and at Congresses of the International Psycho-Analytical Association, Jung became increasingly aware that his conceptions differed from Freud's. Yet, at Freud's urging, he assumed the permanent presidency of the Association in 1910. Jung resigned from the office in 1914, seven months after his differences with Freud came to a culmination over Jung's publication of *Wandlungen und Symbole der Libido* (*Transformations and Symbols of the Libido*, translated by Beatrice Hinkle as *The Psychology of the Unconscious*; revised and republished as CW5, *Symbols of Transformation*), which was discussed at the stormy meeting of the Association in Munich in 1913. In August 1914, Jung resigned as a member of the Association. After the 1913 meeting, Jung and Freud never met again.

Like several other major turning points in his life, Jung's break with Freud stemmed, in part at least, from a dream. On the trip to Clark University, the two men were together every day for seven weeks and analyzed each other's dreams. Freud's attempt to interpret one of Jung's dreams as wish fulfillment conflicted with Jung's view that the dream contained collective content.[6] By contributing both to the development of Jung's theory of the unconscious and to his controversy with Freud, the dream was instrumental in the subsequent break.

After the Munich meeting, Jung's work, including his theory of dream interpretation, rapidly lost its Freudian cast and began to reveal more fully his interest in archetypal symbolism. He was able to pursue freely his unique approach to the contents of the unconscious mind. It is doubtful that Jung ever had been a "disciple" of Freud.[7] He had been a fellow worker in depth psychology who, by independent investigation of unconscious phenomena, had come close to Freud's views for a time in the course of his own development.[8]

After the break with Freud, Jung went through a period of what he termed "inner uncertainty" or "disorientation" (MDR, p. 170). For about six years he spent a great deal of time working on his own dreams and fantasies, translating their images into the language of consciousness and incorporating them, as far as possible, into the daily routines of his life (see MDR, Ch. VI). Ellenberger (1970) called these years the period of Jung's "creative illness" (p. 672) because the investigation of his inner reality led Jung to develop many of his psychological theories. Between 1919 and 1944, when he was halted by a severe illness, Jung wrote most of his major works, many in the form of individual essays, which were collected later into volumes of the *Collected Works*. He also conducted a large psychotherapeutic practice, held seminars in German and in English, and made numerous long journeys, including several to the United States. A continuing interest throughout his active life was the building and occupying of his famous "tower" at Bollingen. He participated in founding the C. G. Jung Institute in Zurich, in 1948, and was its first president, serving until 1950, when he retired from active participation in the Institute (Hannah, 1976). After 1945 and until his death in 1961, Jung saw a decreasing number of patients and concentrated primarily on his work on the psychological meaning of alchemy, which culminated in the writing of *Mysterium Coniunctionis* (CW14).

Jung's capacity for stirring his analysands and pupils to their depths produced tales about him that make sound godlike. But those who knew him tend to agree that he was an intensely human person. In physical appearance he was tall, broad-shouldered, strong, and healthy looking, with a "cheerful open face" (Bennet, 1962, p. 5). He was a mountain climber and expert sailor, and always lived next to a river or a lake. He was a good listener and conversationalist who did not waste time in trivialities, and he had a keen sense of humor that was equalled, perhaps, by his quick temper. Jung valued his family, yet he had a great need for solitude; he spent weeks at a time away from his wife and children, often in his house at Bollingen, much of which he built himself. His power of concentration was prodigious, as can be inferred from his encyclopedic knowledge and the quantity of his writings. His openness to new ideas reflected the undogmatic attitude which is expressed in his oft-quoted statement, "I am not a Jungian." His fascination with his own inner life, so apparent in *Memories, Dreams, Reflections*, affected profoundly all aspects of his psychological theories; it was especially evident in the large amount of time and effort he spent studying archetypal materials.

Dreams and Jung's Theory of Personality[9]

All of Jung's theories are attempts to illuminate the workings of the human psyche. Most are closely related to his work on dreams. This work was based on his empirical method, which he defined as "the observation of phenomena" (CW11, par. 2), as opposed to "ideologism" (CW6, par. 518). His data often were the unconscious materials, such as dreams and hallucinations, of his patients. The frequently heard assertion that Jung was "mystical" ignores this empirical base and the distinction between nonrational methods, of which Jung has been accused unjustly, and nonrational data, in which he took great interest (see Dallett, 1973).

The most widely accepted and validated of Jung's theories, probably, is that of the attitude types, extraversion[10] and introversion. Jung designated these categories as types, but he treated them more as personality dimensions, especially with his recognition that everyone has some of each (CW6, pars. 563, 621) and that they can change over the course of a person's life. Although other psychologists (Cattell, 1957; Eysenck & Eysenck, 1969) have defined the categories somewhat differently,[11] the terms and their general conceptualization are Jung's. Jung defined extraversion as "an outward-turning of *libido*," by which he meant psychic energy; that is, "Everyone in the extraverted state thinks, feels and acts in relation to the object" (CW6, par. 710). Conversely, introversion is defined as "an inward-turning of *libido* . . . . Everyone whose attitude is introverted thinks, feels, and acts in a way that clearly demonstrates that the subject is the prime motivating factor and that the object is of secondary importance" (CW6, par. 769).

Jung developed the concept of attitude types from his experiences with patients, "with men and women of all social levels, . . . personal dealings with friend and foe alike, and . . . a critique of [his] own psychological peculiarity" (CW6, p. xi.). The concept was generated out of his perplexity over the controversy between Freud and Adler. Here were two intelligent men, both of Jewish background, both living in the same urban invironment (Vienna), both treating what were basically the same kinds of patients, yet one concluded that sexual conflict was the basis of neurosis and the other concluded that the will to power was the basis. Jung's intense interest in this controversy, elaborated in *Two Essays on Analytical Psychology* (CW7), was rooted in the pain of his own disagreement and break with Freud. He concluded in the first of the two essays that the two points of view arose out of Freud's and Adler's different perspectives of the world: extraversion (Freud)[12] and introversion (Adler). Because of the difference in perspectives, neither man could understand the other's point of view.[13]

The attitude categories are "just two among many peculiarities of human behavior" (CW18, par. 499), Jung concluded. The "functions"–sensation, thinking, feeling, and intuition–also distinguish people because in each person one function is better developed than the others. Jung defined the functions as follows:

> *Sensation* (or sense perception) tells you that something exists; *thinking* tells you what it is; *feeling* tells you whether it is agreeable or not; and *intuition* tells you where it comes from and where it is going. (CW18, par. 503)

Jung observed clinically that when thinking is the best developed function in a particular individual, feeling (the opposite of thinking in Jung's typology) tends to be the least developed, and vice versa. A parallel situation exists for sensation and intuition. The best developed function is known as the "superior" and its opposite as the "inferior" function. Jung described the attitude and function types in detail in Chapter 10 of *Psychological Types* (CW6).

The types are related to dreams through specific images. For example, in a dream, a human figure with an opposite temperament from the dreamer, and usually of the same sex, may represent the dreamer's inferior attitude or function.

Along with the psychological differences among people, described as attitude and function types, there are commonalities in the psychic structure of all. Each personality is composed of some consciousness—the ego and the contents readily accessible to it—and a great deal that is unconscious, chiefly the *shadow*, the *persona*, and the *anima* or *animus*. Each of these contents often may appear as figures in dreams, and each is capable of endless variations, forms, and blendings. A short definition of each term must suffice here.

Ego (Latin: "I") was for Jung the center of the individual's field of consciousness, that which provides the unity and continuity for the personality.[14]

Shadow is made up of the qualities one prefers to hide, those that are unadapted and awkward. It includes the individual's potential, in an undeveloped form. The ego perceives the shadow as inferior and even entirely bad, but much of it is only embarrassing.[15]

Persona (Greek: "mask") is the term that Jung applied to those aspects of the personality by which one adapts to the outer world, the face one shows that is presentable and acceptable to others.[16]

Anima and *animus* (Latin: [f. & m.] "soul") are the aspects of the psyche that carry one's image of the other sex. To Jung all human beings incorporated both masculinity and femininity (which he saw as rooted in the principles of logos [structure] and eros [relatedness] rather than in social roles). The unconscious feminine part of the male is the anima, and the unconscious masculine side of the woman is the animus. The anima is likely to be experienced negatively as moodiness, positively as creativity; the animus is likely to be experienced negatively as opinionatedness, positively as constructive initiative.

Self "designates the whole range of psychic phenomena in man [conscious and unconscious]. It expresses the unity of the personality as a whole" (CW6, par. 789), and should not be confused with ego, which is the center of a person's consciousness only. Jung used the term Self[17] also in a transpersonal sense as the reflection of a larger totality—God.

Completing this brief statement of Jung's personality theory is a description of the mechanism that Jung called "projection." It designates the tendency to perceive a part of one's own psyche[18] as belonging to another person.[19] It can operate in relation to the positive or negative expression of any facet of the personality: an attitude; feeling; quality; or ability, developed or undeveloped. It is through projection that dreams frequently help to reveal a person's psychic structure, in indicating what one is projecting onto others.

The shadow, animus, and anima were hypothesized originally by Jung at least partly on the basis of dreams. All of them, along with the Self, are likely to appear in dreams in personified form (see Mahoney, 1966). The persona is likely to appear in the dream as the clothing or some other outward aspect of the dreamer. The image of the dreamer is known as the "dream ego" (see Ch. 3). A male figure in a woman's dream is assumed to be an aspect of the animus; a female figure, of the shadow. In a man's dream, the female and male figures belong to anima and shadow, respectively.

Some of the seemingly individual figures of the unconscious, such as the shadow, animus, anima, and even the persona (which *"feigns individuality"* [CW7, par. 245]), are determined only partly by the individual's personal experience; the remaining determinants are archetypal. Thus, each figure has some common and some individual characteristics. Because of their special importance in dream interpretation, the concepts of archetypes and the collective unconscious require more detailed treatment than the psychic structures already presented.

Archetypes and the Collective Unconscious: An Exposition

In Jung's conception of the human psyche, a relatively small portion[20] of it is conscious; the rest is unconscious. The unconscious portion is composed of two types of contents: that which has been part of the individual's experience and subsequently has been forgotten or repressed, and that which was never conscious, that is, which comes from the heritage of humanity. Jung called the first the personal unconscious and the second, the collective (universal, rather than personal) unconscious, which he described as *archetypal*. The concept of archetypes is so controversial and so crucial to Jung's approach to dreams that it is important to clarify what the concept is and what it is not, how he derived it, the evidence that supports it, and its implications.

An archetype is not a specific image or motif.

> It would be absurd to assume that such variable representations could be inherited. The archetype is, on the contrary, an inherited *tendency* of the human mind to form representations of mythological motifs—representations that vary a great deal without losing their basic pattern. There are, for instance, numerous representations of the motif of the hostile brothers, but the motif remains the same . . . . " (CW18, par. 523)

Similarly, an archetype is not an idea which has been acquired by humanity. It is, rather, a "possibility of representation" (CW9-I, par. 155), that is, a predisposition to an image, a common psychic structure that parallels the common human physical structure. Its existence is analogous to "the axial system of a crystal, which, as it were, preforms the crystalline structure in the mother liquid, although it has no material existence of its own" (CW9-I, par. 155). Thus, the archetype itself cannot be experienced; all we can know of it is its effects on dreams, other mental contents, emotions, and actions.

Jung's first intimations of the existence of this collective material issued from some of his dreams. He stated that his "intellectual life had its unconscious beginnings" (MDR, p. 15) at age three or four when in a dream *he descended a stone stairway into a hole in the ground. At the bottom, behind a heavy green curtain was a rectangular chamber with an arched ceiling of hewn stone. In the center of the flagstone floor a red carpet ran from the entrance to a low platform. A wonderfully rich golden throne stood on the platform, with a red cushion on the seat. Standing on the throne was what appeared to be a tree trunk twelve to fifteen feet high and about one and a half to two feet thick, reaching almost to the ceiling. It was made of skin and naked flesh, and on top there was something like a rounded head with no face and no hair. On the very top of the head was a single eye, gazing motionless upward. He heard his mother's voice call out, "That is the man-eater!"* (D2). For years, he was haunted by this dream. Much later, he came to realize that what he had seen in the dream was a phallus, and only after decades did he understand that it was a ritual phallus and an archetypal image.

Jung found that he virtually was forced into hypothesizing the collective unconscious. Indeed, he maintained that anyone going through his clinical experiences would reach the same conclusions. In addition to many of his own dreams, some of the dreams and hallucinations of his patients contained images which were unlikely to have been a part of the individual's personal experience. A crucial incident is described several times in the *Collected Works*. One account is as follows:

> One day [in the hospital] I came across [a patient] there, blinking through the window up at the sun, and moving his head from side to side in a curious manner. He took me by the arm and said he wanted to show me something. He said I must look at the sun with eyes half shut, and then I could see the sun's phallus. If I moved my head from side to side the sun-phallus would move too, and that was the origin of the wind.
>
> I made this observation about 1906. In the course of the year 1910, when I was engrossed in mythological studies, a book of Dieterich's came into my hands. It was part of the so-called Paris magic papyrus and was thought by Dieterich to be a liturgy of the Mithraic cult. It consisted of a series of instructions, invocations, and

visions. One of these visions is described in the following words: "And likewise the so-called tube, the origin of the ministering wind. For you will see hanging down from the disc of the sun something that looks like a tube." (CW8, pars. 317–318)

Although the first edition of the book had appeared in 1903, the patient could not have read it because he had been committed several years earlier.[21]

The "people's tales" (those authored by a people, rather than by an individual)—myths, legends, and fairy tales—are often said, by Jung also, to be the equivalent of the dreams of an individual, that is, products of the unconscious. Similar motifs which have not been transmitted consciously exist in the tales of peoples separated by time, geography, and culture, and in the dreams of individuals. Jung hypothesized that these common motifs arise out of a common mental substratum, the collective unconscious. With the increase in our knowledge, including the anthropological, of other peoples and cultures, it has become increasingly difficult to demonstrate that a particular image in a dream is not based on something the dreamer has learned. In the first decades of the twentieth century, however, before the great leaps in the development of communications, Jung had the opportunity to find dream motifs that paralleled mythological motifs which the dreamer could not have learned.

An example is a dream told to Jung by an uneducated Negro in the American South,

in which occurred the figure of a man crucified on a wheel. [Jung argued that] it would have been most probable . . . that he should dream of a man crucified on a *cross*. The cross would have been a personal acquisition. But it is rather improbable, that he should dream of the man crucified on a *wheel*. That is a very uncommon image. Of course I cannot prove to you that by some curious chance the Negro had not seen a picture or heard something of the sort and then dreamt about it; but if he had not had any model for this idea it would be an *archetypal image*, because the crucifixion on the wheel is a *mythological motif*. It is the ancient sun-wheel, and the crucifixion is the sacrifice to the sun-god in order to propitiate him, just as human and animal sacrifices formerly were offered for the fertility of the earth. The sun-wheel is an exceedingly archaic idea, perhaps the oldest religious idea there is. We can trace it to the Mesolithic and Paleolithic ages, as the sculptures of Rhodesia prove. Now there were real wheels only in the Bronze Age; in the Paleolithic Age the wheel was not yet invented . . . . The Rhodesian sun-wheel is therefore an original vision, presumably an archetypal sun-image. But this image is not a naturalistic one, for it is always divided into four or eight partitions . . . .

In the dream . . . , the man on the wheel is a repetition of the Greek mythological motif of Ixion, who, on account of his offence against men and gods, was fastened by Zeus upon an incessantly turning wheel. (CW18, pars. 81–82)[22]

It is unlikely that the dreamer had studied Greek mythology or that he had seen representations of Greek mythological figures, including Ixion. Jung concluded that the dream image was a product of the collective unconscious.

Many persons acknowledge the similarity of motifs in disparate cultures at different times but still argue that archetypes do not exist. To such persons Jung replied,

> Certainly they do not exist, any more than a botanical system exists in nature! But will anyone deny the existence of natural plant-families on that account? Or will anyone deny the occurrence and continual repetition of certain morphological and functional similarities? It is much the same thing in principle with the typical figures of the unconscious. They are forms existing *a priori* . . . . (CW9–I, par. 309n)

Jung likened the archetypes, "*typical modes of apprehension*" (CW8, par. 280), to the instincts, which to him were "*typical modes of action*" (CW8, par. 273) based on physiological urges.

The basic structure of the human brain can be perceived as generating archetypal patterns: general modes of perception that provide the elements and perhaps set the limits within which human beings are capable of thinking, perceiving, and receiving communications. When Penfield (1952) applied electrical stimulation to the brains of human subjects, he found that

> The responses from stimulation of sensory areas follow what may be called inborn patterns. They are the same regardless of what an individual's past experience may have been. On the other hand . . . . responses from the memory cortex are of an entirely different order. They are made up of the acquired experience of that particular individual.
>
> It is the difference between a simple sound and a conversation or a symphony. It is the difference between the sight of colored squares and the moving spectacle of friends who walk and talk and laugh with you. The one is a simple element of sensation. The other is a recollective hallucination. (p. 181)

Although not using the word "instinct," the rapidly developing field of ethology is providing evidence for innate behavior potentials which may be examples of archetype-like predispositions. Some of the ethologists' most relevant findings give evidence of "imprinting," the phenomenon in which an experience of a young animal at a critical period in its life affects its lifelong social behavior by determining its primary affective attachment. Imprinting is known best, probably, through the work of the Austrian zoologist, Konrad Lorenz. He showed that goslings become attached—as evidenced by what or whom they follow—usually to their mothers but, actually, to whatever object is in their line of vision at a critical time, about 15 to 17 hours after hatching. Some goslings were imprinted on adult males of their species; others, on Lorenz himself. The phenomenon can be observed most clearly, of course, in young birds which can be kept apart from their mothers in the first few days of life. Something similar seems to happen, however, in other animals, including some mammals, and is conceivable in human beings.

The idea that the human mind has an evolutionary history was just as reasonable to Jung as the accepted theory of the body's history. That we do not "know" about our unconscious does not invalidate its existence. Millions of people in the world do not "know" that they possess vermiform appendices, branchial arches, or thymus glands, but their ignorance does not negate the organs' existence. These organs and our entire bodies, in fact, are in their current forms because of our biological evolution. Indeed, the vestiges that exist tell us of changes that have occurred in the human body over the aeons.

The human brain also has evolved over the millenia, and with the changes came new dimensions of the mind: "... there is no doubt that the strengthening of mental power came with the vast expansion of the cerebral cortex of New Brain in man" (Hawkes, 1963, p. 165); but since the brain retains vestiges of its past forms, some of the potential for images produced by minds when the brain was less developed also must be vestigially present.

Citing the aesthetic sense evident in the finest hand-axes dating back to the end of the Paleolithic Age, anthropologist Jacquetta Hawkes concluded that

> ... their satisfying proportions show that already a quarter of a million years ago the imaginative mind had its own sense of rightness in pure form which, whatever its source, still holds good for us today ....
>
> ... there is a widely held and also strongly contested view that human beings are born with certain innate mental forms which have come into being through the experience of the evolving species. They are inherited just as the similarly evolved bodily parts are inherited, but as they are mental they tend to be expressed in cultural forms, most obviously in religious myths, which although they differ in outward form with the tone of the culture concerned, often appear to have an underlying unity that is world-wide and timeless ....
>
> Although many people cannot accept this idea of the inheritance of mental forms, it is surely far more likely than that we are born with a mental carte blanche .... (Hawkes, 1963, p. 167)

The evolution of the human mind has permitted people in different parts of the world who were not in communication with each other to "invent" the same artifacts. For example, the wheel appeared in the Mediterranean area during the Bronze Age when it was put to use for vehicles pulled by animals. In Central America, the Mayans (or their predecessors) also invented the wheel but, since they had no draft animals, the wheels were used for toys.

> ... When two peoples at some distance from one another possess some peculiar implement, design, myth, in common it may well have been transferred by trade, migration or a spreading influence. These contacts should always be looked for, but if they cannot be detected, then there remains the alternative that the trait represents two independent expressions of a common mental pattern. (Hawkes, 1963, p. 168)

The springs of human greatness, according to Hawkes, are "the development and exercise of the combined mental powers of intellect and imagination" (1963, p. 164). We can attribute the increase in human mental powers to evolutionary changes in the brain, but to what do we attribute imagination? To what do we attribute the exercise of the imagination, which is what we call creativity? Curiosity is a trait shared by primates, other animals, and humans, but only humans use curiosity creatively, that is, translate curiosity by imagination into artifacts, symbols, or concepts.

All humans display some degree of creativity—whether in problem solving, the arts, or solely in dreaming. That creative forces are released during dreaming sleep is evidenced by the experiences of artists, writers, scientists, and other persons who have "slept on" a problem and awakened in the morning with a solution or an understanding of the procedures to follow to reach a solution.

Creative works, whether inventions, intellectual productions, or works of art, all appear to result from the interaction between environment and genetic endowment. But even with the continuing advances in mapping the relevant part of the genetic endowment, the human brain, no one yet has identified the seat of creativity. The genetic endowment necessary for creativity is considered by some scholars and scientists to be the collective unconscious. The creative person has an especially ready access to this inner resource. (See Neumann, 1959, for a fuller discussion of the collective unconscious as the source of creativity.)

Thus the concept of the collective unconscious offers an explanation for creativity. Since it has not won general acceptance, the term "collective unconscious," coined by Jung, may be semantically unfortunate. Living as we do in an age of individualism, we have lost sight of the commonalities which bind all of humanity into one species, and of the history that links us irrevocably to our common origins and development. Perhaps if Jung had used a term more compatible with individualism, such as "creative unconscious," his concept would be accepted more readily. Whatever it may be called, Jung's concept of the collective unconscious connects contemporary humans with each other, the past, and the future.

Although few other dream theorists acknowledge the existence in dreams of archetypal material as such, several do so implicitly. Psychologist Calvin Hall, for example, stated that "there is no theme of mythology or literature which fails to be represented in the dreams of people living today" (1953, p. 20).

Research psychologists have found evidence that psychological mechanisms impose perceptual structure on stimuli of at least two kinds. One is binocular perception of visual stimuli. Psychologist John Ross's subjects, for example, perceived square targets as "more perfectly square, with more perfect edges than any real square" (1976, p. 86). Even in infants, there seems to be a perceptual structure imposed by psychological mechanisms. J. A. Fodor and his associates (1975) found that infants of 14 to 18 weeks can discriminate between syllables that have a similar consonant sound and those that do not have such similarities. Both of these sets of data seem to provide further support for the concept of the archetype, which Jung defined as a predisposition to an image.

Many scholars in other fields than psychology hold Jung's approach to be an outstanding contribution to their efforts to understand human nature. For example, Hawkes apparently found Jung's approach fruitful for her anthropological studies and interpretations, and linguist Noam Chomsky has postulated language as a faculty which, from his description, can be regarded as archetypal. He wrote, "The language faculty may be regarded as a fixed function, characteristic of the species, one component of the human mind, a function which maps experience into grammar" (quoted in Trotter, 1975). Chomsky hypothesized a specific property of grammar

> that is unlearned and universal to all grammars, a precondition of learning. If [such a] property ... can be discovered, it would suggest the existence of a genetically determined human language faculty [and that] language might have a partially determined structure as a matter of biological necessity, much as the general character of bodily organs is fixed for the species. (Trotter, 1975, p. 333)

The similarity between the Chomsky-Trotter hypothesis of a language faculty and Jung's idea of a psychic structure as the basis for archetypes is striking.

Joseph Campbell, writer and lecturer on mythology, wrote,

> Jung was not only a medical man but a scholar in the grand style, whose researchers, particularly in comparative mythology, alchemy, and the psychology of religion, have inspired and augmented the

findings of an astonishing number of the leading creative scholars of our time. (1971, p. vii)

Campbell is one of those scholars; his far-ranging interests are of psychological significance in the explorations of the hypothesis of the collective unconscious.

A scholar in still another field has attested to the value of Jung's work in his realm of interest, history. Arnold Toynbee, trying to solve problems of the cultural inequality of various extant human societies, found the nineteenth-century "scientific" explanations useless. He wrote,

> The breakdown of these . . . drove me to turn to mythology. I took this turning rather self-consciously and shamefacedly, as though it were a provocatively retrograde step. I might have been less diffident . . . if I had been acquainted at the time with the works of C. G. Jung, they would have given me the clue. (quoted in Bennet, 1967, p. 78)

The concept of archetypes is probably a basis for the frequent accusations that Jung was "mystical" and, consequently, lacked scientific precision. It is ironic, therefore, that considerable support for Jung's view can be found in the writings of perhaps the greatest scientist of the twentieth century—Albert Einstein. He wrote of "universal elementary laws from which the cosmos can be built up by pure deduction," and added, "There is no logical path to these laws; only intuition, resting on sympathetic understanding of experience, can reach them" (quoted in Pirsig, 1974, p. 114). Such "universal elementary laws" can be understood as principles of organization for mental contents and other phenomena. Thus, Einstein could have used the term "archetype" rather than "universal elementary law."

Poincaré, the French mathematician and physicist, seemed to have a similar idea in his "subliminal self," which selects the combinations of facts relevant to the solution of a problem on the basis of a mathematical beauty or harmony which is "at the center of it all" (quoted in Pirsig, 1974, pp. 267–268).

Other Jungian Concepts

Perhaps Jung's most controversial hypothesis is that of *synchronicity*, which he defined as an "acausal connecting principle," or "a *meaningful coincidence* of two or more events, where something other than the probability of chance is involved" (CW8, par. 969). That is, events are synchronistic if they are connected by meaning and in time but not by causal relation.

Although it is derived in part from the theory of the collective unconscious, synchronicity is related only tangentially to dream interpretation; that is, although one of the synchronistic events may be a dream, the interpretation plays little or no role in the synchronicity.

Jung used the term *libido* to mean psychic energy in general, not in the early Freud's sense of specifically sexual energy.[23] In Jung's terms, psychic energy can be measured indirectly in terms of psychological values. The concept of psychic energy is relevant to dreams in that energy is necessary for the "action" from the unconscious to initiate the compensation that dreams provide in relation to the conscious situation of the dreamer (see Ch. 7). A release of energy may be a result, moreover, of experiencing the dream images or their interpretation. This release often results from the removal of repression from a content of the unconscious.

Jung's psychological theory centers around his concept of *individuation*,[24] the process of psychological development by which a person becomes an undivided (i.e., whole or integrated, as well as unique) personality. In the process, the individual's third and fourth functions become somewhat developed and, by confronting successive pairs of opposites (e.g., light and dark), one realizes and progressively integrates unconscious contents, such as the shadow and the animus or anima. Since dreams contribute to experiencing these unconscious parts of the psyche, they give impetus to the individuation process. Jung saw unattended dreams as moving chaotically or in a circle, which gives way to the spiral of the individuation process when attention is given to them.

Religion proved to be a crucial problem for Jung's patients, especially in the second half of life (after age 35 or 40). He agreed with Otto (1958) that religion is an experience described as "numinous," that is, beyond the comprehension or understanding of humans, and not a dogma, creed, or institution; it can be experienced as good, but sometimes as evil. Jung defined religion as

> a peculiar attitude of mind which could be formulated in accordance with the original use of the word *religio*, which means a careful consideration and observation of certain dynamic factors that are conceived as "powers": spirits, daemons, gods, laws, ideas, ideals, or whatever name man has given to such factors in his world as he has found powerful, dangerous, or helpful enough to be taken into careful consideration, or grand, beautiful, and meaningful enough to be devoutly worshipped and loved. (CW11, par. 8)

By "religion," Jung seemed to mean also the quest for meaning and the awareness of one's own limitations, especially mortality.

The implications of this explanation are that Jung considered religion to be an essential aspect of human life and not an optional practice.[25] He developed this view of the importance of religion on the basis of its frequency in his patients' dream material. The view is supported by archaeological evidence indicating that as long ago as Paleolithic times humans needed religious beliefs.

Although religion has been characterized as arising sometimes from feelings of helplessness before the vicissitudes of existence, sometimes from the need to define the place of humanity in the order of the universe, and sometimes from the desire to unify the social unit in which people live, anthropologists have found that virtually no established social group ever existed without some beliefs and practices which could be designated as religious. The need to believe in powers greater than humans is apparently as old as humanity, and Jung recognized the universality of this need. He warned that psychotherapy can be "faulty" (CW8, par. 686) if the religious content of dreams is not recognized. His view of religion is integral to his view of the individuation process as the ego's giving way to the centrality of the god-image, the Self.

Jung's view of religion as a necessity for human beings is closely related to his understanding of the archetypal basis of many dream images. He wrote,

> The most important symbols are collective ... [and] are found principally in the religions. The believer assumes that they are of divine origin—that they are revealed. The sceptic thinks they are invented. Both are wrong. It is true that ... such symbols have for centuries been the object of careful and quite conscious elaboration .... But, on the other hand, they are *représentations collectives* dating from dim and remote ages, and these are "relevations" only in the sense that they are images originating in dreams and creative fantasies [which] are ... spontaneous manifestations and [not] arbitrary and intentional inventions. (CW18, par. 481)

Notes

[1] For more complete accounts of Jung's life, see Bennet (1962); Campbell (1971); Ellenberger (1970); Hall & Nordby (1973); Hannah (1976); Jung (MDR); and van der Post (1975). According to Stern (1976), Carl was the Jung's second child; the first-born, a boy, had lived only a few days.

[2] "In the first dream *I was in a dark wood that stretched along the Rhine. I came to a little hill, a burial mound, and began to dig. After a while I turned up, to my astonishment, some bones of prehistoric animals. This interested me enormously, and at that moment I knew: I must get to know nature, the world in which we live, and the things around us.*

"Then came a second dream. Again *I was in a wood; it was threaded with watercourses, and in the darkest place I saw a circular pool, surrounded by dense undergrowth. Half immersed in the water lay the strangest and most wonderful creature: a round animal, shimmering in opalescent hues, and consisting of innumerable little cells, or of organs shaped like tentacles. It was a giant radiolarian, measuring about three feet across. It seemed to me indescribably wonderful that this magnificent creature should be lying there undisturbed, in the hidden place, in the clear, deep water. It aroused in me an intense desire for knowledge,* so that I awoke with a beating heart. These two dreams decided me overwhelmingly in favor of science, and removed all my doubts" (MDR, p. 85). Later, through his work on alchemy, Jung discovered that the image of the radiolarian was archetypal (von Franz, 1975, p. 31).

In an earlier work (CW9–II, par. 208), Jung had recounted the same dream and its effect on the dreamer with some differences in detail and without identifying himself as the dreamer. He identified the water creature as a mandala, however.

[3] Earlier word association tests had been developed between 1879 and 1907 by Galton, Wundt, Kraepelin, and Münsterberg (see Anderson & Anderson, 1951).

[4] Test behavior includes such observable phenomena as posture, facial expression, stammering, and perseveration.

[5] In Jung's *Collected Works*, Volume 2 is devoted to his research on the Word Association Test. A less formal account appears in *The Tavistock Lectures* (CW18, pars. 97–160).

[6] The dream was of *a house that Jung did not know, but was "his house." The upper of the two stories was furnished in rococo style; the lower floor had medieval furnishings. There was also a cellar containing the remains of a primitive culture, including two human skulls* (MDR, pp. 158–159). In looking for the wish fulfillment, Freud assumed that the two skulls represented wishes for the death of two persons close to Jung. In contrast, Jung associated the skulls with two he had studied in paleontology, and he saw the house as an image of the psyche that included beneath twentieth century culture a primitive level "which can scarcely be reached or illuminated by consciousness" (MDR, p. 160). This dream was his "first inkling of a collective a priori beneath the personal psyche" (MDR, p. 161). The concept of the collective psyche, or unconscious, was the subject of the book, *The Psychology of the Unconscious*, that so alienated Freud.

[7] Although Jung referred to himself as a "pupil of Freud's" (CW4, par. 553) and, in some of his letters to Freud, declared his allegiance and referred to the psychoanalytic group he had organized as "Freudian" (FJ, 46J), a persistent theme throughout the correspondence is Jung's doubts about the way Freud overgeneralized his theories, especially the theory that all neuroses had their roots in polymorphous, perverse, infantile sexuality.

[8] After the break with Freud, Jung began to be accused of anti-Semitism. Thus the way was prepared for the further accusation of Nazi sympathizer, during the Hitler era. For varying points of view on this issue, which is not relevant to this book, see Ellenberger (1970), Jaffé (1971), Jurgevich (1974) and Stern (1976).

[9] For a more complete account of the development of Jung's theories, see von Franz (1975).

[10] In most American non-Jungian psychological literature, the preferred spelling of the term is "extroversion." The spelling "extraversion" was "agreed on with Jung himself" according to Gerhard Adler (1977, p. 117), one of the editors of the *Collected Works*, and is usually used in England and by most American Jungians.

[11] Eysenck and Cattell both described extraversion–introversion as a dimension of personality based on the factors of which the dimension appears empirically to be composed. Eysenck (1969) found that extraverts are high on two factors, sociability and impulsiveness; introverts are low. Cattell (1957) found five such factors: *affectothymia* (similar to Eysenck's sociability), *surgency* (similar to Eysenck's impulsiveness), *nonconformity, self-sufficiency,* and *parmia* (roughly, a "happy-go-lucky" attitude to life). The Minnesota Multiphasic Personality Inventory (nd) contains a Social Introversion scale, which is considered to indicate pathology, but the trait is defined as an absence of extraversion, not as the positive quality it was in Jung's thinking.

[12] Jung wrote much later, in 1957, "My characterization of Adler and Freud as, respectively, introverted and extraverted does not refer to them personally but only to their outward demeanor. The question of the real personal type still remains open" (Let-2, pp. 349–350).

[13] Ellenberger (1970) considered some of the differences in background between Freud and Adler to be "deep-reaching" (p. 572) and due to the different attitudes of the groups of Austrian Jews to which they belonged: Freud's forebears were from Galicia and south Russia, Adler's, from the "comparatively privileged community of Kittsee, in the province of Burgenland" (p. 572). These facts, however, would not preclude their having differences in temperament as individuals.

[14] Freud saw the ego as a synthesis of contents of the id, superego, and external world.

[15] The shadow includes the part of the psyche which Freud called the "id."

[16] Roughly equivalent to Freud's superego.

[17] Jungians disagree on whether to capitalize "Self;" the translators of the *Collected Works* did not do so. (Jung wrote mainly in German, in which all nouns are capitalized.) I do so, because in non-Jungian personality theories "self" carries meanings different from Jung's usage.

[18] Jung used "psyche" and "psychic" interchangeably with "personality."

[19] Jung's definition of projection is somewhat broader than Freud's, which seems to refer only to one's own wish or impulse attributed to another.

[20] That which Freud characterized as the "tip of the iceberg."

[21] Jung had the impression at the time, and even as late as 1931, that "the Greek text [was] first edited in 1910" (CW8, par. 319). He learned later that the 1910 edition was the second.

[22] Jung gave no further information on the dream in this passage or in CW5, par. 184, where he mentioned the same dream image.

[23] In Freud's later work he came close to Jung's usage.

[24] Other psychologists, including Freud, have used the term, but to denote a concept closer to Jung's "ego development."

[25] Freud saw religion as an "illusion," in that he considered wish fulfillment to be a prominent factor in its motivation.

Chapter 3

THE NATURE
OF DREAMS

Like Freud before him, Jung hypothesized that dreams are generated by psychically determined activity in the unconscious. The two men differed in their interpretations of many dream images, however, because they had partially different concepts of the unconscious. To Freud, all unconscious contents were repressed material. To Jung, repressed contents (perceptions, thoughts, values, emotions) accounted for only some of the unconscious contents. In addition to the repressed material, Jung wrote, the unconscious

> ... contains all those psychic components that have fallen below the threshold, including subliminal sense-perceptions. Moreover we know, from abundant experience as well as for theoretical reasons, that the unconscious also contains components that have *not yet* reached the threshold of consciousness. These are the seeds of future conscious contents. (CW7, par. 204)

If Freud's concept of the unconscious were true, Jung argued, the lifting of repression would result in paralysis of unconscious productivity and dreaming would cease. Yet, he observed that no matter how much repression is released, dreams and fantasies persist. On the basis of this observation, he deduced that an underlying process continuously generates dreams and fantasies, only a small proportion of which come into cognitive awareness, and, hence, that the unconscious contains more than repressed material.

Elaborating poetically, Jung wrote:

> The dream is a little hidden door in the innermost and most secret recesses of the soul, opening into that cosmic night which was psyche long before there was any ego-consciousness, and which will remain psyche no matter how far our ego-consciousness extends. . . . It remained for the rationalism of our age to explain the dream as the remnants left over from the day, as the crumbs that fall into the twilit world from the richly laden table of our consciousness. These dark depths are then nothing but an empty sack, containing no more than what falls into it from above . . . . It would be far truer to say that our consciousness is that sack, which has nothing in it except what chances to fall into it. (CW10, pars. 304–305)

Thus, while not denying that some contents pass from consciousness into the unconscious, Jung hypothesized that all psychic contents, including dreams, have their roots in the ever-productive collective unconscious. This hypothesis seems to be based on the assumption that all behavior and ways of perceiving experience must be potential within the person before they can become actual, and these potentialities are contents of the collective unconscious.

The dream, then, if Jung's view is correct, is not necessarily a wish fulfillment, as Freud had it. Nor is it a reflection only of the dreamer's personal experience. Rather, it is a product of the collective unconscious also and, as such, it is characterized by an objectivity that provides whatever is necessary for psychic balance, regardless of the ego's wishes. Indeed, in his later works, Jung often used the term "objective psyche" as a synonym for "collective unconscious."

According to Freud, the meanings of dreams are disguised (by the manifest content) in order to preserve sleep. Jung saw this explanation as an oversimplification. He acknowledged that dreams preserve sleep, so far as is possible; he noted also that they sometimes interrupt sleep. The psychophysiological evidence that dreaming (REM) sleep is frequent during the night affirms that the dream does not waken the dreamer during or after most dreams; whether the dream actually protects one from waking is probably impossible to determine with our present state of knowledge. Jung suspected that the completion of the dream message sometimes wakens the dreamer. This view is supported by the subjective experience of many persons, an experience recognized by both Jung and Freud, of waking spontaneously with the memory of a dream (sometimes, but not always, anxiety producing) and the impression that it had just occurred. Foulkes (1966), a non-Jungian investigator of dreams, hypothesized that it is the atypically unpleasant dreams that interrupt sleep.

Just how the unconscious contents are translated into dreams, we do not know; we know only the resultant images. Although the dreamer is unable to produce a dream as one can make up a story, Jung's assertion that the dreamer is *totally* unable to control the dream content is not supported unequivocally by the evidence. Few dreamers claim to have dictated the images they wanted to appear in their dreams, but some report experiences of consciously intending or "asking the unconscious for" a dream that would respond to a current problem, and then having such a dream. Dream experimenters report similar responses when they attempt to determine the images or emotional tone of their subjects' dreams. When Foulkes and Rechtschaffen (1964), for example, exposed subjects to a violent Western film or to a quiet romantic comedy before sleep, the subjects reported few unchanged film sequences in their subsequent dreams. The emotional tone of the dreams seemed to be influenced, however, in that the dream content following the Western film was judged as more vivid, imaginative, and emotionally charged than the dream content following the comedy. Specific images (e.g., persons, trees, horses) have been introduced to dreams by post-hypnotic suggestion before sleep (Stoyva, 1965). Patricia Garfield (1974) presented anecdotal evidence that a dreamer, by conscious intent, can introduce specific images into dreams. (Even she did not claim, however, that an entire dream text can be dictated by consciousness.) When such autosuggestion appears to be effective, Jung accounted for it by the explanation, it "suits" the purpose of the unconscious. (VS1, p. 14)

Unknown also is the process by which a dream enters consciousness. Jung seemed to think that a "small portion of consciousness ... remains to us in the dream state" (CW17, par. 113). This remnant may be possible because of the existence of the dream ego, which is a "limited and curiously distorted ego" (CW8, par. 580). It is experienced when one of the dream figures is identified as the dreamer. (The dream ego seems to represent the ego that is the center of consciousness plus "some factors outside the scope of consciousness," according to Marjasch [1966a, p. 75].) The dreamer appears as a person, in most dreams, but sometimes in the form of "emotional contents" (VS1, p. 41). The implications of the absence of a dream ego are unknown, but could be studied. Dreams differ from conscious contents[1] in their lack of logical coherence and continuity of development. Jung hypothesized that a reason for the difference is that dreams are produced, not by the cortex, which sleeps, but by the sympathetic nervous system, which functions constantly. His hypothesis is supported by experimental studies, postdating his work, which found that the cerebral cortex is not necessary for the state of sleep—REM—with which most dreaming is associated. The part of the brain necessary for REM sleep is the pons, one of the brain's most primitive structures (Witkin & Lewis, 1967; these authors cited Jouvet, 1962, and Jouvet, Valatx & Jouvet, 1961).

Another difference between dreams and conscious contents is what Jung called the "irrationality" of dreams.[2] (Jung frequently used the word "irrational" where "nonrational" might be more precise.) To be sure, conscious contents are not always rational, in the sense of being logical, sensible, or even accurate perceptions of the world, but dream images often are especially nonrational in that they are not subject to physical or time limitations and they frequently depict creatures not now found in the world of nature. For example, dreams are common of humans flying without wings or falling from great heights without injury. Nonrational, however, does not mean "unnatural." Jung insisted that dream images are the natural products of the psyche, just as baby birds, however strange appearing, are the natural offspring of their parents.

Dreams are irrational also in that very few "form logically, morally, or aesthetically satisfying wholes" (CW8, par. 532). Past, present, and future seem often to blend together in a dream. This phenomenon is possible, probably, because the unconscious contains timeless contents that have not yet appeared in consciousness. (This hypothesis may help to explain anticipatory as well as prophetic dreams; see Ch. 11.) Despite the nonrational quality of dreams and, hence, their similarity to psychotic mental content,[3] dreams are normal and not pathological.

The Sources of Dream Images

Dreams are composed of images that arise from a variety of sources. The idea is popular that dreams are determined by somatic factors, such as the position of the dreamer's body, indigestion, fever, pain, and other physical stimuli, such as noise, light, cold, and heat. Jung acknowledged that some images are so influenced (e.g., a bell may be incorporated in the dream if an alarm clock rings) but he insisted that images are determined mainly otherwise, that is, psychically.

Psychophysiological studies tend to support Jung's conclusion. In a study by Dement and Wolpert (1958), neither dreaming sleep nor dream images were produced by sounds, lights, and tactile stimulation presented to the dreamer during non-REM sleep. Even during REM sleep, external stimuli had to be startling in order to have a marked effect on the content of the dreams that were occurring. A pure tone of 1000 cycles per second was judged to be incorporated into subsequently elicited dreams only 9% of the time; a flashing 100-watt light, 23%; and a spray of cold water on the sleeper's skin, 42%. The awakening stimulus, a bell, never was incorporated into the dreams.

A source of dream images more prolific than physical stimuli during sleep is the dreamer's everyday environment. Jung mentioned, for example, that the dreamer's occupation appears frequently in dreams: A musician dreams of performing, an architect of buildings, and a teacher of classrooms. No data seem to be available on the frequency of dreams depicting the dreamer's occupation, but the immediate environment of some dreamers, the laboratory in which the dream took place, was reflected in as many as 30% of laboratory dreams, according to some studies (Domhoff & Kamiya, 1964; Whitman, Pierce, Maas, & Baldridge, 1962).

A popular idea that most dreams arise out of anxiety was not borne out in Jung's experience, nor has it been in mine. Jung hypothesized, moreover, that emotion-arousing pre-sleep stimuli appear in dreams only in distorted form, "as a sort of language . . . that expresses some psychological problems in [the dreamer]" (VS1, p. 14). Experimental studies tend to confirm this hypothesis. Witkin (1969) found heightened emotion in reported dreams but no clear carry-over of images from emotion-arousing films of subincision rituals and human birth shown to the subjects. Breger, Hunter, and Lane (1971) obtained similar results with dreamers in stressful situations, such as the anticipation of surgery.

Subliminal perceptions seem to be another source of dream images. They include, according to Jung, subliminal thoughts and feelings as well as sense-perceptions that are too weak to reach cognitive awareness. Possible evidence for the incorporation of sense perceptions in dreams is provided by the "Poetzl phenomenon," described in 1917 by Otto Poetzl, a Viennese physician acquainted with Freudian theory.

> Using a *tachistoscope* . . . he showed unfamiliar color slides to normal subjects, who recorded all they said they were able to perceive. The subjects were then asked to "watch" their hypnagogic and nocturnal dreams on that night. The next day, they returned to the laboratory and drew simple sketches of particular dream fragments . . . . None of the consciously perceived aspects of the slide could be seen in the dream sketches; [there were seen] only those elements that the subject had *not* reported seeing immediately subsequent to the tachistoscopic presentation. (Foulkes, 1966, p. 149)

The Poetzl research has been faulted for its nonquantitative and subjective method and its "susceptibility . . . to influence by the preconceptions of the experimenter" (Foulkes, 1966, p. 150). Subsequent studies purporting to replicate Poetzl's findings have been criticized equally severely. Even with careful experimental designs and better controls, further attempts to replicate Poetzl's findings have failed (Johnson & Ericksen, 1961; Pulver & Eppes, 1963; Waxenburg, Dickes, & Gottesfeld, 1962). Foulkes concluded from his own research that the Poetzl phenomenon is possible but probably infrequent.

Nevertheless, Foulkes's data do little to cast doubt on Jung's claim that dreams incorporate subliminal perceptions, because Jung took into account a selective factor, the conscious situation of the dreamer.

Jung recorded a man's dream that appears to reflect such subliminal perceptions. The dreamer was a businessman who was offered a deal that seemed honorable on the surface. The following night he dreamed that *his hands and forearms were covered with black dirt* (CW10, par. 826). He learned later that the deal would have involved him in fraud. It is likely that subliminally he had perceived something in the demeanor of the person with whom he was dealing that reflected the dishonesty of the offer when it was made, but he had not been able to admit the perception to his cognitive awareness.

In addition to current and anticipated waking events, memories of past waking experiences often appear as dream images. They may be memories that were once conscious, perhaps in childhood, but subsequently were forgotten. Some memories may be represented because they are related to unacceptable impulses and, hence, are painful, or because they are not sufficiently important to be remembered consciously. Penfield (1952) and others have demonstrated that the brain retains many memories that are not available to consciousness. Patients whose temporal cortices were stimulated electrically remembered experiences which they had not been able to recall previous to the electrical stimulation. After the electrodes were withdrawn, the subject could remember the general outlines of the recalled experience but not the details.

Sometimes, however, readily available memories appear as dream images, such as memories of traumatic events (e.g., war experiences) which are repeated over and over in dreams.

In addition to the sources of dream images in the environment and experiences of the individual dreamer mentioned thus far, there is a further source, which is limitlessly creative, according to Jung: the collective unconscious. In addition to being ultimately the source of all psychic material, the collective unconscious supplies specific contents which are more than personal, and which never had been conscious. Because of it, the dreams of many people, even people who are living in a given historical period, can be expected to represent the full range and variety of human behavior and experience, from the bizarre to the banal, including "ineluctable truths, philosophical pronouncements, illusions, wild fantasies, memories, plans, anticipations, irrational experiences, even telepathic visions" (CW16, par. 317).

The Language of Dreams

The language of dreams, according to Jung, is at least as complex and varied as the language of consciousness. Dream language is made up largely of nonverbal images that vary in complexity and vividness more dramatically than corresponding waking experiences.

On a relatively simple level, dream language is often figurative, that is, akin to figures of speech. For example, in day-to-day conversations we may characterize a person as a "snake-in-the-grass," "pig," or "pussycat," to mean that he or she is perfidious, unmannerly, or gentle. Similarly, in a dream, the unconscious may use the image of a lion, the king of beasts, to characterize power. Sometimes the dream makes a pun; for instance, an image may depict "pray" to suggest "prey."

On the next level of complexity is the metaphor. For example, a dream image of crossing a bridge can be a metaphor for making an important transition; or an image of imprisonment likens the dreamer's situation to one of severe restriction. Thus, abstract thoughts are expressed through concrete imagery.

Some dreams contain images that are fantastic and even physically impossible, such as the dream of the 16-year-old boy in which *he was being followed by the devil and, in "deathly terror, he leaps into the air and hangs there suspended"* (CW7, par. 285). Jung relished such picturesqueness in dream language. He found it more vivid than abstract statements because it is not limited by the conscious mind and can draw upon a greater wealth of associations.

Color contributes to the dream language by its presence or absence, hue, and intensity. (Some dreams seem to be in black and white, as are many photographs, or in sepia.) Jung found that emotionally intense dreams are likely to be remembered as dreamed in color, but to my knowledge, no one has tested this hypothesis.[4]

Other empirical studies, based on dreams recorded upon waking, have attempted, with some success, to discriminate persons who did and did not remember dreams to have been in color, on such dimensions as sex, Jungian typology, and anxiety level. Fortier (1952; cited by Suinn, 1967) found "color dreamers" to be more responsive to their environment and apt to have richer affectional relationships than people whose dreams were reported as not being in color. Hall (1951) found no difference between color dreamers and non-color dreamers. Suinn (1966, 1967), found some differences by sex (women have more dreams in color) and Jungian personality type (e.g., introverted and feeling types have more color dreams), but not by anxiety level. Tatibana (1938; cited by Suinn, 1967) found that people who dream more in blue hues are quiet and calm, and those who dream more in red are more excitable and lively.

It may not be necessary to carry this research further, because empirical studies have shown that as many as 83% of REM dreams were reported in color if subjects were questioned discreetly in sufficient detail, following a

REM period (Kahn, Dement, & Fisher, 1962) and before they engaged in any bodily movement. Improved research methodology may make it possible to demonstrate that all dreams are in color. The hypotheses that should be tested then, are that various colors reflect different emotions, and that varying intensities of color reflect varying degrees of emotionality.

Another characteristic of dream language is exaggeration: Images of ordinary objects or people may appear as fascinating or threatening, and real-life situations may take on exaggerated proportions or otherwise differ in detail from actual situations. Still another characteristic is iconoclasm: Dreams challenge cherished convictions and values. For example, in Jung's childhood dream of the *phallus with a single eye* (D2), the iconoclasm lay not in the sexual nature of the image, but in the image as an exalted pagan symbol in the dream of a Christian pastor's son.

In some dreams, the figures are like those of fairy tales—helpful animals, for example. Other images can be recognized as belonging to the mythological language of dreams but only after the time-influenced terms are translated into the timeless images. Thus, an airplane may stand for an eagle that can carry a woman on its back, an automobile or railroad train may be equivalent to a dragon, and an injection may represent a mythological snakebite.

Although most dreams are made up of visual imagery, there are exceptions, which Jung did not mention. Persons blind from birth tend to dream in all sensory modalities other than visual (Hartmann, 1967, pp. 131, 141) during REM sleep. An occasional nonvisual, even nonsensory, dream can present itself to anyone. An example is the dream of a middle-aged woman, which she was able to report only in the form of a poem:

I am . . .
But to know that I am.
To know consciously that I exist
As an entity which extends
Beyond the restrictive enclosures
Of my day-to-day mind.
In fact, previously unknown to me,
I have always existed in This Other.
Now, slowly, I am conscious
That I am trying to draw This Other
Into the Now. (It seemed outside of time, and I am within it.)
I am trying to draw it within my Body,
But I cannot.
I am aware that I am in my own
consciousness again.
I am again, part of the Life with Time and Space.
I am still upon the earth.
Who am I? (MAM Files)

The question frequently arises of whether any dreams are typical, or whether, at least, some motifs are typical. (A motif is a repeated image or idea; hence, a dream can have several motifs.) Identical groups or even pairs of dreams are rare. However, a given image may recur frequently in the dreams of one person, and some similarity can be found between the motifs of one dreamer's dreams and those of another. Examples are the motifs of falling, flying, being threatened by dangerous animals, and running hard but getting nowhere. The relative rarity of images repeated exactly from one dream to another is a consequence of the fact that any object or figure that exists or can be imagined is available as a dream image; therefore, the possible variety and number of images are literally infinite.

Dream Mechanisms

Although Jung maintained that "the dream follows no clearly determined laws or regular modes of behaviour" (CW8, par. 535), he acknowledged that there are mechanisms that help to form the dream language. However, he placed much less emphasis on them than did Freud, who saw the mechanisms as essential to the dream work through which the latent dream content is translated into the manifest dream. To Freud, the mechanisms were four in number: censorship, condensation, displacement, and distortion. Jung's list included six: contamination, condensation, doubling or multiplication, concretizing, dramatizing, and archaic mechanisms. (These mechanisms are described, solely and only briefly, in MPI-II, pp. 203–204, but mentions of them are scattered through the *Collected Works*.)

Contamination is the relating of apparent unconnected objects and ideas to each other by a chain of associations that operates when the limitations of consciousness are relaxed in sleep. Jung gave the example of starting with a table. "A cloth, for instance, has a direct relation to it, but it seems a far cry from a table to Julius Caesar; the sequence, however, leads us there quickly if we know it" (MPI-II, p. 203). Sometimes contamination reveals that the members of a pair of opposites are in some sense identical, as are some opposites in various languages. In Latin, for example, "altus" means both "high" and "deep"; in English, "scan" means "to examine closely" and "to look over hastily."

Condensation is a stronger form of contamination; it not only connects but combines apparently unrelated objects and ideas. Through condensation, otherwise neutral images can assume powerful emotional significance in a dream. A woman who is familiar to a dreamer because she passes his house every day, but otherwise is unknown to him, might appear in a dream wearing some clothing of the dreamer's sister. Thus, the image of the stranger in the street is condensed with that of the sister. The interpretation, then, would be based on the dreamer's associations to both his sister and the stranger.

Doubling, or *multiplication*, is the reverse of condensation. The same image may be repeated or may occur in double form (e.g., twins) for emphasis, or perhaps to indicate the partially completed emergence of a content from the unconscious; and identical images may reflect duality, such as the opposition of positive and negative. Similar images may show different aspects of the same problem; for example, two persons of the same sex and age but with different faces and clothing. An extension of multiplication is the occurrence of several episodes in one dream. Jung did not discuss this phenomenon but a Jungian analyst (Edinger, 1972) stated that "when a dream has several scenes they can usually be best understood as varying ways to describe the same central idea" (p. 23).

Concretizing is the use of figurative language, including the presentation of complexes in personified form.

Dramatizing is the expression of a content in story form.[5]

Archaic mechanisms translate unconscious contents into archetypal forms (see Ch. 6).

How Do We Know that Dreams Have Meaning?

The most important question relating to the nature of dreams may be whether dreams are meaningful. Illustrating the meaningfulness of dreams is easy; demonstrating that all dreams have meaning is difficult and perhaps impossible. However, Jung brought considerable evidence to bear on this question.

For centuries dreams were regarded as the voices of gods. For example, both Old and New Testaments report numerous "visions of the night," in many of which God spoke to a human. (For a full discussion, see Kelsey, 1968.) Although late twentieth century people are less likely to describe such dreams as of divine origin, the assumption is common that dreams have meaning,[6] albeit in varying ways. Perhaps most common among Western peoples is the belief that a dream may foretell a concrete event.

The Senoi people of the Malay Peninsula discuss their dreams daily, on the assumption that "everything that appears in dreams is filled up with your own spirit or force, and that you must control your own psychological resources or they will hurt you or your associates" (Stewart, 1954, p. 392).[7] Other preliterate[8] tribes take dreams so literally that a person may apologize for injuring a neighbor in a dream.

The high value that preliterate people place on dreams may be justified, as Jung pointed out, by the fact that they live very close to danger. If a man wakens in a nervous state, for example, he may slip later while crossing a river on a tree trunk and drown or be eaten by a crocodile. He knows that his "life depends on being at one with himself" (MPI-II, p. 159); consequently, if his dreams are unfavorable, he refuses to do anything that day. The existence of such a belief in the meaningfulness of dreams, moreover, gives them a certain efficacy.

A spontaneous assumption that dreams have meaning is reflected by the persons in therapy who tell their dreams without being asked. Jung found that people who came to him often had begun to write down their dreams long beforehand. This behavior could be attributed to the influence of Freud and Jung on popular cultural assumptions, but the positive response of an individual to such an assumption depends, according to Jung, on an inner readiness for it. (Some patients find dreams meaningful only after some striking experiences with their own dreams, and some never do.) The increasing popularity of books on dreams reflects further the widespread belief in the meaning of dreams.

Jung's conviction that dreams are meaningful was rooted in his premise that much significant mental content is unconscious. "Without [the unconscious], the dream is a mere freak of nature, a meaningless conglomeration of fragments left over from the day" (CW16, par. 294).

Many dreams, of course, are not readily comprehensible to the person attempting to interpret them. Jung argued that the problem is similar to that of any scientist engaged in the work of investigating natural phenomena: one must assume that a phenomenon under investigation has meaning before one can attempt to comprehend the facts. This assumption is supported by clinical experience. In analyzing tens of thousands of dreams, Jung found that some message can be gleaned from nearly every dream, and often the message is more significant than would be anticipated from a superficial appraisal. A dream that at first appears to be silly, absurd, or just unintelligible leads, sometimes, to important revelations about the dreamer.

In addition to clinical experience, other supports can be cited for the notion that dreams have meaning. One is the presence of repeated motifs in a dreamer's series of dreams; the repetition gives the impression that the motifs, whether in familiar or unfamiliar images, are demanding attention to something specific in the dreamer's life. Another possible basis is the discovery, discussed earlier in this chapter, that dreams cannot be influenced to any considerable extent by autosuggestion, and can be influenced only to a limited degree by external suggestion, even posthypnosis.

More than an impression of the meaningfulness of dreams is found in many persons' experiences of solving intellectual problems in dreams. Historical examples are numerous of scientific and intellectual leaders in various fields who had such an experience once or, in some instances, many times: the philosopher and mathematician René Descartes; the Danish scientist Niels

Bohr (discoverer of the type of atom that bears his name); Friedrich August Kekulé, the German chemist who discovered the formula for benzene and revolutionized organic chemistry; and Robert Louis Stevenson, to whom the plot of Dr. Jekyll and Mr. Hyde was revealed in a dream after years of searching for a story that would describe his strong sense of man's double being. Jung added some experiences of "ordinary" people to these examples, such as those of an accountant who had tried unsuccessfully for several days to untangle a fraudulent bankruptcy.[9] Retiring after working until midnight on the case, he got up during the night, made notes at his desk, and returned to bed. In the morning he did not remember his nocturnal behavior but he discovered on his desk, in his handwriting, a series of notes that solved the situation (CW8, par. 299).

Sometimes, a dream that is not understood at the time it occurs proves to be the preparation for a subsequent event. A few weeks before the sudden death of her husband, a woman dreamed that *she was looking at him, and saw his face change until it looked very similar to her father's. She was horrified* (MAM Files). Since her father had died suddenly a few months earlier, the dream seems to have been an expression of the unconscious "intended" to prepare her for the second shock, and it reflected an unconscious knowledge of the seeds of death already present in her husband's body.[10]

Further evidence for the meaningfulness of dreams can be seen in Jung's perception that uninterpreted "dreams can be 'understood' to a certain extent in a subliminal way" (CW18, par. 476). For example, a dream can have a profound positive or negative effect on the dreamer's waking mood. Jung cited the example of a patient who dreamed of *a lame sheep and a pregnant lamb, both of which were in danger of dying* (D3). After the dream, the patient felt a great weariness, as if in response to the condition of the lamb and the sheep.[11]

The meaning of dreams can be demonstrated even more dramatically when the unconscious expresses itself in a physical way after a dream's message is ignored. The self-destruction of Jung's mountain-climber acquaintance, who dreamed that *he stepped out into empty air* (D1) and then literally did so, is an example.

Of all the reasons and evidence for the meaningfulness of dreams, perhaps the most convincing are the data that verify specific dream interpretations (see Ch. 16).

The search for meaning in dreams is rooted, no doubt, in the wonderment of human beings at the workings of the mind. The mind continues to function in some form during sleep, as evidenced by the findings that when sleepers are awakened, whether during REM or NREM sleep, they nearly always report that something has been going on in their minds. With our present limited knowledge of the mind and its functioning, it is certainly premature to discard its activities during sleep as meaningless. Rather, the probability of our gaining further knowledge of the mind by the study of dreams and dreaming seems very high.

A possible challenge to the premise that dreams are meaningful is in the selection of dreams that are remembered. Studies by Domhoff and Kamiya (1964) and Hall and Van de Castle (1966b; cited in Domhoff, 1969), for example, show that dreams remembered in the morning—"home dreams"—are different from those garnered via awakenings in the dream laboratory. Home dreams tend to contain more emotional themes, such as aggression, sexual interactions, and misfortunes. A difference was found by Domhoff (1962; cited in Domhoff, 1969) and Schonbar (1961) between the dreams of "poor" and "good" recallers; the dreams of the "poor recallers" were more emotionally neutral than those of the good recallers. Yet, not remembering some dreams does not invalidate the significance of those that are remembered; it may be that we are incapable of remembering all our dreams or that we remember only those dreams that occur under certain conditions, such as at certain times in the sleep cycle.

Notes

[1] Jung sometimes referred to the dreams themselves as "conscious contents" (CW8, par. 443), apparently in recognition of the fact that the dreamer could not be aware of them if they were still totally unconscious. It is necessary, however, to distinguish them from mental contents that ordinarily are considered conscious. (The latter cannot be called "waking contents" because waking fantasies and visions are considered to be unconscious contents.)

[2] Designated by Freud as "primary process" thinking.

[3] Dreams also share with psychotic content their basis in an "abaissement du niveau mental" (lowering of consciousness) (Janet, 1903; cited by Jung, CW3, par. 12n.)

[4] Jung wrote also,

> The question of colours or rather absence of colours in dreams, depends on the relations between consciousness and the unconscious. In a situation where an approximation of the unconscious to consciousness is desirable, or vice versa, the unconscious acquires a special tone, which can express itself in the colourfulness of its images (dreams, visions, etc.) or in other impressive qualities (beauty, depth, intensity).
>
> If on the other hand the attitude of consciousness to the unconscious is more or less neutral, or apprehensive, there is no marked need for the two to make contact, and the dreams remain colourless. (Let-2, pp. 299–300)

The hypotheses in the foregoing statement seem far too complex for testing at present, even clinically.

[5] Jung actually included as concretizing the expression of the unconscious

in stories, and defined dramatizing as "a mechanism which dramatises everything that happens" (MPI-II, p. 204). Because Jung presented these comments orally, I assume that he spoke loosely and I modify his definitions accordingly.

[6] Empirically, there is some correlation between this assumption and certain kinds of pathology. The Minnesota Multiphasic Personality Inventory (nd) scores on the "Mania" scale a *yes* response to the statement, "A person should try to understand his dreams and be guided or take warning from them."

[7] The Senoi method of dream interpretation is similar to Jung's subjective and constructive approaches (see Chs. 10 and 11).

[8] Anthropologists say that there is no adequate term for the peoples Jung referred to as "primitive." To him, the term was not deprecatory but a psychological as well as anthropological description, meaning human nature uncontaminated by cultural errors and repression. Nevertheless, I am following the practice of many anthropologists in using the term "preliterate."

[9] In a bankruptcy case, the attorney for the person petitioning for bankruptcy must present to the court a financial statement to prove that there is no fraud. Accountants prepare and examine the statement.

[10] An alternative interpretation is the dreamer's fear of being "abandoned" by her husband as she had been by her father's death. This interpretation is unlikely to be valid, however, since no evidence—conscious or unconscious—arose to indicate that she felt abandoned by her father. She had had hostile feelings toward him most of her life and felt more relieved than grieved by his death.

[11] One could take the view that the mood produced the dream, rather than vice versa. It may be that both the mood and the dream images were rooted in the same unconscious contents.

Chapter 4

THE JUNGIAN APPROACH TO DREAM INTERPRETATION: AN OVERVIEW

Dream interpretation is as difficult as it is rewarding. Jung considered it an art, like diagnosis, surgery, and therapeutics in general, which can be learned "by those whose gift and destiny it is" (CW17, par. 198). From this statement, it would appear that Jung believed that the role of a Jungian analyst could be filled only by those persons who are peculiarly gifted, presumably in intuition and mental imagery.[1] However, in another work Jung wrote, "No sixth sense is needed to understand dreams" (CW8, par. 543). Although intuition and mental imagery are valuable in the work of a Jungian analyst, persons with varying degrees of the two traits and widely differing talents have become effective analysts and successful dream interpreters. As in any psychotherapeutic practice, the particular personal gifts or qualities that are required for Jungian analysts would seem to be integrity, compassion, and courage, in addition to intelligence.

How a Jungian Learns to Analyze Dreams

The interpretation of dreams is a very important part of the training of Jungian analysts, and especially at the C. G. Jung Institute in Zurich,

Switzerland. (Other Jungian training centers are in England, France, Germany, Israel, Italy, and the United States; e.g., Los Angeles, New York City, and San Francisco. Some centers emphasize dream interpretation less than the Zurich Institute.) Dreams are analyzed in nearly all therapy sessions, both in the trainee's personal analysis, and in work with patients. The work on dreams in personal analysis helps the trainee to gain self-understanding, which is essential because "No one who does not know himself can know others" (CW10, par. 325). This work is incidentally helpful, also, in learning to interpret the dreams of others and, along with the dream analysis integral to case discussions, provides the trainee with a great deal of valuable experience in the interpretation of dreams.

My exposure to dream interpretation began with a New York analyst four years before I enrolled in the Institute in Zurich, and the analysis and interpretation of dreams were a major study during the four-and-one-half years I was in the training program. (The minimum time required for training is three years.) Of the analysts with whom I underwent analysis, three (two in New York and one in Zurich) had had part or all of their analyses with Dr. Jung; the fourth had had his analytic training with some of Jung's students who had become senior analysts at the Zurich Institute.

Following Jung's tutelage, most Jungian analysts encourage analysands to record their dreams. (See Faraday, 1974, and Garfield, 1974, for details on keeping a dream diary.) In addition to the dreams themselves, the dreamer records the personal associations to each dream, whatever archetypal amplifications become available (most of them from the analyst's knowledge), and, after the analytic sessions, whatever interpretations have been developed. Some Jungian analysts work best by listening to oral accounts of dreams; others ask their analysands to provide written reports of their dreams and personal associations. (It is important in either case for the dreamer to keep a written record of all remembered dreams.) I prefer to see as well as hear the dream text.

As a trainee at the Institute, I recorded many more dreams than could be discussed in analytic sessions. Since I gathered amplifications for all my recorded dreams, I amassed even more experience in amplification than in interpretation. About half-way through my Zurich analysis, I began to attempt to interpret my own dreams. Although many of these interpretations were not subjected to my analyst's scrutiny, they all added to my experience. (At that time, the Institute required 300 hours of personal analysis; I had many more. The usual frequency of sessions was two per week.)

The systematic training specific to dream interpretation was provided along with the Institute's offerings in psychological theory, approaches to psychotherapy, and underlying areas of knowledge. This general background was built up through courses and independent preparation for the

Propadeuticum, a set of eight oral examinations in areas of knowledge important in the work of a Jungian analyst. A trainee sat for these examinations after a minimum of a year and a half at the Institute. The subjects least specifically relating to dream interpretation were, "Basic Principles of Analytical Psychology," "Theory and Technique of the Association Experiment and Theory of Complexes," "Comparative Theories of Neurosis," and "Basic Principles of Psychiatry, with Special Regard to Psychopathology."

The *Propadeuticum* also included examinations in "The History of Religions" (including mythology), "Primitive Practices," and "The Psychology of Fairy Tales," all of which are useful for amplifying archetypal material. The remaining propadeutical examination, "The Theory of Dream Interpretation," required the candidate to demonstrate understanding of the various procedures which are discussed in this book.

Both before and after the *Propadeuticum*, I attended lectures dealing with the amplification and interpretation of myths and fairy tales, and I participated in seminars on dream interpretation itself and on the analysis and interpretation of dreams which were presented as parts of case studies. Some of the seminars were led by Zurich analysts; others, by visiting analysts from the United States, England, and other countries. In additional seminars, trainees presented psychological interpretations of fairy tales as practice in the amplification and interpretation of archetypal material in its purest form.

After successful completion of the *Propadeuticum*, trainees began their work with patients. Thus, with the help of my supervising analysts,[2] I worked with my analysands on their dreams and, in case conferences with other trainees, led by a training analyst, I participated in the interpretation of analysands' dreams presented by all the trainees.

The final examinations at the Institute contributed to, as well as tested, one's capability in interpreting dreams by requiring two actual interpretations, one of a dream and one of a fairy tale. In addition, examinations were given in "The Individuation Process and Its Symbols" and "Practical Application of Knowledge to an Individual Case"; both required that considerable attention be given to dream images. Thus the training program at the Zurich Institute qualified graduates to use the interpretation of dreams as a major tool in psychotherapy. (The remaining final examinations covered "Psychiatry, with Special Regard to Differential Diagnosis," "Interpretation of Pictures from the Unconscious," and "Discussion of the Diploma Thesis." My thesis was entitled, *The Christian Concept of Sin as an Approach to the Shadow*.)

Since establishing my analytic practice in 1965, I have continued my systematic studies in dream interpretation through intensive work with my analysands on their dreams, wide reading among dream theorists of many psychological schools, formal study of personality psychology at the

University of Minnesota, and preparation of my doctoral dissertation (Mattoon, 1970), which was the first draft of this book. Although I was a qualified psychotherapist upon graduation from the Zurich Institute, I undertook the doctoral program in the research-oriented field of Personality Psychology (not in the practice-oriented field of Clinical Psychology) to give me a broad base in the world of non-Jungian psychology, and to qualify for certification and, later, licensing as a Consulting Psychologist by the State of Minnesota.[3]

Steps in Interpreting A Dream

The Jungian method of dream interpretation, which is presented in detail in the following chapters, is used, with variations, by virtually all Jungian analysts. The variations occur primarily in the part of the procedure that is emphasized. For example, one analyst will rely more on an intuitive impression of the dream's meaning; another, on gathering detailed amplifications. Always, however, the conditions of the immediate therapeutic situation determine the completeness of the procedure and of each interpretation.

The major steps in the Jungian approach to dream interpretation are as follows:

1. State the dream text in terms of *structure*;[4] examine for completeness.
2. Establish the *dream context*, the situational material in which the dream is embedded. The context is composed of:
   a. *Amplifications* of the dream images, which may include
      (1) *Personal associations*,
      (2) *Information from the dreamer's environment*, and/or
      (3) *Archetypal parallels*;
   b. *Themes interconnecting* the amplifications, and
   c. The immediate and long-term *conscious situation* of the dreamer;
   d. The dream *series* in which the dream occurs.
3. Review the appropriate attitudes to bring to dream interpretation:
   a. Nothing can be assumed regarding the meaning of the dream or of specific images.
   b. The dream is not a disguise but a set of psychic facts.
   c. The dream probably does not tell the dreamer what to do.
   d. Awareness of the personality characteristics of the dreamer and the interpreter.
4. Characterize the dream images as *objective* or *subjective*.
5. Consider the dream's *compensatory* function.
   a. Identify the problem or complex with which the dream is concerned.
   b. Ascertain the relevant conscious situation of the dreamer.

    c. Consider whether the dream images and the psychic development of the dreamer require a *reductive* or *constructive* characterization.

    d. Consider whether the dream compensates by opposing, modifying, or confirming the relevant conscious situation; or

    e. Whether the dream is non-compensatory: *prospective, traumatic, telepathic*, or *prophetic*.

  6. Hypothesize an interpretation by translating the dream language in relation to the relevant conscious situation of the dreamer, test it against the dream facts, modify where necessary, and state the interpretation briefly.

  7. Verify the interpretation.

Variations in Approach

Like other Jungian analysts, I attempt to observe all the steps in the outlined procedure of dream interpretation. In some ways, however, my approach to the process is rather different from that of some of my colleagues because of differences in temperament or differing conceptions of the theory.

In my view, dreams are a highly accessible source of unconscious material and, thus, dream interpretation is a basic tool in the analysis and treatment of patients. Nevertheless, there are other sources of information from the unconscious: emotions, overt behavior, bodily symptoms, the various forms of active imagination, and waking fantasies. (All of these sources can reflect the phenomenon of transference, which is considered by most Freudian and some Jungian analysts to be central to the analytic process.) Like all Jungians, I consider analysis to be a unique process through which the conscious and unconscious contents can be brought together and reconciled. Some Jungians seem to see dreams as pre-eminent in producing the desired synthesis. For me, the various sources of unconscious material contribute in varying proportions for different patients. Diversity in concept of the role of the dream and its interpreter, in my view, do not produce irreconcilable differences in the concept of the analytic process.

I am also at variance with some of my colleagues in the way I develop a hypothesis about the dream's meaning. Like Jung, many Jungians depend heavily on intuition for such hypotheses. Jung made little mention of his use of intuition in dream interpretation, probably because it came so naturally to him.[5] Intuition also appears to come naturally to the approximately 85% of Jungian analysts for whom intuition is the first or second function (Bradway, 1964; Bradway & Detloff, 1976; Plaut, 1972.) These analysts may have an intuitive idea about the dream's meaning soon after hearing it for the first time. Because I am of a different temperament (probably sensation-thinking), my hypotheses come to mind much later—usually after I have worked step-by-step through the dream context and the other procedures leading to interpretation. Whatever the timing of the interpretive hypothesis, a more or less systematic testing process is necessary to verify it.

A third difference is that I am more likely to assume initially that an image arises out of the dreamer's personal experience; only if no such basis can be found do I take the image as primarily archetypal. To be sure, a seemingly highly individual experience, such as falling in love, can have archetypal proportions; nevertheless, the related dream images usually can be amplified from personal experience. Jung himself, I have concluded from my study of his works, sought out archetypal parallels as enrichment to, rather than a substitute for, the personal associations (see Ch. 6). Furthermore, after the images have been amplified, the dream still must be interpreted in relation to the dreamer's conscious situation, that is, to current life experience. The archetypal nature of dream material may reveal the problem to be a general human one but it does not remove the material from the dreamer's individual life. Unless a dream interpreter moves only with great care into archetypal amplifications and non-personal interpretations, he or she may overlook dream messages that are crucial to the dreamer's life.

Notes

[1] Elsewhere, Jung stated more poetically, "[The richness of dreams] reveals itself, one might say, only to him who understands the language of animals and plants" (CW18, par. 1282).

[2] An experienced analyst who trains new analysts is known as a "training analyst," a "senior analyst" and a "supervising analyst."

[3] Minnesota licenses a person with a Ph.D. in psychology and certain other qualifications as a "Consulting Psychologist." An M.A. in psychology is necessary for licensing as a "Psychologist."

[4] In presenting this overview of the Jungian approach to dream interpretation, I have found it necessary to use terms which are explained in subsequent chapters. In order to make the overview useful to the reader, therefore, all terms defined in later chapters are in italics. The reader can use this chapter as an outline, and refer back and forth. The subsequent chapters in this book take up the topics which are listed here and others, each in as much detail as possible.

[5] Jung seemed to experience a large range of degrees of difficulty in dream interpretation: "In very many cases a single glance at the dream and the assembled material suffices to give us at least an intuition of its meaning, and no special effort of thought is needed to interpret it. In other cases it requires much labour and considerable experience" (CW17, par. 115).

Chapter 5

THE DREAM CONTEXT: INDIVIDUAL AMPLIFICATIONS[1]

The dream context includes individual and archetypal amplifications, themes interconnecting the amplifications, information about the dreamer's conscious situation, and the dream series. Before the context can be considered, however, the dreamer must ascertain the dream text, that is, the actual images dreamed.

Identifying the Dream

Sometimes the dreamer has no difficulty in recounting a perception of the dream. At other times, he or she doubts that all the material reported is actually part of the dream text or is under the impression that only a portion is remembered.

Two kinds of material may contaminate the dream text. The first, supplemental waking or half-waking images which are relevant to the dream,[2] intrude upon the dream as it reaches the dreamer's consciousness. Although Jung recognized the possibility that such images can change a dream substantially, he considered the additions in general to be part of the dream material because, like the basic dream, they arise from the unconscious.

The second kind of material that sometimes is added to the dream is introduced later as the dreamer rehearses the dream and, especially, in telling it to another person. Some dreamers tend to elaborate on the images and sequence of events they remember. For example, they may weave in waking experiences or images from other dreams. The interpreter then cannot be sure which segments of the material were experienced while the dreamer slept, and which were added subsequently. In my experience, this conscious contamination can be avoided almost entirely if the dreamer, upon awakening, writes the dream.[3] If any confusion remains regarding a statement or a description of an image, it usually can be dispelled by asking the dreamer whether the questioned detail was actually dreamed or added later. With a little practice, nearly all dreamers can answer this query.

By contrast, some dreamers have difficulty recounting their dream experiences and, hence, bring fragmentary dream texts. The interpreter can help them to give more complete accounts by asking what happened next, or by requesting clarification of elements which are vague or mentioned only in passing. The dreamer, when asked, often can remember more details than were given in the original account. It may be fruitful, also, to ask for specific aspects of the dream which seem to be missing or incomplete, such as the setting of the dream or the identity of a figure. The questions, of course, should be phrased in words that are comprehensible to the dreamer; for example, "Where did the dream seem to occur?" communicates more clearly than, "What was the dream setting?"[4]

Sometimes the vagueness of a dream is reflected in the statement that the dreamer "thinks" an image was thus and so. In such instances, Jung advised assuming that the report is correct. If the dreamer offers two or more accounts of a dream image, and is uncertain which is correct, the interpretation should take all of them into account. For example, if the dreamer remembers an image as either a dog or a cat, associations to both are needed, and the apparent meaning of each animal should be tested in the hypothesized interpretation.

Jung advised asking how the dreamer feels about the dream and its individual images. Because the dreamer's feeling after waking may be different from the feeling experienced during the dream, I find it useful to ask for both reactions. Many dreamers neglect to specify these feelings along with the dream text.

It is a common occurrence for a dreamer to report that the text that was written down is only a part of a much longer dream, the rest of which has been forgotten. Some dreamers are bothered enough to call even a 300-word dream text a "dream fragment." Since psychophysiological studies show that dreaming sleep occupies about one-fifth of sleep time, it is probable that only a small fraction of the dream material is remembered by any dreamer. For purposes of interpretation, however, I see no alternative but to work with the available material. As the dreamer gains experience in recording dreams, the accounts tend toward more completeness.

In this book, I sometimes recount dreams in different words at different times, especially when they are given in abbreviated form. This practice does not seem to me to carry much risk of inaccuracy because the words merely describe the images that formed the dream experienced by the dreamer, and more than one set of words can describe the same image.

The Structure of Dreams

Although the forms of dreams can range from single images to long, detailed narratives, many dreams have a story-like nature, which was characterized by Jung as a "drama taking place on one's own interior stage" (Let-1, p. 355). The drama is presented, in general, through a structure[5] common to many dreams, with varying degree of completeness. Many dream texts have so few of the necessary elements that they must be considered fragments, or more like still photographs than motion pictures. Nevertheless, the structure of a great many dreams is fairly complete and can be divided into component parts that enhance understanding of the "plot" development and the dream's emphasis, and expedite identification of the missing content.

The first part of the dream account is the *exposition*. It usually includes a *statement of place* or setting (*"I was on parade"*), a statement about the *protagonists* or dramatis personae, and the *initial situation* of the dreamer (*"with a number of young officers and our commander-in-chief was inspecting us"*). A statement of *time* may be included, such as time of day or season of the year.

The second phase gives the *development* of the plot (*"Eventually he came to me, but instead of asking a technical question he demanded a definition of the beautiful"*). The third phase is the *culmination* or *peripeteia*, in which something decisive happens, or a marked change occurs, either favorable or unfavorable. (*"I tried in vain to find a satisfactory answer and felt most dreadfully ashamed when he passed on to the next man, a very young major, and asked him the same question"*). Then comes the fourth phase, the *lysis*, which is the solution or result (*"This fellow came out with a damned good answer, just the one I would have given if only I could have found it"*). (Description of structure: CW8, pars. 561-564; CD38, p. 27; DA1, p. 177. Dream text: CW17, par. 187).

Amplification

A dream cannot be interpreted from its text alone, however; its symbolism must be translated, like an unknown language (see Ch. 9), by means of the context. In order to make such a translation, each image must be "amplified," because "a dream is too slender a hint to be understood until it is enriched by the stuff of association and analogy and thus amplified to the point of intelligiblity" (CW12, par. 403).

Although some dream images are relatively fixed and amplified by arche-typal parallels (see Ch. 6), most are idiosyncratic to the dreamer and must be amplified by personal experiences, facts regarding the environment, and other dreams of the dreamer. Whatever their sources, all of the amplifications to a particular image are used to enlarge the store of information about the image.

The dreamer supplies most of the information regarding experiences and dreams not discussed in therapy sessions, while the interpreter has approxi-mately equal access to information from the environment, and from other dreams that have been considered in therapy. The interpreter, especially one who has been trained as a Jungian analyst, can be expected to have greater knowledge of myths, cultural and religious customs, and historical events. Through the analytic sessions, also, the interpreter becomes sufficiently familiar with the dreamer's experiences to contribute occasionally to the personal associations.

Personal Associations

The importance of personal associations for Jung was reflected in his insistence on "making sure that every shade of meaning which each salient feature of the dream has for the dreamer is determined by the associations of the dreamer himself" (CW8, par. 542). Jung's method of gathering the dreamer's personal associations, moreover, is integral to his conviction that the dream is not a disguise but means what it says (see Ch. 9). As a help in understanding what Jung meant, it is useful to trace the change in his thinking regarding the appropriate method of associating to the dream elements.

During most of the period of his friendship with Freud, Jung followed the older man's method of free association to dream elements. Free association yields associations to the dream elements and then, successively, associations to the associations. But this method, Jung found, leads only to the identifica-tion of the dreamer's complexes which may or may not have been suggested in the original dream images.[6] (Fritz Perls called this process "free dissocia-tion" [Faraday, 1972, p. 146] .) In one of his last works, Jung recounted the cognitions that led him to abandon free association as a tool in dream interpretation.[7]

> . . . A friend and colleague of mine, travelling for long hours on a train journey through Russia, passed the time by trying to decipher

the Cyrillic script of the railway notices in his compartment. He fell into a sort of reverie about what the letters might mean and—following the principle of "free association"—what they reminded him of, and soon he found himself in the midst of all sorts of reminiscences. Among them, to his great displeasure, he [discovered] those old and disagreeable companions of sleepless nights, his "complexes"—repressed and carefully avoided topics which the doctor would joyously point to as the most likely causes of a neurosis or the most convincing meaning of a dream.

There was no dream, however, merely "free associations" to incomprehensible letters, which means that from any point of the compass you can reach the centre directly. Through free association you arrive at the critical secret thoughts, no matter where you start from, be it symptoms, dreams, fantasies, Cyrillic letters or examples of modern art. At all events, this fact proves nothing with regard to dreams and their real meaning. It only shows the existence of associable material floating about. (CW18, pars. 424–425)

From these and other comments, we can discern that Jung had several objections to Freud's method of free association. First, it does not take advantage of the unique contribution of dreams to gaining information from the unconscious; while free association to dreams is likely to lead to one or more complexes, it has no advantage over free association to any other mental content or external stimulus in identifying complexes. Second, free association to a dream can lead to a complex that may or may not be the one with which the dream is concerned; or it may lead to several, without designating the relevant one. Third, and probably most important, free association does not reveal what the dream says about the complex(es) to which it leads, and the dream's message may be lost completely.

Although Jung rejected free association, he elicited contents beyond those immediate (direct) to the dream images. I designate these further associations as "elaborations" of the direct associations. Sometimes, the dreamer elaborates these associations spontaneously. If this is not done, the interpreter often must ask for elaborations in order to have enough information to hypothesize a meaning for the dream image under consideration.

An example of an elaboration that often must be requested is one associating the age of a child, for example, a four-year-old, to the image in a dream. Elaborations of this association include facts regarding the period of the dreamer's life about four years before the dream, and the dreamer's memories of experiences at the age of four.

Direct associations accompanied by spontaneously offered elaborations are found in the amplifications to a dream Jung cited:

"I was standing in a strange garden and picked an apple from a tree. I looked about cautiously, to make sure that no one saw me" (D4).

To the image of *picking an apple from a tree*, the dreamer associated the scene in the Garden of Eden[8] and a boyhood memory of plucking some pears from a neighbor's garden. The dreamer offered also elaborations: He "had never really understood why the eating of the forbidden fruit should have had such dire consequences for our first parents . . . . Another [elaboration] was that sometimes his father had punished him for certain things in a way that seemed to him incomprehensible. The worst punishment had been bestowed on him after he was caught secretly watching girls bathing" (CW8, pars. 458–45.).

Although the memory of watching the girls bathing is several steps removed from the dream image of picking the apple, the last elaboration is related directly to the dream image. True free association would go farther afield: the name of one of the girls the dreamer had seen, news the dreamer had heard of her moving to another city, an experience he had in that city, and so on. Thus the last association is not related directly to the dream image. In Jung's method, associating to the images and elaborating the associations should continue until the meaning of each element in the dream can be determined, but the interpreter must restrain the dreamer from leaving the dream text and elaborating associations beyond those that are necessary to understand the dream image.

A helpful way to understand Jung's method of direct association and to distinguish it from free association is the notion of circumambulating the image (which applies also to other kinds of Jungian amplification). Free association leads by "zig-zag" lines (CW18, par. 434) away from the dream image; circumambulation makes possible looking at the image from all sides, and describes a metaphorical circle, the content of which suggests the meaning of that image. In the case of a human figure, for example, the relevant associations would include the dreamer's perception of it as a male or female, its name, occupation, interests and personality characteristics, the role it plays in the dreamer's life, and any of the dreamer's specific experiences in which the figure has played a part. Elaborations might include like-named figures in the dreamer's life, attitudes toward any of the facts or perceived characteristics associated to the figure, and the significance to the dreamer of the recounted experiences.

A comparison of interpretations of dreams on the basis of free association with interpretations on the basis of direct association might be a valuable empirical study to test the hypothesis that the two interpretations of the same dream would differ markedly.

The significance of the dreamer's personal associations is accentuated by the idiosyncratic nature of dream elements.

> If, for instance, someone dreams of a table, we are still far from knowing what the 'table' of the dreamer signifies, although the word

'table' sounds unambiguous enough. For the thing we do not know is that this 'table' is the very one at which [the dreamer's] father sat when he refused the dreamer all further financial help and threw him out of the house as a good-for-nothing. (CW8, par. 539)

It is essential that the dreamer give associations only to the images as they actually appear in the dream. Jung warned, "When somebody dreams of a 'deal table,' it is not enough for him to associate it with his writing desk which does not happen to be made of deal" (CW16, par. 320). Instead, it is important for the dreamer to associate to a table specifically of deal.

Sometimes, however, the dreamer departs from direct associations to the dream, and persists in introducing "irrelevant" facts, thoughts, or feelings. (They differ from free associations in that the "irrelevancy" appears not to relate to the direct associations or to the dream. The links from the dream through a chain of free associations can be traced.) The analyst, whose first responsibility is therapy, and only secondarily dreams, must attend to the "irrelevant" material, even though it seems unrelated to the dream, because, as a result, the patient may be enabled to arrive more quickly at recognition of a problem area. Later, a connection to the dream may be found. Often, for example, the "irrelevant" material identifies the conscious situation on which the dream is commenting.

Many dreamers find it difficult to associate to dream images. The kinds of difficulties seem to vary in part according to the dreamer's emotional and intellectual temperament. Some dreamers, Jung found, tend to give theory-based explanations,[9] such as that a long, cylindrical object is a phallus. Others frequently give "coincidents or coexistences" (DA1, p. 120),[10] which are associations naming items that may occur with the dream elements. For example, to a particular wall, some dreamers might associate the chair that stands near it.

Still other dreamers, in my experience, are likely to overgeneralize. One dreamer, for instance, found it hard to say anything about a person whose image appeared in a dream other than that he was "nice." (It is my impression that she was overwhelmed with the complexity of people and, therefore, could not describe a personality to her satisfaction.)

Virtually all dreamers, however, can learn to associate to dream images in a way that is helpful to the interpretive process.[11] Jung suggested an approach that I have found helpful with dreamers who give theory-based explanations: Using the example of the deal table as the dream image, he recommended saying to the dreamer, "Suppose I had no idea what the words 'deal table' mean. Describe this object and give me its history in such a way that I cannot fail to understand what sort of a thing it is" (CW16, par. 320). Another approach I have found productive in eliciting associations to human figures in dreams is to ask the dreamer to tell some experiences with the dream figure. Every dream interpreter who uses Jungian-type direct associations no doubt finds ways to release the flow of associations from the dreamer. Ingenuity, not a set of rules, is needed to elicit from different dreamers associations to a seemingly infinite variety of images.

In addition to the problems of temperament, there are other difficulties for some dreamers in providing associations. Jung mentioned the possibilities of the dreamer's being "baffled," having "resistances," and "emotions prevent[ing] associations" (DA1, p. 82). That is, the dreamer may be too anxious or angry to be aware of the associations or to share them with the interpreter. These emotions may be aroused by the specific dream images, the complex on which the dream is commenting, the presence of the interpreter, or the associations themselves. Jung recommended that the interpreter respect the dreamer's resistances and not attempt to break them down. Thus, it may not be possible at a given time to interpret the particular dream around which the resistances have arisen. In such a case, it is possible that the dreamer will return to the dream later; or a subsequent dream referring to the same problem may be less threatening and, hence, possible for the dreamer to associate to. Then, the way would be opened to considering the problem reflected by both dreams.

Information from the Dreamer's Environment

Information beyond the personal associations of the dreamer is required for the amplification of some dreams. This information may affect the dreamer without being known to him or her, or it may be drawn from a store of generally available knowledge. Jung gave an example of information not consciously known to the dreamer prior to the dream: A young man developed a neurosis, one symptom of which was an inability to swallow, shortly after he became "happily engaged . . . to a girl of 'good' family. In his dreams, *she frequently appeared in very unflattering guise.* The context showed that the dreamer's unconscious connected the figure of his bride with all kinds of scandalous stories from quite another source" (CW8, par. 542). Although the young man resisted the notion that his dreams were based on fact, he agreed to follow Jung's recommendation and initiate some inquiries. On doing so, he found that the dreams were reflecting aspects of the girl's reputation which the young man had not known. "The shock of the unpleasant discovery did not kill the patient but, on the contrary, cured him of his neurosis and also of his bride" (CW8, par. 542).[12]

Sometimes, information needed to amplify the dream has been known to the dreamer but forgotten by his conscious mind. One woman dreamed in July that *she visited her aunt, expecting the aunt to be pleased to see her, but found her curt and crabby. She did not invite the dreamer to sit down, and seemed to change into different people* (MAM Files). The dreamer had been unaccountably depressed for several days before the dream. In asking for associations to the aunt, the analyst, who knew the aunt was dead, asked when the death had occurred. The dreamer replied, "Oh, last fall sometime." The analyst's notes from previous sessions revealed that the death had occurred the previous July. The dreamer recalled that she had been sad after her aunt's death, but not as deeply as her feeling for her aunt warranted. The dream was interpreted as an explanation for her depression: She still had a need to realize and accept her grief, which was renewed around the anniversary of her aunt's death. The interpretation evoked some of the tears that had not been shed a year earlier. The information that had been "forgotten" by the dreamer was that the anniversary date was a few days after the dream.

Other information associated to dreams goes beyond the personal experience and knowledge of the dreamer. Some is found in the "store of general conscious knowledge" (CW18, par. 588). Jung used the hypothetical example of a dream in which the number 13 occurred. He wrote,

The question is: Does the dreamer habitually believe in the unfavorable nature of the number, or does the dream merely allude to people who still indulge in such superstitions? The answer will make a great difference to the interpretation. In the former case, the dreamer is still under the spell of the unlucky 13, and therefore will feel most uncomfortable in Room No. 13 or sitting at a table with thirteen people. In the latter case, 13 may not be more than a chiding or disparaging remark. In one case it is a still numinous representation; in the other it is stripped of its original emotionality. (CW18, par. 588)

Sometimes, a knowledge of the particular culture that has shaped the dreamer's thought patterns is a necessary amplification to a dream image. Jung cited one of his dreams in which an image concretized a colloquialism from a specific culture:

A certain Mr. X was desperately trying to get behind me and jump on my back. (CW18, par. 463)

The dream had translated the Austrian colloquialism, "Du kannst mir auf den Buckel steigen (you can climb on my back), [into a pictorial image that] means, 'I don't give a damn what you say' " (CW18, par. 463). The dream was a response to the man's twisting one of Jung's remarks into a travesty of its meaning.

Although the interpreter as well as the dreamer can contribute to the amplification of a dream, Jung recommended that the interpreter "check the flow of [his] own associations and reactions" (CW18, par. 483) in order not to interfere with those of the dreamer. Sometimes the interpreter can offer supplementary associations which are valid if they are based on knowledge that is common to a great many people, including the dreamer. A relevant instance would be a dream in which a well-known public figure appears, and the dreamer is not able to recall generally known facts about the figure. The interpreter can supplement the dreamer's associations, but should do so sparingly, and a little at a time.[13]

The interpreter also may offer a personal association which the dreamer could have made but which did not come to mind. For example, one day a male analysand reported a dream in which

> *A tall middle-aged woman comes up to me. She is somehow unhappy with me. I finally take the woman and spank her.* (MAM Files)

He recognized her as Mrs. E., a woman who had asked him for counseling help, and he associated her with a woman he had known under similar conditions in the past and whom he had felt like spanking. The interpreter remembered, and reminded the dreamer, of his statement a few weeks earlier, that Mrs. E. was a woman who complained of many problems, and that the day before the dream he had recited (like her) a long list of problems which were besetting him. Recognizing that the dream image of Mrs. E. represented his tendency to rehearse problems, the dreamer understood the dream as a message to take a firmer attitude toward this tendency, that is, to "spank" his inner figure that encouraged him to complain.

In both situations, general knowledge and information specific to the dreamer, the interpreter must not insist on an amplification that does not seem to the dreamer to be pertinent.

When to Amplify with Archetypal Parallels

When dreams have archetypal content, amplification includes parallels: similar images in similar background situations drawn from mythological and ethnological literature (see Ch. 6). Before archetypal parallels are considered, however, the interpreter must explore all possibilities for personal associations. If any are overlooked, the interpretation may be distorted or even wrong. For example, a middle-aged man dreamed that *he arrived at a very old butcher shop. A young man came in, asking for a hog which he was to cut up for someone, and needing directions for cutting it* (MAM Files). The interpreter thought of the hog (pig) as sacred to Demeter, a mother-goddess, but refrained from mentioning it until the personal associations had been gathered. The dreamer remembered having been attacked by hogs in the farmyard of his home when he was 4 or 5 years old. The personal association emphasized the remaining child-like fears, which could have been overlooked, distorting the interpretation, if only the mythological parallel had been considered. (The dream image of the young man preparing to cut up the pig suggested the solution: The hero part of the dreamer overcame, the threatening maternal part. The need for directions [presumably from the dream ego] for cutting the hog suggested that the ego must provide the thought [analyzing, that is, cutting] processes. The dreamer's fears made it necessary for him to discover his heroic side in order to accomplish the task posed by the dream.)

In other instances, archetypal amplification is more appropriate (see Ch. 6). A controversial example was Jung's dream in December 1913, that *he caused the death of Siegfried* (D5). At first he felt that if he did not understand the dream he must kill himself. But then he saw what he considered to be the true meaning of the dream:

> Siegfried . . . represents what the Germans want to achieve, heroically to impose their will, have their own way . . . . I had wanted to do the same. But now that was no longer possible. The dream showed that the attitude embodied by Siegfried, the hero, no longer suited me. Therefore it had to be killed . . . my heroic idealism had to be abandoned, for there are higher things than the ego's will, and to these one must bow. (MDR, pp. 180–181)

Nandor Fodor (1971) interpreted the dream otherwise:

> Siegfried was [Jung]. The father of Siegfried was Sigmund. He was then Sigmund's son. Freud had treated him like a son, and Siegfried was a play on Sig Freud. It was Freud whom he killed in the dream, a dramatization of his death wish and remorse at carrying out the unconscious aggression against the father of psychoanalysis who wanted to make him his Crownprinz and heir. In his megalomania he wanted to step into Freud's place without delay and owe him nothing. (p. 23)

This example demonstrates that there can be a marked difference in interpretation between that using the mythological parallel of the hero Siegfried and the personal association of the name of Freud.[14]

Therapeutic Value of Individual Amplifications

The individual amplifications alone can be therapeutic, sometimes even before an interpretation is attempted. Jung cited the dream of a female patient who was skeptical of dream analysis. Early in her treatment, she dreamed that

> She was in a hotel in a strange city. Suddenly a fire broke out. Her husband and her father, who were with her, helped her in the rescue work. (CW4, par. 537)

She associated the fire with the recent fire-destruction of a hotel in which she had had a rather frivolous love affair. From this association, the fact came out that she had had quite a number of casual sexual relationships. (This fact is an elaboration that borders on free association, the use of which carried over into Jung's early post-Freudian period; the dream was included in a 1913 lecture.) Jung pointed out her frivolous attitude, and the patient was able to begin to question some of her attitudes.

A full interpretation of the dream, in Jung's view, would have been likely to have less value because of her skepticism about dream analysis. He did not specify why he saw the situation that way, but one can imagine that a full interpretation might have pushed her to realize the intensity of her sexual problem, as suggested by the fire, and the importance of her husband and father in helping her to deal with it. Her resistance to so much psychic knowledge all at once might have delayed her accepting any of it.

My experience bears out the therapeutic value of amplifications, especially personal associations, in that they point to problem areas in the dreamer's life, which have not been faced. For example, a father might dream of a toy to which he associates his daughter. In mentioning the child, the dreamer focuses on her and may become aware of the inappropriate demands he has been making on her.

Themes Interconnecting the Amplifications

Although Jung specifically mentioned the interconnections among amplifications only in passing (e.g., CW16, par. 319), he used them as guides in ascertaining which amplifications are relevant, and in identifying the attitudes and events in the conscious situation of the dreamer which are linked emotionally to the complex or complexes on which the dream is commenting. Common factors or themes may be found in the amplifications to various elements. Such a common theme constitutes an interconnection, which provides a degree of objectivity in ascertaining the interpretive relevance of the multiple associations to each image. A man's dream, for instance, might depict three human figures: a young woman he once nearly married, a friend who is in the process of divorce, and the minister who performed the dreamer's wedding ceremony. Although he has other associations to all three figures, and there may be archetypal parallels, the common theme is marriage. In interpreting the dream, one would look for possible problems in his marriage and his attitude toward it.

Notes

[1] Although Jung often used the term "amplification" to mean only archetypal parallels, he illustrated the concept also with personal associations

(CW18, par. 174). I have chosen the broader usage as one that subsumes personal associations, information from the dreamer's environment, and archetypal parallels.

[2] These additions to the dream are similar to what Freud called "secondary elaborations."

[3] This discovery, surprising to me, was made when I searched my files for examples of contaminated dream texts written down by the dreamer, and found none. Additions seem to be made to the dream fairly often when it is told orally.

[4] Some dream interpreters insist that the dream be told in the present tense. I find this requirement to be based on an idiosyncratic view of dreams.

[5] Jung described the structure only once in the *Collected Works* (CW8, pars. 561-564) and twice, more briefly, in CD38, p. 27 and DA1, p. 177. He made very little use of structure in connection with other aspects of his theory. In one of his last works, however, he stated that "very often dreams have a very definite, as if purposeful, structure, indicating the underlying thought or intention though, as a rule, the latter is not immediately comprehensible" (CW18, par. 425). This statement was changed (evidently by someone other than Jung) in *Man and His Symbols* to the statement, "A story told by the conscious mind has a beginning, a development, and an end, but the same is not true of a dream" (MHS, p. 28).

[6] In a 1916 work, Jung went even further and stated that "the entire psychic content of a life could ultimately be disclosed from any single starting-point" (CW8, par. 454). The statement about identifying complexes seems more representative of his thinking, however.

[7] Although Jung rejected the concept of free association, he continued to use the term (CW17, par. 114) while he was clarifying his method of ascertaining the dream context.

[8] The Garden of Eden could be considered an archetypal amplification (see Ch. 6) but, in this instance, the interpretation would not be affected.

[9] Jung attributed theory-based "associations" to thinking types (DA1, p. 120).

[10] Jung attributed coincidence and coexistences to sensation and intuitive types (DA1, p. 120).

[11] In a seminar Jung stated, "If the rational type tries to have irrational associations they are always false, they do not fit, so I ask [them] to just tell me what [they] think about it" (DA1, p. 120). Since I find the generalization untrue, the advice unproductive, and both out of harmony with Jung's other statements on the matter, I omit them from the text.

[12] According to Barker (1972), the young man was a university student who was unable to study for his final examination; a private detective discovered that the fiancée was a prostitute. "The relief from the uncertainty set him free to work, and he passed his exam" (p. 25).

[13] In one essay, Jung included as associations analogies from "primitive psychology, mythology, archaeology, and comparative religion" (CW16, par. 96), but did not specify any way in which they could be used other than as archetypal parallels (see Ch. 6).

[14] Another possible view of the difference between Fodor's and Jung's interpretations of the dream is that interpretation by an objective person may be more reliable than the dreamer's idiosyncratic interpretation. It also may

display the difference between an intuitive interpretation and one based on the steps of the process, according to which personal associations are considered fully before archetypal amplifications are undertaken. Nevertheless, the "personal associations" are Fodor's, not the dreamer's, hence they cannot be assumed to be definitive.

Chapter 6

THE DREAM CONTEXT: ARCHETYPAL AMPLIFICATIONS

The basis for Jung's conception of archetypes is presented in Chapter 2. Here, the discussion is limited to materials that are useful for amplifying archetypal dreams and approaching their interpretation.

A purely archetypal dream is rare; hence, the use of the term "archetypal dreams" is somewhat misleading. Dreams containing archetypal content nearly always have some personal content also. "Archetypal images" and "archetypal motifs" are more accurate designations of the material to which Jung referred frequently in making use of transpersonal amplifications. Therefore, in practice, the term "archetypal dreams" means dreams that contain one or more archetypal images and, thus, require archetypal amplifications.

Unlike a non-archetypal dream, which usually focuses on the dreamer's immediate psychic situation, an archetypal dream may be concerned with the "fate" of the dreamer (MRI-II, p. 198).[1] The dream seems to come from a "different level" (CW17, par. 209) of the unconscious.[2] Even if the dream is not understood, it enriches the individual's experience; Jung described such dreams as "stand[ing] out for years like spiritual landmarks" (CW17, par. 208).

The feeling that archetypal dreams are highly significant may impel some dreamers to hide them as if the dreams were "precious secrets" (CW17, par. 208). Jung saw this behavior as appropriate because of the importance of the dreams to the dreamer's psychic balance.

Paradoxically, many people seem to have a strong impulse to tell their archetypal dreams, perhaps, initially, in order to assimilate the emotion experienced. The impulse to tell was considered by Jung to be as appropriate as the impulse to conceal, because these dreams have a general meaning; each reflects and compensates "an eternal human problem that repeats itself endlessly, and [is] not just a disturbance of personal balance" (CW8, par. 556). It brings the "problems posed by mythology . . . into connection with the psychic life of the individual" (CW11, par. 450). Mythology originates in the universal problems of mankind: the quest for food, mating, procreation, cultural initiation, parent-child relationships and responsibilities, the relation of the individual to the universe, and the fears of war, illness, death, and natural catastrophes. Thus, in contrast to an ordinary dream, which is valid only for a particular person at a particular time, the archetypal contents of a dream are significant to the lives of many people across a broad spectrum of time. Thus the sharing of an archetypal dream can be of help to people who are facing a problem similar to the dreamer's.

Recognizing Archetypal Material

Some Jungian analysts (e.g., G. Adler, 1961; Harding, 1965; Hillman, 1975; and Neumann, 1964) hypothesize that all products of the psyche spring from an archetypal base. They seem to mean that the potential for an image or a form of behavior must exist in a person before it can be manifested. Based on this premise, the root of all dream images indeed may be archetypal. However, this idea has little practical effect as it does not preclude personal amplification.[3] At the same time, amplification of archetypal images solely on a personal level is likely to result in incorrect interpretation, can lead to frustration and failure in therapy, and may retard the dreamer's psychological development. Thus the distinction between archetypal and personal amplifications has important consequences.

The dreams that Jung called "archetypal" are those that are known to preliterate peoples as "big dreams." The images, which can be grotesque, may include objects, figures, and experiences not encountered in ordinary life, such as dragons, strange masks, helpful animals, hidden treasure, gods and demons, and alchemical processes. Furthermore, an archetypal dream gives the impression that it is a spontaneous product of the unconscious which is trying to convey some extraordinary message. The dreamer may sense the importance of the dream and be emotionally stirred or even fascinated by it; he or she may see in the dream some suggestion of enlightment, warning, or supernatural help because of the striking resemblance of the images to mythological and religious motifs. It is likely to have a numinous quality.

Perhaps the clearest criterion for recognizing archetypal images is a cosmic quality. Jung classified as cosmic qualities temporal or spatial infinity, movement at tremendous speeds or for enormous distances, astrological associations, changes in the body's proportions, or qualities of the dreamer's dream behavior: flying through space like a comet; thinking one is the earth, the sun, or a star; being inordinately large or dwarfishly small; dying; coming to a strange place; being a stranger to oneself; confusion; madness; or feelings of disorientation, dizziness, or euphoria.

In addition to archetypal situations, there are archetypal figures: "the chief of them being, according to [Jung's] suggestion, the *shadow*, the *wise old man*, the *child* (including the child hero), the *mother* ("Primordial Mother" and "Earth Mother") as a supraordinate personality ("daemonic" because supraordinate), and her counterpart the *maiden*, and lastly the *anima* in man and the *animus* in woman" (CW9-I, par. 309).

But not every archetypal image is bizarre or impressive. Sometimes it is identified by its reiteration so often in a series of dreams—perhaps a few hundred—that it can be recognized as typical. (The further significance of recurring motifs is discussed in Ch. 8.) Some archetypal motifs can be recognized empirically by their similarity to motifs in mythology, folklore, religion, philology, and ethnology, especially when they are found in such sources frequently. An example of such a typical image is the water motif. In addition, the possibility that an image is archetypal should be explored if the dreamer has no personal association to it, or if personal associations are available but the image still is not understood.

Some archetypal images give no recognizable clues. Despite his extensive knowledge of the sources of amplifications, Jung said that there were instances when he failed to recognize the source of an image immediately. The only advice he could offer was to give "special attention" (CW9-I, par. 338) to the possibility of archetypal parallels.

When and to Whom Archetypal Dreams are Likely to Appear

The recognition of archetypal dreams is aided by knowing when and to whom such dreams are likely to appear. Jung's experience indicated that they tend to appear at important junctures of a person's life, such as early childhood, especially from the third to sixth years; puberty; early adulthood; the beginning of the second half of life (from age thirty-five to forty); the climacteric; before death, and at other times of crisis. Archetypal dreams are characteristic also of the individuation process, especially during the second half of life; during this period, special care must be taken to use an archetypal approach when it is indicated, in order not to limit possibilities for psychological development.

The preliterate people whom Jung visited in East Africa believed that "big" dreams are dreamed only by "big" men, such as medicine men and chiefs, and even these individuals stopped dreaming big dreams when Europeans took charge of the government, and usurped the authority of the medicine men and chiefs. But Jung found that among Europeans, people in all walks of life had archetypal dreams. They can be dreamed by "simple people, more particularly when they have got themselves, mentally or spiritually, in a fix" (CW10, par. 324). As with other dreams, an archetypal dream is likely to be compensatory (see Ch. 11), and "the more general and impersonal the condition that releases the unconscious reaction, the more significant, bizarre, and overwhelming will be the compensatory manifestation" (CW7, par. 278).

One of the "fixes" a person in psychotherapy may experience is that of the therapy's becoming "stuck," that is, failing to move forward. Although any dream may be useful at such a time, Jung found that if the situation is serious enough, or if the patient is not open to a needed religious orientation, archetypal dreams are likely to appear; they suggest a way of moving ahead in a direction that would not have occurred otherwise to the dreamer or the therapist.

Archetypal dreams are likely to occur also in the dreams of "people who are inwardly cut off from humanity and oppressed by the thought that nobody else has their problems" (CW10, par. 323). Some of these people, and others who have archetypal dreams, are neurotics with a severe one-sidedness of personality, and psychotics, especially schizophrenics. The frequency of archetypal dreams is likely to increase shortly before the onset of a psychosis or heavy neurosis. This increase may be the harbinger of the coming breakdown (Jung reported such a case in "An Analysis of the Prelude to a Case of Schizophrenia," the subtitle of CW5, *Symbols of Transformation*) or it may be part of the cause, especially of a schizophrenic breakdown, in that the dreamer begins to identify with the unconscious contents and, eventually, becomes possessed by them.

At the other end of the scale of psychic states in which collective compensations appear is a fairly high degree of self-knowledge and emotional maturity; that is, when the dreamer has integrated much of the personal unconscious and is in the advanced stages of the individuation process. Then his dreams begin to reflect his wider consciousness of objective interests and the dreams begin to reflect a wider consciousness of objective interests and the world at large, perhaps philosophical or religious problems, such as the contemplation of death, rather than the limited world of the ego. Or the dreamer's behavior affects others. In stressing the appearance of archetypal dreams during the individuation process, Jung seemed to see individuation as a relatively infrequent phenomenon. It is probably the advanced stage of individuation that is infrequent, however, since nearly all dreams are compensatory, and hence, work toward wholeness, that is, individuation.

Sometimes a person in analysis has a paucity of archetypal dreams and may feel deprived because ordinary dreams are assumed to be superficial, and archetypal dreams a mark of individuation. The reason for the paucity, Jung warned, may be the failure to analyze the "small" dreams, which can result in the inhibition of "big" dreams. In my experience, however, it is possible for psychological development to occur, including the encounter with general human problems, with few or no archetypal dreams. Further, the desire for archetypal dreams in itself will be a hindrance to the individuation process if it results in ignoring the psychic material presented by nonarchetypal dreams.

In any case, transpersonal interpretation of a dream should be sought only after all other possibilities have been exhausted. Interpreters who think that Jung always preferred collective over personal interpretations will find it useful to know that he wrote, "The collective unconscious influences our dreams only occasionally" (CW17, par. 208). He cautioned that archetypal concerns are legitimate only when they

> arise from the deepest and truest needs of the individual; illegitimate when they are either mere intellectual curiosity or a flight from unpleasant reality . . . . People who go illegitimately mooning after the infinite often have absurdly banal dreams which endeavor to damp down their ebullience. (CW7, par. 288)

Jung's hypotheses regarding the greater incidence of archetypal dreams under specific conditions could be tested empirically. The one study I have found (Kluger, 1975) indicates that "vivid" dreams—those that leave a vivid impression on the dreamer—contain a significantly higher proportion of archetypal content than a control sample of everyday dreams.

Amplifying Archetypal Dreams

For the amplification of archetypal dreams, archetypal parallels are needed in addition to personal associations. The use of such parallels is based on the understanding that for the psychic elements common to all humanity—archetypes—amplifications from all of human experience are relevant to the dreams of any one person, just as the individual's entire life experience potentially provides personal associations to each of that person's dreams.

The interpreter looks for amplifications in mythology, history of religions, archaeology, the practices of preliterate peoples, alchemical treatises, and indeed, "all branches of the humane sciences" (CW8, par. 527). Jung likened this process to a "comparative anatomy of the psyche" (CW18, par. 522). The archetypal parallels usually are supplied from the interpreter's store of knowledge or from information sought out during or between psychotherapy sessions. Discovering the relevant parallels may require extensive research; some of the results of such research form the major content of several volumes of Jung's *Collected Works* and the works of many Jungian writers (e.g., Harding, 1935; Kirsch, 1973; Whitmont, 1969). Occasionally, of course, the dreamer is able to make a contribution out of personal knowledge of these subjects. The process may yield a wealth of amplifications. As in any investigation of historical or empirical material, the method does not work automatically; the skill of the investigator is necessary to sift and examine the archetypal parallels for relevance to the dreamer's conscious situation and comparison with the dream images.

There are times, indeed, when archetypal amplifications must be used sparingly because the collective unconscious is dangerous to the dreamer. One of Jung's patients, for example, had

> a richly developed, indeed positively luxuriant fantasy life, ... Her powers of fantasy [were] a symptom of illness in that she [reveled] in them far too much, but [allowed] real life to slip by. Any more mythology would [have been] exceedingly dangerous for her, because a great chunk of external life [stood] before her, still unlived. She [had] too little hold upon life to risk all at once a complete reversal of standpoint. (CW7, par. 161)

Jung made no distinction in the usefulness of amplifications already known to the dreamer and those not known,[4] on the ground that those which are known are remembered by "something deep in his unconscious. . . . This part of the unconscious evidently likes to express itself mythologically, because this way of expression is in keeping with its nature" (CW8, par. 308).

An example of a dream amplified archetypally is that of a 27-year-old army officer who had the puzzling symptom of a pain in the left heel. The officer dreamed, after he had been in analysis for some time, that "*he was bitten in the heel by a snake and instantly paralyzed*" (CW8, par. 305). Jung assumed that the dreamer probably had learned at some time of the Biblical story of the serpent who was made the enemy of woman and her offspring, with the decree, "You shall bruise his heel" (Genesis 3:15). The relation of the injured heel to the mother in the Genesis story had its parallel in the dreamer's history: He had been pampered and, hence, weakened by his mother; indirectly, therefore, she had lamed him. A further archetypal parallel, probably not known previously to the dreamer, was introduced by Jung from the ancient Egyptian hymn that used to be recited or chanted for the cure of snakebite:

> [Isis] . . . wound not the living snake about her face,
> But threw it in a coil upon the path
> Where the great god was wont to wander. . . .
> Then the noble worm stung him. . . .
> (CW8, par. 307)[5]

Both the Genesis story and Egyptian hymn parallel the dream: A male is bitten by a snake because of the acts of a woman. Thus, amplifications supply the essential fact that is missing in the officer's dream: A woman was the agent of his paralysis. Moreover, the example passes Jung's test: The parallel images must have the same context to have the same "functional meaning" (CW9-I, par. 103). That is, because the snakebite is in the heel in both the dream and the Biblical story, it has the same functional meaning in each. In the Egyptian hymn it can be inferred that the snakebite is in the foot, and that the functional meaning may well be the same. The Biblical and Egyptian accounts have in common further that a woman brought about the snakebite. Thus, the dream image was amplified: Evidently in the dreamer's life, too, a woman was instrumental in the "snakebite." Accordingly, the common context made possible the interpretation that Jung gave the dream.

The Significance of Archetypal Dreams

The effect of archetypal dreams is not automatic. In fact,

> The most beautiful and impressive dreams often have no lasting or transformative effect on the dreamer. He may be impressed by them, but he does not necessarily see any problem in them. The event then naturally remains "outside," like a ritual action performed by others. These more aesthetic forms of experience must be carefully distinguished from those which indubitably involve a change of one's nature. (CW9-I, par. 211)

However, the analysis of archetypal dreams can be therapeutic, more than the analysis of nonarchetypal dreams, in two ways: by helping the dreamer to be less isolated and by advancing the dreamer's psychic wholeness. In the first instance, the dreamer is forced to realize that other human beings have similar problems and that "every subjective difficulty has to be viewed from the standpoint of the [general] human situation" (CW10, par. 323). In the second instance, the wholeness of the dreamer is enhanced and consciousness "is brought into harmony with the . . . natural law of his own being" (CW16, par. 351).

The young officer's dream of *being bitten by a snake* (CW8, par. 305), is a useful example, again, in that the patient was "shown that his particular ailment [was] not his ailment only, but a general ailment—even a god's ailment" (CW18, par. 231). Such knowledge can have a curative effect by overcoming the isolation and shame a person may experience as a result of a psychic disturbance.

Jung reported that the young man had first experienced his difficulties in the form of severe pains in the region of the heart and a

> choking sensation in the throat, as though a lump were stuck there. He also had piercing pains in the left heel. There was nothing organically the matter with him .... As the anamnesis revealed nothing, I asked about his dreams. It at once became apparent what the cause was. Just before the beginning of his neurosis, the girl with whom he was in love jilted him and got engaged to another man. In talking to me he dismissed this whole story as irrelevant—"a stupid girl, if she doesn't want me it's easy enough to get another one. A man like me isn't upset by a thing like that." But now the affects came to the surface. The pains in his heart soon disappeared, and the lump in his throat vanished after a few bouts of weeping. "Heartache" is a poeticism, but here it became actual fact because his pride would not allow him to suffer the pain in his soul. (CW8, par. 303)

The pain in his heel, however, did not disappear. When Jung turned again to the patient's dreams, the man brought the one in which "*he was bitten in the heel by a snake and instantly paralyzed*" (CW8, par. 305). The pain was interpreted by the dream: His heel hurt because it had been bitten by a snake. Jung acknowledged that nothing rational could be made of this interpretation. The neurosis itself, however, was the "nearest analogy [to the dream] .....When the girl jilted him, she gave him a wound that paralyzed him and made him ill" (CW8, par. 306).

Amplifying the dream with the Biblical story of Eve and the ancient Egyptian hymn of Isis raised the heel symptom

> to the level of a mythological event, as though this would in some way help the patient. This may strike us as flatly incredible. But the ancient Egyptian priest-physicians, who intoned the hymn to the Isis-serpent over the snake-bite, did not find this theory at all incredible; and not only they, but the whole world believed, as the primitive today still believes, in magic by analogy or "sympathetic magic."
> We are concerned here, then, with the psychological phenomenon that lies at the root of magic by analogy .... What is stirred in us is that faraway background, those immemorial patterns of the human mind, which we have not acquired but have inherited from the dim ages of the past.
> If this supra-individual psyche exists, everything that is translated into this picture-language [is] depersonalized .... Not as my sorrow,

but a pain without bitterness that unites all humanity. The healing effect of this needs no proof. (CW8, pars. 312–316)

In this instance, the young man's isolation resulting from his inability to acknowledge his emotions was overcome by nonrational experience which helped him to discover his grief and through it, his link to humanity.

Archetypal images can have negative effects, also. Jung found that if the images were not understood there was a danger of the dreamer's being possessed by them. An example is the unhappy history of Nietzsche who identified with archetypal images and fell into a psychosis. Alternatively, an attitude of acceptance of a negative image, such as a pursuing animal, may change it into something benign, after which it probably will disappear.

Although each person's dreams relate almost exclusively to the dreamer, Jung recognized that occasionally an archetypal dream has a collective significance, that is, it reflects the psychic state of an entire nation or group of nations. In his memoirs Jung described a twice-repeated vision (which he considered the equivalent of a dream) which came to him in October 1913. While he was alone on a journey,

I saw *a monstrous flood covering all the northern and low-lying lands between the North Sea and the Alps. When it came up to Switzerland I saw that the mountains grew higher and higher to protect our country. I realized that a frightful catastrophe was in progress. I saw the mighty yellow waves, the floating rubble of civilization, and the drowned bodies of uncounted thousands. Then the whole sea turned to blood.* This vision lasted about one hour. I was perplexed and nauseated, and ashamed of my weakness.

Two weeks passed; then the vision recurred, under the same conditions, even more vividly than before, and the blood was more emphasized. *An inner voice spoke. "Look at it well; it is wholly real and it will be so. You cannot doubt it.".* . . .

I asked myself whether these visions pointed to a revolution, but could not really image anything of the sort. And so I drew the conclusion that they had to do with me . . . and decided that I was menaced by a psychosis . . . .

. . . in the spring and early summer of 1914, I had a thrice-repeated dream that *in the middle of summer an Arctic cold wave descended and froze the land to ice. I saw . . . the whole of Lorraine and its canals frozen and the entire region totally deserted by human beings. All living green things were killed by frost.* This dream came in April and May, and for the last time in June, 1914.

In the third dream *frightful cold had again descended from out of the cosmos.* This dream, however, had an unexpected end. *There stood a leaf-bearing tree, but without fruit (my tree of life, I thought), whose leaves had been transformed by the effects of the frost into sweet grapes full of healing juices. I plucked the grapes and gave them to a large, waiting crowd . . . .*

On August 1 the world war broke out. Now my task was clear: I had to try to understand what had happened and to what extent my own experience coincided with that of mankind in general. (MDR, pp. 175-176)

Jung mentioned one other dream that was significant for a collectivity of people. This one, recorded by Knud Rasmussen,[6] was the dream of an old Eskimo medicine man which enabled him to lead his tribe from the island of Greenland across Baffin's Bay to North America. The dream depicted a far country with plenty of seals, whales, and walruses at a time when there was a shortage of food in Greenland because of the rapidly increasing size of the tribe. At first, the entire tribe believed him and followed him out on the ice. Halfway over, however, certain old men began to voice their doubts, with the result that half the tribe turned back; they perished. The half that followed the medicine man reached the North American shore safely and thrived there.

Notes

[1] Jung used the expression "the fate of the ego" (MPI-II, p. 198), but the context indicates that he meant the dreamer as a person.

[2] As an extrapolation of his view that "all the activities ordinarily taking place in consciousness can also proceed in the unconscious" (CW8, par. 299), Jung posed the question of "whether the unconscious has dreams too" (CW8, par. 301). He indicated that it does; such a dream "probably derives from some deeper layer that cannot be fathomed rationally; . . . This part of the unconscious evidently likes to express itself mythologically, . . ." (CW8, pars. 306, 308). By distinguishing this "deeper level" from that in which "the repressed affects lie" (CW8, par. 309), he implied that he was designating, in unusual language, the collective unconscious and the personal unconscious as alternative sources of dreams.

[3] In an early work, Jung made a distinction between the parallels useful for reductive interpretation: those "drawn from biology, physiology, literature, folklore, and other sources," those useful for "constructive treatment of an intellectual problem": philosophical parallels; and those useful for the "intuitive problem": parallels in mythology and the histories of religions (CW6, par. 703). Because he made no further mention of this categorization, despite his extensive discussions of archetypal amplification, and because amplification precedes selection of reductive or constructive interpretation, I am omitting the categorization from the established body of theory.

[4] Jung made a point, in some of his examples of archetypal images, of giving evidence that the mythological parallels could not have been known to the dreamer, but he did so to prove the existence of archetypes, not to amplify images for interpretive purposes.

[5] From Erman, Adolf, *Life in Ancient Egypt* (Trans. by H. M. Tirard), London, 1894, pp. 265-267 (modified).

[6] Knud J. V. Rasmussen (1879-1933), Dane, part Eskimo, explorer and authority on Greenland Eskimo; he published several studies of the Eskimo.

Chapter 7

THE DREAM CONTEXT: THE CONSCIOUS SITUATION OF THE DREAMER

Although it arises out of the unconscious, the dream's content is specified by the conscious situation of the dreamer: the events, emotions, thoughts, fears, hopes, and conflicts of the dreamer's waking life. The dream "is not a reflection of unconscious contents in general, but only of certain contents, which are linked together associatively and are selected by the conscious situation of the moment . . . the dream contains [the] unconscious complement [of the conscious situation]" (CW8, par. 477). At least one dream experimenter has agreed with Jung: Cartwright (1969) found that "dreams . . . relate directly to present concerns" (p. 111).

Because of the importance of the dreamer's conscious situation, "it is practically impossible and it is certainly not desirable, to interpret dreams without being personally acquainted with the dreamer" (CW17, par. 187). The conscious situation, in Jung's view, includes the happenings in the dreamer's life the previous day or two, especially those that have had or might be expected to have a marked emotional impact. A dream of more far-reaching significance may reflect a conscious situation that embraces the days, weeks, or even months preceding the dream. It is necessary, of course, for the dreamer to give as much information as possible about the conscious situation so that the facts relevant to the dream are available for the interpretation.

The relevant conscious situation is usually an experience that impinges on a complex, or a problem on which the dreamer has made a wrong or inadequate conscious judgment. The judgment may be in the form of a decision, an attitude toward another person, or a self-evaluation. Moreover, to Jung, "the treatment of dream symbolism demands that we take into account the dreamer's philosophical, religious, and moral convictions" (CW16, par. 339), but he did not say how. I suggest two ways, each balancing the other: (a) challenging previously unexamined convictions and (b) respecting solidly founded convictions.

Jung seemed to use the terms "conscious situation" and "conscious attitude" interchangeably. Very often they are the same; an attitude almost always is an element in a conscious situation. However, concrete facts—actions or other events; such as success or failure in an attempted enterprise, illness, or an impending change in occupation or residence—also are included in the conscious situation, as are the problems that brought the dreamer into therapy.

Whatever the problematical conscious situation, it constellates in the unconscious certain contents which then appear in the dream. That it is essential for the interpreter to know the conscious situation is illustrated by the case of a young man who brought the following dream to Jung:

> *My father is driving away from the house in his new car. He drives very clumsily, and I get very annoyed over his apparent stupidity. He goes this way and that, forwards and backwards, and manoeuvres the car into a dangerous position. Finally he runs into a wall and damages the car badly. I shout at him in a perfect fury that he ought to behave himself. My father only laughs, and then I see that he is dead drunk.* (CW16, par. 335)

In the conscious situation, the dreamer had a good relationship with his father and admired him as a highly successful man. However, the father was "still too much the guarantor of his existence" (CW16, par. 336). By assailing the young man's view of his father, the dream forced the dreamer to become conscious of himself as a separate person who did not need his father's guaranty of existence. Knowledge of the conscious situation prevented an erroneous interpretation that would have impugned the father's character.

The importance of knowing the conscious situation can be seen further in the fact that the same dream can have quite different meanings for different dreamers. Jung stated that two men, one young, one old, brought him essentially the same dream:

A company of young men are riding on horseback across a wide field. The dreamer is in the lead and jumps a ditch of water, just clearing it. The others fall into the ditch. (CW18, par. 519)

The image is that of the dreamer's overcoming an obstacle that defeats others. For the young man, who was cautious and introverted, the dream indicated possibilities in life which he was not realizing. For the old man, who was an invalid and did not follow medical instructions, the dream seemed to mean that he had an illusion of his capacities, far above what was true for his age and situation.

There may be exceptions to the rule that a knowledge of the dreamer's conscious situation is necessary for interpretation. Jung seemed to think so, "particularly with people who know nothing about psychology" (CW17, par. 187), evidently people who are not psychologically oriented. He used the example of the dream of an old general whom he met on a train. The general had dreamed that *he was asked for a definition of the beautiful. He was not able to answer, but a young major gave a very good answer* (CW17, par. 187). Jung asked what the major looked like. The general answered, "He looked like me, when I was a young major" (CW17, par. 187). The general's reply was, in my view, a clarification of the dream text. Thus, on the basis of the text, Jung was able to give a broad interpretation: "Well then, it looks as if you had forgotten or lost something which you were still able to do when you were a young major" (CW17, par. 187). Only then did Jung obtain any personal knowledge of the dreamer: The general "thought for a while, and then he burst out, 'That's it, you've got it! When I was a young major I was interested in art. But later this interest got swamped by routine" (CW17, par. 187). This confidence was composed of a personal association to "the beautiful," the general's interest in art; and a statement about his conscious situation, that he was swamped by routine. A rough interpretation of the dream, however, had been made on the basis of the text alone.

Another possible exception to the "rule" of the dreamer's supplying the conscious situation, as well as personal associations, occurs in the dream series Jung presented in *Psychology and Alchemy* (CW12). He interpreted some dreams of a patient not directly under his care, declaring that the activity was not really an exception because "the series is the context which the dreamer himself supplies" (CW12, par. 50). That is, Jung seemed to treat the series as the conscious situation.

The conscious situation of the dreamer pertains to archetypal dreams just as it does to personal dream images. That is, the same range of possibilities applies. The major variation is likely to be in the proportion of occasions when the relevant conscious situation extends beyond the brief period of a day or two preceding the occurrence of the dream. As with all dreams, however, archetypal dreams are meaningless without reference to some aspect of the conscious situation of the dreamer.[1] For example, a mandala as a symbol of wholeness may appear as a compensation for a fragmented ego or as an aid to a well-advanced individuation process.

Archetypal dreams, according to Jung, "are no longer concerned with personal experiences, but with general ideas" (CW8, par. 555), the problems of people in general, including "a sense of historical continuity" (CW16, par. 99). Nevertheless, usually, "the archetype . . . cannot be explained in just any way, but only in the one that is indicated by that particular individual" (CW18, par. 589). Exceptions are the dreams for which the conscious situation is the collective situation of a group of people, such as a nation.

Although the conscious situation relevant to a particular dream is only one aspect of a dreamer's complex life, Jung gave no general rules for identifying it. In many of his examples, however, he appeared to follow the practice of asking the dreamer, after the amplifications had been gathered, to describe the experiences and mental preoccupations of the day before the dream. Sometimes the dreamer's or the interpreter's intuition selects the relevant experience or preoccupation. One or another "just seems" to be related to the dream. More often, in my experience, an additional guideline is helpful: reflection on which predream experience or thought has had an emotional impact on the dreamer or, on recall, arouses the most emotion. The emotion may be evident directly, in anxiety or sadness, for example, or it may be evident indirectly, in resistance to further discussion or depreciation of the importance of the matter in question. Sometimes it proves to be an experience which the dreamer had "decided not to mention" in the session.

In addition to the methods already mentioned for ascertaining the relevant conscious situation, I have found that the actual images in the dream may give clues. If a woman dreams about her husband, for example, the dream may reflect the fact that a problem has arisen between them which she has been avoiding.

Sometimes the relevant conscious situation becomes apparent by the fact that the therapy session centers around a particular problem. In addition, I usually ask for the dreamer's impression of the relevant conscious situation. Then I try out the various possibilities, including the problem or topic with which the session began.

It is evident, by now, that Jung set very high standards for relevance in establishing the context of a dream, both in amplification and in identifying the conscious situation of the dreamer. Nevertheless, he insisted that examination of the context is "a simple, almost mechanical piece of work which has only a preparatory significance" (CW8, par. 543). Whatever the basis for identifying the relevant conscious situation, the conclusion must be tested in the process of dream interpretation, the guidelines for which are discussed in the following chapters.

Note

[1] Although Jung indicated that archetypal dreams have "no relation . . . to the conscious situation" (CD38, p. 5) of the dreamer, he seemed to mean here what he wrote elsewhere: that archetypal images are not derived from the dreamer's conscious experience.

Chapter 8
DREAM SERIES

The dream context has been treated thus far as if each dream were a discrete event. Indeed, the interpretive process for every dream is begun as if the dream were an isolated experience: (a) The dream text is stated in terms of structure and examined for completeness, and (b) the dream context is established. During the latter process, however, similarities between the dream under analysis and preceding dreams may be noted—in images, themes, amplifications, and conscious situation. Jung seemed to consider the dreams preceding a given dream to be part of its amplification, especially if motifs recurred. He used dreams following the given dream as tests of verification (see Ch. 17) to confirm or correct an interpretation. Thus, the preceding, current, and subsequent dreams may be said to constitute a series. Technically, any succession of dreams is a series, but Jung used the term to mean a succession of dreams related to each other by one or more of the particular factors that are discussed in this chapter.

Series are important, among other reasons, because they demarcate dream units, a process that is comparable to identifying the dream. Sometimes a person may remember only bits and pieces of dreams that have occurred during a single sleep period or the period between therapy sessions, but if these bits and pieces are taken together, they can be considered to constitute the equivalent of one or more complete dreams. (In my experience, it is not unusual for a dreamer to recall many fragmentary dreams and only a few that approach completeness.)

In more complete dreams, the series may help to identify important motifs. Some dreams in series are like variations on a common theme or episodes of a continuing serial. From his experience with tens of thousands of dreams, often including many from one person, Jung concluded that if one could know all of a person's dreams, a definite line of connection nearly always would be found. (This conclusion probably was the basis for his statement, "I attach little importance to the interpretation of single dreams" [CW16, par. 322].) This hypothesis is difficult to substantiate, because one does not remember all one's dreams and the succession of different themes may obscure the connections. Nevertheless, it is useful to seek recurring motifs.

If successive dreams are connected, it may be because each dream "is just one flash . . . of psychic continuity that became visible for a moment" (CW18, par. 181). Jung found that when the process of psychological development known as individuation is incorporated in this psychic continuity, dream series often reveal the process at work. Even when the individuation process is obscured by the compensatory effect (see Ch. 11) of an isolated dream, it can be traced, often, through a series of dreams over time.

Identifying a Dream Series

Jung sometimes indicated that a dream series might be comprised of a certain number of successive dreams (e.g., 10, 20, or 100), but he did not recommend the selection of an arbitrary number to define a series. Rather, he apparently considered a series as consisting of the number of individual dreams it took to put a specific facet of the dreamer's life into perspective: from relatively few dreams to 100 or more. Sometimes, a dream series is identified by the repetition of a dream. More often, a specific motif appears in a series of dreams over a period of time. Again, a series of dreams may comment on a given problem in the dreamer's life.

In my experience, additional criteria may be used to identify a dream series: (a) If the dreamer remembers few dreams, the series may be composed of all dreams that occur during therapy. (b) If the dreamer's life is in transition—changing jobs or locations, marrying or being divorced, or making an important decision—all the dreams during the period of transition (including anticipation and aftereffects), may form a series.

In addition, the dreams of one night are assumed by many dream interpreters to focus on one theme. This is a useful hypothesis in interpretation, but it has not been demonstrated empirically, to my knowledge. One relevant study (Dement & Wolpert, 1958b), however, found that nearly every dream had elements in common with one or more of the dreams of the same night, usually those immediately preceding or following. The common elements varied from trivial details to similarity in plot. Nevertheless, "each dream seemed to be a self-contained drama" (p. 569), and only occasionally did "a coherent dream thought [seem] to be maintained in all dreams of a sequence" (p. 578). These findings do not support or preclude the possibility that dreams of the same night comment on different aspects of the same problem.

The order of a dream series is not necessarily chronological. In the metaphor that Jung used, dreams may radiate out from a psychic center in a circular or spiral fashion. Determining the connection among the dreams, then, is analogous to the geometric process of finding the center of a circle from a combination of points on its perimeter. Each dream in a series reflects the comment of the unconscious on the problem or situation from a different perspective.

Practical Use of Long Dream Series

As a practical matter, a series of 100 dreams, or even 20, is unlikely to be interpreted in detail. Instead, a long series can serve as a resource for amplifying the few dreams that are analyzed in some detail, even without the interpreter's thinking of the category "dream series." In considering the context of a particular dream, the interpreter or the dreamer may recall previous dreams that contained similar motifs or focused on the same problem, or interpretations that seemed to link to the dream under consideration. The use of the dream series consists, then, of keeping in mind, as much as possible, the dreamer's dream history. The limitations of this practice are obvious: a person remembers only a small proportion of each night's dreams; there is not enough time in therapy sessions to discuss all the dreams recalled and recorded by the dreamer; and the dreams previously discussed are not all remembered.

Sometimes, the interpreter can interpret a dream from a person unknown to him or her if a series of 10 to 20 dreams is available as the context. This procedure was used in the long series interpreted by Jung in *Psychology and Alchemy* (CW12).

The most feasible way available, so far, to take into account a large number of the dreams of one dreamer seems to be the method of content analysis devised by Hall and Van de Castle (1966a). To my knowledge, this method has not been used in the context of psychotherapy, but it might be possible to do so. In this method, dream images—specific figures, types of characters, and actions—are grouped into categories and the frequencies are calculated. By comparing the frequencies of the categories at various periods in the dreamer's life, the psychological changes in the dreamer over time may be indicated. Such an analysis is unlikely to reveal the day-to-day compensation, but it is a possible means of discerning significant personality change.

Recurring Dreams

Sometimes, a dream series is determined not by number but by content. Such a series may be made up of recurrences of one dream. A recurring dream is likely to impress the dreamer with its vividness, frequency, or both. Such a dream is "of special importance for the integration of the psyche, [it refers] to something that has been in existence for a long time and is particularly characteristic of the mental attitude of the individual" (Let-1, p. 93). Jung mentioned three possible alternative purposes that may be served by recurring dreams. The first, compensation, differs from the compensatory function of a single dream only in its persistence and, hence, emphasis on a continuing defect in the dreamer's conscious attitude. Such a dream ceases to occur, according to Jung, when it has been understood. A second type of recurring dream is the "traumatic dream": the trauma has been assimilated, the dream ceases to occur (see Ch. 12). A third type of recurring dream may anticipate an important development in the dreamer's psyche (see Ch. 12).

If people's memories serve them correctly, nearly everyone has experienced at least one recurring dream in childhood (see Ch. 13). In adulthood such dreams seem to be relatively rare. Only one example of a patient's recurring dream (as distinguished from recurring images or motifs) is included in Jung's works. He reported it in part as follows:

> [The dreamer's] father, long dead, had not really died but lived in sad and reduced circumstances. A meeting with the father was always frustrated by his father's hopelessness about himself and his wish to disappear. (Let-1, p. 52n.)

(The account implies that some details may have varied, but that the successive dream texts were similar enough to qualify as recurrences of one dream rather than of several motifs.) Jung seemed to put this dream into the compensatory category of recurring dreams. He wrote to the dreamer,

> On the subjective level the "father" is an imago: the image of your relationship to the father and to everything he stands for. In your dream this imago is dark, on the point of disappearing; that is to say a different attitude to the father imago is brewing (and to everything it stands for). (Let-1, p. 52)

In my analytic practice, I have encountered only one instance of an adult's recurring dream, and it had ceased to occur years before the dreamer first consulted me. It seems to fall into Jung's third category of recurring dreams, that of anticipating a future important event, or perhaps two such events:

> *I would be getting dressed to go out and only be able to find black or dark clothes to wear. Finally I would choose something just to be able to keep my appointment in time. When I arrived at my appointment it would be a funeral. The man laid out would be my husband. It would be a very sunny day. As the minister would be praying I would look at the crowd of men that surrounded the gravesite. They were all dressed in black suits with terribly white collars and bands. The sun would hit the front white part so harshly the reflection blotted out all the faces. As soon as the minister pronounced the Amen to the prayer, one of the men would step out of the crowd and come and take my arm, leading me to the car. In the shade of the car I would see it was my husband. He would smile at me and say "Let's start all over again," and we would drive off.*
> (MAM Files)

The dreamer's husband had actually died, suddenly and inexplicably, about a year after the last occurrence of the dream. Many of the persons present at the funeral were his fellow students at a theological seminary who came dressed in clerical garb: black suits with white collars and bands. For a long time after her husband's death, the dreamer assumed that the dream had been anticipating that event; later, she understood the dream differently. Several years before he died, her husband had coerced her into moving from her much-loved home to a distant city so that he could attend the seminary. At the time, she felt that she had "died." Later, she found herself to be a more independent person. The dream can be understood as compensatory, prospective, or both. A compensatory interpretation would stress the dream's proposing the need for the death of an old attitude, represented by the husband, and the adoption of a new attitude, that of making a fresh start.[1] A prospective interpretation would include the anticipation of both the husband's death and the dreamer's "new start," which may have begun before the dream stopped occurring. The cessation of the dream seems to confirm that the dreamer already had embarked on her "new start."

Recurring Motifs

Much more common than the recurring dream is the recurring motif. Sometimes, the major purpose of the repetition of a motif seems to be emphasis; the motif appears repeatedly in approximately the same context and with the same meaning for the dreamer. The repetition seems to be necessary to make the point clear enough for the dreamer to accept. For example, a young women dreamed twice, at an interval of about six weeks, that *her unmarried sister was pregnant and asked the dreamer to help her.* In the first dream, *the sister refused to have an abortion or to give up the baby for adoption.* In the second, *the parents came and kept .telling the pregnant young woman what to do. At the end, the dreamer said something to her mother about her failure to relate to her "mean old man" (meaning her animus), and her dad's failure to relate to his "bitchy woman"* (MAM Files). (The phrase, "meaning her animus," was part of the dream text. The dreamer had read a great deal of Jungian literature and knew the terminology well.) The dreamer, less of a conformist than her sister, always had been more at odds with their parents. The dream image of the sister was interpreted as that part of the dreamer's personality that did conform to the parent's wishes. The pregnancy in the two dreams seemed indicative of a new life developing in the part of the dreamer that was like her sister. The sister's dream situation was unconventional, that is, nonconforming, and the dream ego helped the sister by standing up to the parental figures. The two dreams seemed to tell the dreamer that there was a possibility of loosening the ties between the conforming part of herself and the parents, but some positive action was needed to complete the separation.

Another purpose served by a dream series with a recurring motif is to recommend, anticipate, or reveal a change in an attitude or a personality characteristic of the dreamer. Jung recorded such an experience of his own:

> I myself dreamt of a motif . . . many times over a period of years. It was that I *discovered a part of a wing of my house which I did not know existed . . . . It contained interesting old furniture, and* towards the end of this series of . . . dreams *I discovered an old library whose books were unknown to me. Finally, in the last dream, I opened one of the old volumes and found in it a profusion of the most marvelous symbolic pictures.*
>
> Some time before this dream, I had placed an order with an antiquarian bookseller abroad for one of the Latin alchemical classics,[2] because I had come across a quotation that I thought might be connected with early Byzantine alchemy, and I wished to verify it. Several weeks after my dream a parcel arrived containing the parchment volume of the sixteenth century with many most fascinating symbolic pictures. They instantly reminded me of my dream library. As the rediscovery of alchemy forms an important part of my life as a pioneer of psychology, the motif of the unknown annex of my house can easily be understood as an anticipation of a new field of interest and research. At all events, from that moment thirty years ago the recurrent [motif][3] came to an end. (CW18, pars. 478–479)[4]

In some dream series, the early dreams are incomprehensible until the later ones are known. Then the series provides the amplifications, that is, the dreams amplify each other, just as myths amplify a dream.[5] The series is "not one text but many . . . , throwing light from all sides on the unknown terms, so that a reading of all the texts is sufficient to elucidate the difficult passages in each individual one" (CW12, par. 50).

The exploration of the meaning of a series of dreams with a common motif was likened by Jung to the task of a philologist faced with a volume in an obscure tongue: Decipher the meanings of recurring words, then of words in combinations, and so on until the entire volume can be read. The dream series, thus, is a text composed of strings of "words" (images) that form "sentences," and of "paragraphs" (episodes or dreams) that form "chapters." Each recurring dream image becomes a "word" in a kind of "private language" for the dreamer, and its meaning becomes clearer as it is used more often.

A relatively simple example is provided by two dreams from the long series that Jung studied without personal contact with the dreamer (CW12). The first reported dream of the series was as follows:

> *The dreamer is at a social gathering. On leaving, he puts on a stranger's hat instead of his own.* (D6)

Jung was able to amplify but not interpret this dream until he had access to another dream much later in the series:

> *An actor smashes his hat against the wall, where it looks like this:* [a diagram of a wheel with eight spokes and a solid black center (CW12, par. 254). (D7)

Jung amplified the hat in the first dream with the dream facts surrounding the hat in the second, and vice versa, then interpreted the image.

> The hat refers to the first dream of all, where *he puts on a stranger's hat*. The actor throws the hat against the wall, and the hat proves to be a mandala. So the "strange" hat was the self, which at that time—while the dreamer was still playing a fictitious role—seemed like a stranger to him. (CW12, par. 255)

An example from my practice was the dream of Willa, a thinking-type young woman:

> *I had decided to murder someone named Alice. I committed the murder and disposed of the body.* (MAM Files)

Alice was the mother of Willa's friend, who had appeared in earlier dreams as the personification of Willa's damaged feeling function. Alice had been rejecting and cruel to her daughter, and thus appeared as the destructive side of Willa's experience with maternal figures. Alice was the image or dream word for "destructive maternal figure." The dream was interpreted as meaning that the dreamer was protecting her feeling function, personified by Alice's daughter, by eradicating from her life the attitude, personified by Alice, that was destructive to it.

Sometimes, a recurring motif takes different forms that reflect various facets of a situation, problem, or personality characteristic in the dreamer's life. For example, one dreamer reported a water motif in 26 dreams extending over a period of two months (CW16, par. 14). Jung saw the series as illustrating the continuity of the unconscious and indicating how the motifs could be interpreted by comparing their various forms and the dream situations in which they occurred.[6] In many of the images, the body of water mentioned was the sea. Jung considered water as "the commonest symbol for the unconscious" (CW9-I, par. 40) and the sea as a relatively fixed symbol that "signifies a collecting place where all psychic life originates, i.e., the collective unconscious" (CW16, par. 15).[7] Another connecting link among the images is water in motion, which Jung saw as meaning "something like the stream of life or the energy-potential" (CW16, par. 15). An additional common characteristic of many of the images in the series is that of traveling: down a river, crossing an ocean, driving to the ship in an automobile, stopping on an island. I would add, tentatively, the interpretation that the water motif reflects the dreamer's "inner journey," which is proceeding in various ways at different times.

In a longer series of dreams, one motif is likely to be superseded by another. In the dreams of the same man, "the water-motif gradually retreated to make way for a new motif, the 'unknown woman,'" (CW16, par. 16) which occurred 51 times in a period of three months. Jung saw the unknown woman as replacing the water motif because "Just as water denotes the unconscious in general, so the figure of the unknown woman is a [feminine] personification of the unconscious, which I have called the 'anima'" (CW16, par. 17). When one motif seems to replace another, both probably should be considered in the amplification supplied by the combined series.

Series Centering on Problems

Recurring dreams and recurring motifs by no means exhaust the possibilities of dream series. Quite often, even without recurring motifs, a series can be identified by the relevance of several dreams to a particular problem in the dreamer's life. In such an instance, the series comments on the problem from various points of view or, perhaps, urges the dreamer in the direction of a particular psychological development. Experimental evidence supporting this view is found in a study by Offenkrantz and Rechtschaffen (1963). Taking as a series the dreams of one night, they found that "all the dreams of a night were concerned either with the same conflict or with a limited number of different conflicts" (p. 507).

Although he did not specify whether the dreams were from the same night, Jung gave an example in which two of a young woman's dreams made different comments on one problem, her attitude toward religion. The first dream "was mainly concerned with . . . *a baptizing ceremony in a Protestant sect that took place under particularly grotesque and even repulsive conditions*" (CW11, par. 162). Jung characterized her associations to the dream as "a precipitate of all the dreamer's disappointments with religion" (CW11, par. 162). This first dream, then, seemed to express her negative view of institutionalized religion.

In the second dream,

> *She was in a planetarium, a very impressive place overhung by the vault of the sky. In the sky two stars were shining; a white one, which was Mercury, but the other star emitted warm red waves of light and was unknown to her. She now saw that the walls underneath the vault were covered with frescoes. But she could recognize only one of them: it was the antique picture of the tree-birth of Adonis.* (CW11, par. 162)

The red waves of light she took to be warm feelings, that is, love, and the star, consequently, to be Venus. The dreamer had seen a picture in a museum of the tree-birth of Adonis.[8] (Adonis was "born of a tree into which his mother had transformed herself" [New Larousse Encyclopedia of Mythology, p. 81].) Adonis, to her, was not only the dying and resurgent god but also a god of rebirth. Thus, the second dream, which included the image of a mandala vision of a world clock (the planetarium), the united divine pair (Mercury and Venus), and the image of renewal (Adonis), together with the first dream formed a statement of contrasting views of religion. The two dreams are also question and answer: Is this the only way religion can be? No, here is an alternative ("which [has] to do with mysterious rites of creation and renewal" [CW11, par. 164]).

Some dream series comment on a specific problem in the dreamer's life, leading the dreamer in the direction of the psychological development required and stimulated by a particular problem. Jung discussed such a series in one of his unpublished seminars. The dreamer was a business man of 45, a husband and father. He had a good intellect; was cultivated, prosperous, and very polite; was careful in manners, speech, and clothing; and was very rational in his views of how one should live.

In the first dreams of the series under consideration, *he is trying to help the child of his sister to pronounce the name of the dreamer's wife, Maria. He says "Mari–ah, ah" (like yawning). The family members present protest this joke.* (D8) Jung interpreted the episode to mean that the man was bored with his wife and, presumably, with his marriage, hence the yawning; his conflict over his feeling of boredom is reflected in the criticism of the dream ego's behavior by other figures in the dream.

In the next dream of the series, the dreamer *pays a call on a poor young woman, a tailoress, who lives and works in an unhealthy setting and is suffering from TB. He tells her that she should work out in the open, adding that she could work in his garden, using his wife's sewing machine.* (D9)

The dreamer associated the young woman's confined setting with his own imprisoned life, and her illness with the popular belief that tubercular people are erotic. Jung interpreted the dream as meaning that the man's erotic feelings toward women other than his wife had not come out into the open. His suggestion that she work in his garden meant "pressing his [erotic] feelings back into his marriage" (DA1, p. 66) although he had become bored with it (as revealed in the first dream). This second dream, then, was focusing attention on the limitation of the dreamer's current emotional life and the inadequacy of his efforts to change it.

A subsequent dream attempted to stimulate the dreamer to accept his erotic feelings so that he could integrate them and become a more nearly whole person. In the dream *he has four chickens. In spite of his efforts to contain them, they escape. He catches them and puts them into the safest place he has. He sees that one does not move and thinks that it is because he has pressed it too hard. He thinks further that if the chicken is dead it cannot be eaten. While he watches, it begins to move and he smells an aroma of roast chicken.* (D10)

The dreamer's associations to the chickens were limited to eating them. Jung saw them as panicky, dumb creatures, "an excellent simile for fragmentary tendencies repressed or never come across by us" (DA1, p. 81), that is, the chickens are an excellent simile for the dreamer's erotic feelings. The fact that the chickens escaped suggests that the dreamer has moved a step beyond the previous dream: Some of his feelings are now out in the open. He returned them to captivity and squeezed one too hard, an indication that he was trying again to press his erotic feelings out of existence (or back into his boring marriage). Nevertheless, as he contemplated the apparently lifeless feeling (chicken), it revived. Its revival was accompanied by an aroma of roasting, which suggested another possibility of development, that of acknowledging and even incorporating his erotic feelings.

Any developmental process can be seen best, of course, after the conclusion of a dream series. For example, the series may reveal a change in the way the dreamer deals with a certain problem situation, such as a difficult task or a complex. Although Jung did not mention the possibility of a change for the worse, it is certainly possible. The dream of the escaped chickens, however, seems to indicate a potential development, or perhaps even the beginning of a realized development, in the dreamer.

In a longer series, psychological development can merge into an individuation process. In Jung's view, "The symbols of the process of individuation that appear in dreams are images of an archetypal nature which depict the centralizing process or the production of a new centre of personality" (CW12, par. 44). He exemplified this view in the series presented in *Psychology and Alchemy* (CW12). (Jung seemed to consider individuation virtually impossible without archetypal dreams. This view remains to be tested.)

The individuation process seems certainly to be enhanced and accelerated by the analytic process, "especially when it includes a systematic dream-analysis" (CW8, par. 552). Jung stated frankly that he did not know whether the individuation process could be observed in a long dream series recorded apart from the analytic process.[9] Research on this question could be a substantial contribution to the work on the efficacy of psychotherapy.

Complications in Considering Dream Series

Complications may arise in trying to interpret dreams in series. One is the result of considering dreams in analytic sessions. A correct interpretation can change the content of subsequent dreams by contributing to psychological development. An incorrect interpretation can have a comparable effect by eliciting a dream that corrects the invalid interpretation. Jung's writings suggest that he recognized the effect of interpretation on subsequent dreams, but he did not present data on his idea or discuss its implications. Although the effects of interpretation on the content of subsequent dreams are difficult to demonstrate empirically, the matter is of great importance. There is little point in interpreting dreams if the interpretation does not affect the dreamer's psychological development which, in turn, should be reflected in the content of subsequent dreams.

Another complication is the possibility of someone dreaming another person's dream. This phenomenon is rare; it is identified primarily through the examination of dreams in series. Jung sometimes found it possible to recognize this phenomenon because the "other person's dream" was an exceptionally strange one among those of the dreamer (Z9, p. 41). I have found the criterion of exceptional strangeness of limited usefulness because there are other bases for a dream's appearing exceptionally strange: archetypal content, psychic trauma, or, simply, obscurity of meaning. The basic criterion I have found useful for identifying "another person's dream" is that the dream can be interpreted best in relation to a person other than the dreamer. The other person is almost certainly someone who, at the time of the dream, is having a strong psychological impact on the dreamer. Often, this is someone with whom the dreamer is involved in an intense relationship. Or the other person may be someone in great difficulty for whom the dreamer has a strong empathy and is expending a great deal of psychic energy. The latter was the case with a psychotherapist who had a dream that did not yield to an interpretation in relation to herself, but was quite comprehensible in relation to J., her patient.

> *I was looking at a strange book. I knew it was G.H.'s will. I noticed written in the frontispiece the name J...S...H... in a sort of German script. The book was made or published in Germany, and it appeared very old, with round, red, glass-like seals, giving it a documentary appearance. Moreover, there was a military feeling about this unusual red and gray book, written in German, which was G.H.'s will, or legacy.* (MAM Files)

G.H., of German extraction, was the former husband of J.; S. was his second wife. The dreamer's association to red and gray was her father's car; he was similar to G.H. in his militaristic attitudes. G.H. had used his will and life insurance to exert power over J., his first wife. When the dreamer saw the patient the day after the dream, they discussed J.'s feeling that it would be nice to be married once again to G.H., because of the economic security entailed, despite her awarness that the marriage had been destructive to her. The dream was comprehensible when considered as belonging to J.; it pushed her to see more realistically G.H.'s propensity to treat his wives in a militaristic way, and to use his last will and testament as a weapon. J. was in great psychic stress at the time of the dream. She had been telephoning the therapist between sessions, and the therapist was deeply concerned for J.'s well-being. Hence the requirements were met for the hypothesis that the therapist had dreamed J.'s dream: (a) There was marked emotional involvement between the two persons at the time of the dream, and (b) the dream was not comprehensible in relation to the dreamer's psychic situation but was comprehensible when it was interpreted as "belonging" to a person other than the dreamer.

The dreams preceding the dream under consideration are always a potential part of its context, and attention should be given to a series, if one or more of the factors Jung discussed is present. Nevertheless, in my experience, a relevant series often cannot be found for a dream. In this case, the interpreter and dreamer proceed to interpret the dream on the basis of the context, as discussed in Chapters 5, 6, and 7. A subsequent dream still may verify or disconfirm the interpretation.

Notes

[1] A Freudian might say that the dream should be interpreted as wish fulfillment—for the husband's death. Such an interpretation would be a special case of compensation, reflecting an unconscious attitude toward the husband. However, the emphasis in the dream on making a fresh start takes it beyond the realm of a pure wish for the husband's death.

[2] Von Franz (1975, p. 202) reported that the book was called *Artis auriferae, quam Chemiam vocant*, Volumnia duo (1593).

[3] Jung wrote "dream" but "motif," which he had used at the beginning of the passage, seems more accurate.

[4] The same dream, in different words, is recounted in MDR, p. 202.

[5] Jung actually wrote, "The series is the *context* which the dreamer himself supplies" (CW12, par. 50; italics added). Amplification is the part of the context to which Jung seemed to refer.

[6] Jung said the motifs can be evaluated "statistically" (CW16, par. 15) but he did not state how to do it.

[7] In another context, Jung wrote, "Water as an obstacle in dreams seems to indicate the mother, or a regression of libido. Crossing the water means overcoming the obstacle, i.e., the mother as symbol of man's longing for the conditions of sleep or death" (CW5, par. 503n). This interpretation seems to be a residue from Freud's influence and, in any case, is not relevant here.

[8] The dreamer used the Roman names, Mercury and Venus, and the Greek name, Adonis.

[9] A possible exception to this statement is the producer of the long series of dreams and visions discussed in *Psychology and Alchemy* (CW12). Jung reported: "In order to avoid all personal influence I asked one of my pupils, a woman doctor, who was then a beginner, to undertake the observation of the process. This went on for five months. The dreamer then continued his observations alone for three months. Except for a short interview at the very beginning, before the commencement of the observation, I did not see the dreamer at all during the first eight months. Thus it happened that 355 of the dreams (or visions) were experienced away from any personal contact with myself. Only the last forty-five occurred under my observation. No interpretations worth mentioning were then attempted because the dreamer, owing to his excellent scientific training and ability, did not require any assistance" (CW12, par. 45).

Chapter 9

APPROACHING
THE INTERPRETATION

When the amplifications to the dream images have been gathered, the interconnecting themes noted, and the dreamer's relevant conscious situation ascertained, the dreamer and interpreter are ready for the next step in the interpretation process: deriving the dream's message. For this step, the interpreter uses a set of tools. These "tools" are basic attitudes toward the dream: avoidance of theoretical assumptions, recognition that the dream images are not a disguise but a set of psychic facts, and awareness of the impact of the personalities of dreamer and interpreter on the process of interpretation.

Avoiding Assumptions

The interpreter must avoid all biases in seeking the dream's meaning. The starting point is the premise that the dream is "a source of information about conditions whose nature is unknown to him, concerning which he has as much to learn as the [dreamer]" (CW16, par. 317). The same images are likely to have different meanings for different dreamers. Similarly, different dreamers may have the same problem but it is expressed differently in each person's dream. Any guiding principle, then, may be used only sparingly and with care.

However great may be the temptation to use a store of knowledge to look for a particular message in a dream, the interpreter must not assume that the dream interpretation can be made to fit any theory of personality. Dream language is obscure and highly individual. Thus, each dream must be regarded as a unique event. This imperative precludes the imposition on the dream of any theoretical presupposition regarding human personality and its implications for the dream's meaning, such as the wish-fulfillment theory, the power theory, or even the theory that the psyche is self-regulating.[1] "A dream ... is a natural product, which is precisely a thing without ulterior motive" (CW11, par. 136). Although there are dreams that, for example, serve as wish fulfillments, not all do so. Rather, the interpretation is contingent on the procedures Jung outlined, if the objective is to ascertain the message from the unconscious. Any assumption about a dream's meaning is a conscious content; imposing it on a dream limits the exploration of the dream's meaning to messages that already are in the dreamer's or interpreter's conscious mind. Thus, biases can prevent the interpreter from becoming open to the limitless possibilities of dreams and their reflections of the richness of the unconscious. The presence of biases can be recognized, often, by the "monotony of interpretation" (MDR, p. 312) experienced by the interpreter. Receptivity to all possibilities is more than a matter of aesthetics; it is required for realizing the validity and the therapeutic value of the interpretation.

Jung found a monotony of interpretation in Freud's view that unraveling the dream work leads to discovery of the instinctual impulse behind the manifest content. Jung insisted, "The fact that the dream as well as consciousness rest on an instinctual foundation has nothing to do either with the meaning of the dream-figures or with that of the conscious contents, for the essential thing in both cases is *what the psyche has made of the instinctual impulse*" (CW9-II, par. 316n).

Also rejected by Jung was Freud's theory that dream interpretation is a process of unraveling the dream work, until the latent content is revealed. Jung saw this theory as predicated on the unsubstantiated assumption that dreams preserve sleep. Moreover, the theory posits the manifest content as symptomatic, and the latent content as pathological; this view is difficult to reconcile with the knowledge that everyone dreams, hence that dreaming—and dreams—are normal phenomena. Further supporting the sufficiency of the manifest content are interpretations, yielded by Jungian dream analysis, that meet the available tests of verification (see Ch. 16).

Underlining his disapproval of applying theory to dream interpretation, Jung warned that any interpretation that meets the expectations of the interpreter or the dreamer should be regarded with suspicion, because such an interpretation is presumptuous and does not overcome the dissociation between conscious and unconscious. A dream should add to the dreamer's conscious knowledge; when it fails to do so, it probably has not been interpreted properly. (Jung acknowledged, however, that the latter statement is theoretical.) Archetypal dreams, especially, must not be subjected to "cramping intellectual formulae [which] rob them of their natural amplitude" (CW16, par. 15).

Psychotherapists, Jung argued, share the dilemma of objectivity with every scientist who investigates any natural phenomenon. When we form hypotheses, we never can be sure whether we are basing them on data or wishful thinking. Jung said that he made it a rule, when confronted with a dream, to say to himself, first of all, "I have no idea what this dream means" (CW8, par. 533). The only assumption he was willing to make was that dreams have meaning. Although he could not prove this assumption—and he admitted that there are many dreams which interpreter and dreamer do not understand—he found it necessary in order to explain to himself why he analyzed dreams at all.

From my detailed study of Jung's extensive work on dream interpretation, I find that he fulfilled well his own dictum not to impose theory on dreams. Despite extensive amplifications, especially in his later works, a close look reveals that he began empirically, with the "dream facts," and drew his conclusions from them. For example, even his controversial conclusion that human beings have a built-in religious need—an instinct for religion, in Jung's terms—grew out of observing actual dreams of his patients. Even if it is true, as has been said, frequently, that people in Jungian analysis have "Jungian dreams"—dreams that bear out Jungian hypotheses (e.g., the collective unconscious)—there was a time when there were no Jungian hypotheses. At that time, Jung developed his psychological ideas from the clinical data (including dreams) available to him.

Dream Images as Symbols

Both Jung and Freud referred to dream images as "symbols" but they used the term differently. According to Jung, Freud used the word "symbol" for what is actually a sign[2] (or analogue); that is, Freud assigned specific, fixed meanings to the images. For example, to Freud a church steeple stood for a penis and nothing more. (It is said that Jung queried, "If a church steeple stands for a penis, how does one interpret [the image of] a penis?")

Jung did not assign a fixed meaning to a dream image; he looked for a meaning that exceeded the obvious and immediate appearance of the image and accorded with the dreamer's experience. To him, a symbol was "the best possible formulation for still unknown or unconscious [psychic] facts" (CW14, par. 772),[3] which could not "be reduced to anything else" (Let-1, p. 143).

Freud's seemingly arbitrary assignment of meanings to dream symbols was not acceptable to Jung's view of scientific method. Highly preferable, to Jung, was interpretation based on amplification by archetypal parallels. He found this comparative research to be "the only possible scientific foundation" (CW17, par. 196) for symbolism.

Experts in fields dealing with symbolism support Jung's understanding. Thass-Thienemann, for example, wrote, "[A] characteristic of the symbol consists of the fact that the symbolic meaning permeates, sometimes consciously, mostly unconsciously, the physical vehicle which is its carrier" (1973, Vol. 1, p. 21).

The distinction between sign and symbol is important to the therapeutic process. Interpreting a dream image as a sign gives it a pre-established, hence an already conscious, meaning. Thus, the unconscious contents are repressed further and the dissociation between conscious and unconscious is perpetuated. Jung found that interpreting the dream images as symbols recognizes their complexity, deepens one's understanding of them, and makes their individual meanings available to consciousness.

The therapeutic process is affected further by the fact that, as a sign, the dream image is considered to be like a neurotic symptom—undesirable. As a symbol, the dream image offers possibilities for psychological development and "facilitates a transition from one attitude to another" (CW6, par. 828). Because a symbol can facilitate such a transition, Jung named it the "transcendent function."

Since phallic objects were frequent in Freud's interpretations, Jung discussed them as examples of the distinction he made between sign and symbol.[4] If a phallic object is taken for a penis, it is a sign and nothing more. As a symbol it implied also, for Jung, the "creative mana, the power of healing and fertility" (CW16, par. 340). Depending on the context, moreover, a phallic image, like any other image, can have various interpretations. For example, a key inserted into a lock would represent, as a sign, a penis entering a vagina; as a symbol, it could suggest the union of opposites, unlocking a secret, or opening a door to success.

In addition to alternative meanings for different dreamers or at different times for the same dreamer, a symbol can have, for the same dreamer at the same time, multiple meanings which are all facets of the same central truth. The symbolic meaning of an oil lamp, for example, could be found in its light, which it casts ahead into the future; its age, which suggests the past; its aesthetic value as a decorative object; its ineffectiveness in comparison with electric light fixtures; and its belonging to a particular person in the dreamer's life. Some combinations of multiple meanings can even appear contradictory, such as the forward- and backward-looking characteristics of the oil lamp. But the possible interpretations still are ways of looking at truth from different perspectives. For one image to convey more than one message reflects the economy of the unconscious.

Jung made a distinction also between "natural" and "cultural" symbols. A cultural symbol could occur in the dream of anyone in a given culture and would carry a relatively fixed meaning. A natural symbol could occur in the dream of anyone anywhere in the world, and it could carry either a relatively fixed or an individual meaning. Jung defined as cultural symbols

> those that have expressed "eternal truths" or are still in use in many religions. They have gone through many transformations and even a process of more or less conscious elaboration, and in this way have become the *représentations collectives* of civilized societies. (CW18, par. 579)

Such a symbol is the cross in Christianity. Natural symbols, on the other hand, Jung wrote, "are derived from the unconscious contents of the psyche, and they therefore represent an enormous number of variations on the basic archetypal motifs" (CW18, par. 578). These symbols are of more concern to the psychotherapist because they are derived, in part, from the unconscious psychic contents of the dreamer. Symbols of the Self, such as mandalas, exemplify natural symbols.[5]

Relatively Fixed Symbols

Jung recommended that the interpreter learn as much as possible about symbolism and then forget it when confronted with a dream, so that the interpretation will be based on the dream context and not on a preconceived idea. Thus he countered Freud's view that symbols are fixed, that is, have fixed meanings. Nevertheless, he acknowledged that some symbols are "relatively fixed." He seemed to mean that they have generally valid interpretations, ascertained by nonpersonal amplifications, which may be modified by personal amplifications and by the conscious situation of the dreamer but not be changed essentially. For example, Jung examined a 17-year-old girl who suffered from symptoms that suggested a diagnosis of progressive muscular atrophy but could have been produced by hysteria. Jung said that the girl showed "signs of hysteria" (CW16, par. 343) but he specified no symptoms that could not have been indicative also of the organic diagnosis. When Jung asked for dreams, the patient replied:

> Yes, I have terrible dreams. Only recently I dreamt *I was coming home at night. Everything is as quiet as death. The door into the living-room is half open, and I see my mother hanging from the chandelier, swinging to and fro in the cold wind that blows in through the open windows.* Another time I dreamt that *a terrible*

noise broke out in the house at night. I get up and discover that a frigl. ned horse is tearing through the rooms. At last it finds the door into the hall, and jumps through the hall window from the fourth floor into the street below. I was terrified when I saw it lying there, all mangled. (D11)

Jung interpreted the dreams to mean that "The animal life is destroying itself" (CW16, par. 348). He saw "mother" and "horse" as relatively fixed symbols, standing respectively for the origin of life and the animal life of the body. Jung deduced that the dream images pointed to a "grave organic disease with a fatal outcome" (CW16, par. 350), a diagnosis and prognosis that were soon confirmed.

Jung seemed to mean that the image of mother is relatively fixed as the giver of birth and the nourisher. In this dream it seems to mean also the continuing life force. The image of horse as animal life can be understood generally as instinctual impulse. In this dream it seems to refer more to the body as a total organism. These modifications are made necessary by the dreamer's conscious situation: the possibility that her symptoms were life-threatening.

The interpretation of a relatively fixed symbol can be modified, also, by a partially individual interpretation, based on personal amplifications. For example, in amplifying "horse," if the dreamer had associated the image with racing, an interpretation including competitiveness or interest in gambling might have been made.

The Dream is Not A Disguise

Jung repeatedly attributed to the Talmud the saying, "The dream is its own interpretation." He seemed to consider this statement to be synonymous with his own that dream language is not a disguise, that it "expresses exactly what it means" (CW17, par. 189). In this tenet he differed from Freud, who held that dream images (the manifest content) conceal the latent content (the hidden, repressed dream thoughts), which Freud considered to be the dream's meaning,[6] hidden because it is painful. Jung insisted that "a dream is quite capable . . . of naming the most painful and disagreeable things without the least regard for the feelings of the dreamer" (CW13, par. 469). He maintained that dream images can be likened to the clouds that cover the sky; they are a natural phenomenon and serve a purpose other than to annoy us or conceal something.

The fact that dreams rise out of a primitive part of the brain makes it not surprising that they use images which may seem strange to the conscious mind. But the manifest dream is what it is, with an underlying plan which, like the facade of a house, reveals the interior arrangement and can be "read" by someone who knows how. "They employ no artifices in order to conceal something, but inform us of their content as plainly as possible in their own way" (CW17, par. 189). Jung claimed, with justification, to follow his version of Ockham's razor ("multiplicity ought not to be posited without necessity"): "Principles are not to be multiplied beyond the necessary" (CW8, par. 450). Thus, the fact that the dream's meaning is not comprehended by consciousness need not be confounded with an hypothesis of latency. Rather, the dream reveals, but the meaning may not be evident immediately.

Apparent disguise arises out of the metaphoric nature of a dream's contents. Jung cited a dream that clearly is not a disguise but cannot be taken literally. The dreamer was a woman "well known for her stupid prejudices and stubborn arguments" (CW18, par. 469). She dreamed that

> there is a great social affair to which she is invited. She is received by her hostess . . . with the words: "How nice that you have come, all your friends are already here and are expecting you." She leads her to a door, opens it, and the [dreamer] steps into . . . a cowshed!
> (CW18, par. 469)

The dream hostess's words reveal the intent of the dream by telling the dreamer that her friends are like cows, that is, "bovine"—stolid, dull—implying that the dreamer is like them.

In sum, the difficulty in understanding dream imagery is not because the dream is hiding something but because thoughts and emotions have been translated into imagery, and because the dream's function is to communicate a content previously missing from consciousness.

Jung encountered problems in applying to human figures his observation that the dream is not a disguise. The issue arose very early in his career, as a result of his accepting too readily Freud's assertion that a dream figure is always a cover for someone else. A woman patient with a strong attachment to Jung had, he believed, erotic fantasies about him, which she did not admit. As he told the story:

> Naturally she was betrayed by her dreams, in which, however, my person was always hidden under some other figure, often rather difficult to make out. A long series of such dreams finally compelled me to remark: "So, you see, it's always like that, the person you are really dreaming about is replaced and masked by someone else in the manifest dream." Till then she had obstinately denied this mechanism. But this time she could no longer evade it and had to admit my working rule—but only to play a trick on me. Next day she brought me a dream in which she and I appeared in a manifestly lascivious situation. I was naturally perplexed and thought of my rule. Her first association to the dream was the malicious question:

"It's always true, isn't it, that the person you are really dreaming about is replaced by someone else in the manifest dream?"

Clearly, she had made use of her experience to find a protective formula by which she could express her fantasies openly in a quite innocent way. (CW4, pars. 645–646)

This incident influenced Jung to deal less dogmatically with the apparent substitution of one person for another in a dream.

He continued to concede that a human figure could be disguised in a dream, but warned against such an arbitrary assumption in the interpretation. He insisted, in general, that if the unconscious wanted to convey the idea that a dream figure is a particular person, it would say so. When a substitution occurs, Jung wrote, it has a purpose, that of making more remote the painful emotions connected with the figure for which the substitution is made.

An example of a substitution for the purpose of depersonalizing the associated affect is Jung's dream of

> an elderly man in the uniform of an Imperial Austrian customs official. He walked past, somewhat stooped, without paying any attention to me. His expression was peevish, rather melancholic and vexed. There were other persons present, and someone informed me that the old man was not really there, but was the ghost of a customs official who had died years ago. "He is one of those who still couldn't die properly." (D12)

Jung had this dream while he was working on *The Psychology of the Unconscious* (CW5, *Symbols of Transformation*), the book that he felt would cost him his friendship with Freud. Jung saw the elderly Austrian man whose] "work had ... obviously brought him so little that was pleasurable and satisfactory that he took a sour view of the world ... [as analogous] with Freud" (MDR, p. 163). The depreciation of the dream figure expressed Jung's need to depotentiate his own affect regarding Freud, who had been so important to him professionally and personally, in order that he could let Freud's influence "die" in himself. Thus Jung was able to understand that his problem, which seemed to be with Freud, was primarily an inner problem (see Ch. 10).[7]

Another purpose for a substitution, not mentioned by Jung, is the reverse of depotentiating the affect. It may be to make the dreamer more aware of the affect and attitude regarding a person in the environment. A dream of a gorilla sitting in the chair of the dreamer's employer, for example, may be saying that the dreamer fears and perhaps loathes the employer.

Occasionally, the substitution takes the form of two or more dream figures that refer to one person who is not the dreamer. (Two or more figures that refer to the dreamer are discussed in Ch. 10). In such a situation, evidently no one dream figure suffices to describe the dreamer's unconscious perception of the person indicated. For example, a man in his early 30s dreamed:

> *D. has set herself up in a brothel of her own, assisted by a portly but friendly woman in her late 50s. I go to see D. but am reluctant. She and I talk at length and she tries for a long time to seduce me. After a great deal of persuasion, we fall into bed together and have a fantastic time. Our time together is at a close. I write a check to her for [X] dollars and she says to the older woman: "Make an appointment for him in two weeks time." D. says that I am to have the appointment even though I might cancel it. I agree it is a good thing—to have an appointment, at least.* (MAM Files)

The number of dollars was the same as the fee the dreamer was paying for therapy. The analyst had been on vacation, and two weeks was the period of time between appointments. After an interruption, the dreamer recently had resumed therapy but still was not firm in his decision. Thus, the context suggested that the dream was concerned with the therapeutic situation. The two women, therefore, seemed to represent two aspects of the analyst (who was in her 40s) as he saw her: a younger, seductive woman whom he paid for giving him emotional satisfaction, and a woman the age of his mother who dealt only with the frequency of appointments. If this analysis of the dream is correct, it is probably that no one figure could have conveyed the same message.

Sometimes, the dream text characterizes a human figure as "unknown." Jung took such designations as stated; Freud, on the other hand, assumed that the figure is actually someone known to the dreamer who is presented in a disguised form. A frequent occurrence in the dreams of many males, for example, is "the unknown female figure whose significance oscillates between the extremes of goddess and whore" (CW9-I, par. 356). This changeable figure is a personification of the dreamer's anima, which is largely unconscious, that is, unknown. The meaning of the image would be changed drastically if the interpreter insisted on identifying the unknown woman with an actual person.

Dream Images as Psychic Facts

Dreams are sources of information about ourselves. Jung wrote, "The best way to deal with a dream is to think of yourself as a sort of ignorant child . . . , and to come to a two-million-year-old man or to the old mother of days and ask, 'Now, what do you think of me?' " (CW18, par. 200). As psychic facts,[8] presented in the form of images, dreams can be likened to physiological facts, such as sugar in the urine or a rapid heartbeat. Physiological facts are difficult to read in isolation because alternative diagnoses are often possible. Psychic facts are equally hard to read and, in Jung's view, equally impartial. The man's dream in which *"his hands and forearms were covered with black dirt"* (CW10, par. 826), for example, presented a very specific psychic fact, namely, that something in his current life situation was dirtying him.

In treating dreams as psychic facts, only the material that is clearly part of a dream should be used in the interpretation. Insisting that the dreamer stay with the dream picture, Jung said repeatedly, "Let's get back to your dream. What does the *dream* say?" (CW18, par. 434).

Psychic facts have definite characteristics, one of which is that the appearance of one image rather than another, similar image, is significant. For example, a dream image of traveling on a bus is different from an image of traveling in an automobile. The bus follows a particular route that is predetermined, it is driven by someone other than the dreamer, and it carries many passengers who are strangers to the dreamer. In one's own automobile, the dreamer has the option of driving it and of choosing the passengers and the route. Glossing over such differences is likely to distort the interpretation.[9]

The dream image as psychic fact requires, also, that each detail be considered; overlooking one detail sometimes makes nonsense of the interpretation. An example is an incorrect name: If someone who looks like my friend Nan appears in my dream, but in the dream she is called Kathy, my associations must include facts and experiences that relate to both Nan and Kathy. Otherwise, the interpretation will not be correct.

Sometimes, in a dream, the important detail is whatever is missing; it can be a part of the image that should have been present, such as an article of clothing, or a person such as a member of the dreamer's family. If I dream of a family celebration and my brother is not present, for example, the interpretation must take into account the affect of his absence or of my omitting from awareness the part of myself which is like him.

It is helpful, also, I find, to attend to whatever in the dream image is different from actual life. For instance, if the dreamer's house contains, in the dream, a piece of the parents' furniture, this image would require a different interpretation from an exact reproduction of the dreamer's house without that piece of furniture.

When a motif is emphasized, particular attention should be paid to it. Emphasis may take the form of doubling the image, for example, depicting a person as twins, or of different entities, such as the motif of water, which may appear in one dream as both a lake and a river.

Still another characteristic of a dream image may be its absurdity; an absurd dream image may indicate that the dreamer is doing something nonsensical in waking life. For example, if someone dreams of wearing an incongruous combination of clothing, the ridiculous image may suggest that there is something absurd in an attitude of the dreamer.

Many dreams include time relations that are confused or would be impossible in waking life. Such dreams were no problem to Jung because, to him, time in the unconscious is eternal. The irrationality of the time sequence is a fact which may indicate that time is of no importance in the dream message, or it may be a comment on the dreamer's problem with time: the passage of time, the use of time, or arriving for appointments on time. In some dreams, the telescoping of time may be a means of juxtaposing facts separated by time.

Since dream images arise from the unconscious, they are not inhibited by the dreamer's conscious prejudices. Jung described some dream imagery as "stop[ping] at no scurrility and no obscenity" (CW9-II, par. 315). During his lifetime, the possibility was greater than now that some people would be offended by certain images, and he tried to prevent a prejudiced reaction by suggesting that dreams "are unconcerned with offensiveness, because they do not really mean it. It is as if they were stammering in their efforts to express the elusive meaning that grips their attention" (CW9-II, par. 315). Although it is possible for some images to "disguise and distort for so-called 'moral' reasons" (CW9-II, par. 315n), as Freud had it, Jung found that more often the offensiveness of the image serves the purpose of shocking the dreamer in a different way.

The following dream, which was offensive to the woman dreamer, is an example of what Jung meant: *A man unknown to the dreamer started to make love to her, suddenly was dead, and was taken into a cubicle. A woman who seemed to be part of the dreamer followed the dead man into the cubicle. The dreamer stood outside, horrified because she knew that the other woman was having sex relations with the corpse* (MAM Files). The corpse seemed to represent the impending death of the dreamer's relationship with a man in her waking life, and the shocking image galvanized her into accepting the end of the relationship, which she had been trying to prolong. By labeling the import of such an image "elusive," Jung seemed to mean that it was difficult to accept. Thus an image that offends the dreamer may be imparting a message that is difficult for the dreamer to accept.

Consideration must be given to the relation among images as well as to each image separately. The order in which the images appear is one aspect of this relation. Jung hypothesized that the sequence may be causal, that is, each image may be the cause of the succeeding one. Incongruity among the dream images is likely to be significant, such as a very intimate scene in a public place. Moreover, when a dream scene changes, it is probable that an unconscious thought has come to a climax or, at least, that a theme of the dream message has been concluded or interrupted.

Sometimes the images are such that they give the dreamer the impression of dreaming that he or she is dreaming. According to Jung, such a dream seems not so real and is diminished in emotional impact. It is important, also, whether the dreamer is "watching . . . the flow of images as one watches the movies, [or is] one of the figures [in the drama]" (VS1, p. 43). The dreamer who is part of the drama is more involved emotionally, hence more affected, even "transformed" (VS1, p. 42).

In considering the relation of dream images to each other, the dream structure can be helpful. Variations in the dream structure, such as the absence of lysis, for example, are significant. Jung cited the dream of a woman patient remembered from her sixth year, which had haunted her all her life.

> *I was standing in a desolate place where only craters were to be seen. At a great distance, my father was standing in one of the craters and calling for help.* (CD38, p. 80)

The setting is a desolate landscape pitted with craters. The protagonists are the father and child. The development of the plot and the culmination are indistinguishable: The father stands in a crater and calls for help. Jung interpreted the dream as indicating impending catastrophe. The interpretation was suggested to him by the absence of a lysis, which expressed the lack of a solution to the depicted situation, which was a frightening one, especially to a young child. Jung's interpretation was confirmed objectively by the patient's becoming overtly schizophrenic shortly after she told him the dream.

In connection with this dream and some others without lysis, Jung was asked, "What is the sense in having dreams which are exclusively catastrophic?" Jung replied, "That is the mystery of dreams, that one does not dream, one is dreamt. We suffer the dream, we do not make it . . . . If a fatal destiny lies before us, the thing leading up to it catches us beforehand in the dream, as it will overwhelm us later in reality" (CD38, p. 82).

Implied in all of these observations is the question of judging whether a dream's message is positive or negative, that is, reflecting the psychological development of the dreamer or the failure to develop. The answer is not simple. Clearly, according to Jung, one cannot assume that a dream always has a benevolent intention, even ultimately. Dream images can be highly agreeable or disagreeable, but neither makes the meaning obviously positive or negative. One's conclusion must be based on the nature of the images and how they are related to each other. For example, although a dream without a lysis (such as that of *the child's father calling for help* (CD38, p. 80) often has a bad prognosis, the absence of lysis may not be negative when the development of the plot is not clearly threatening.

In general, a dream that shows something in a negative light is meant negatively. Conversely, positive assurance can be accepted as such. However, Jung found that "it rarely happens that [a dream is] either exclusively positive or exclusively negative" (CW11, par. 53).

It is possible for the context of a dream to demand an evaluation that is quite different from the apparently obvious one, which is based on the dreamer's feeling-response during or following the dream; that is, an image that would be considered bad if it were enacted in conscious experience may mean something good in the life of the psyche. For example, an unmarried woman dreamed that *her nephew had died* (MAM Files). The boy, the only son of her only brother and the darling of the family, represented the carrier of the family tradition. Since the dreamer tended to conform too much, the image of the death of the boy, which would have been a catastrophe in waking life, was interpreted positively as an indication of the death of her tendency to be tradition bound. The interpretation was confirmed when the dreamer was able to discover and affirm more of an individual point of view that was independent of values derived from her family's tradition.

By the same token, a "good" image may have a negative meaning. Jung warned that an exceedingly beautiful image, for example, may indicate the dream's attempt to make something disagreeable look agreeable, because it is what the dreamer unconsciously wants.[10] He reported the following dream from a male patient: The dreamer

> was rummaging about the attic of his house, looking for something. In one of the attic windows he discovered a beautiful cobweb, with a large garden-spider in the centre. It was of a blue colour, and its body sparkled like a diamond. (D13)

The dreamer tended to identify with the Self, that is, he claimed for his ego the infinite possibilities of the Self. This attitude compensated the weakness of his ego and the isolation of the dreamer from his fellow human beings. Therefore, the beautiful mandala image of the cobweb in the dream had a negative import: The ego could be immobilized by becoming lost in the overwhelming unconscious forces intrinsic to the Self.

The discrepancy between the way the dreamer feels about the dream images and events, and their interpretation in a positive or negative light, is often increased, in my experience, by the fact that woven into the dream is an evaluative response that is characteristic of the dreamer in waking life. He or she is happy, sad, repelled, or attracted by the dream experiences as would be the case if they actually happened. Often the dream can be understood more readily if such responses are ignored, on the ground that they are accretions from consciousness. (They differ from the nonevaluative supplemental images mentioned in Ch. 5.)

Further, sometimes the dream images are ambiguous with regard to positive and negative meanings because they are bipolar and oscillate between the two poles.

The Dream Does Not Tell the Dreamer
What To Do

A fact is not the same as instructions on what to do about it or the situation from which it arises. Jung stated specifically, indeed, that a dream does not tell the dreamer what to do. It may or may not present a choice of possible solutions, but it leaves to consciousness the decision on the appropriate action to take. Jung saw this characteristic of dreams as analogous to a compass that tells the traveler the direction of magnetic north but not the path to follow.[11]

Nevertheless, in some instances, the dream appears to carry implicit advice. An example reported by Jung is the dream of an ambitious professor in which *a train was about to be derailed* (D14). Since the train seemed to represent the dreamer's current life plan, the obvious way for him to avoid disaster was to change his plan.

Occasionally, a dream seems to give the dreamer explicit directions, as, for example, when a disembodied voice commands a certain course of action. Since a dream is usually compensatory and not oracular, however, the dreamer must make a judgment in each instance on whether to follow the instructions and, if so, how literally.

The Personalities of Interpreter and Dreamer

Because dream interpretation is a human activity, it is subject to all the possibilities of human error. Even with assumptions excluded, the interpreter must be aware of another possible pitfall, his or her own psychological bent. In suggesting meanings of the dream images, the interpreter must have sufficient self-knowledge to minimize becoming entangled in personal biases.

More specifically, the interpreter of dreams is required to be engaged in the process as a whole person and not just with the superior function, or with knowledge alone. Although it seems, often, that dreams are interpreted mainly by intuition, the other three psychological functions—thinking, sensation, and feeling—are essential also. Intuition may provide interpretive possibilities, but the other functions are needed to test the hypothesized interpretations. Sensation supplies amplifications and, later, tests the interpretation against the original dream images. Thinking is required to analyze the dream into its component parts and to test whether the interpretation can be deduced reasonably from the context that has been established. Feeling, stressed by

Jung as "a certain 'intelligence du coeur' " (CW8, par. 543), is necessary to choose between alternative approaches, such as reductive and constructive, and to evaluate the relevance of the amplifications to the images and of the interpretation to the conscious situation of the dreamer.

Permeating all the functions is the emotional impact a dream carries for the dreamer. The interpreter who experiences vicariously some of this impact has enhanced comprehension of the dream's meaning and value.

In this process, however, the interpreter must not succumb to being overwhelmed by the emotions that the dream images arouse. Required is a "special 'canniness' which depends on a wide understanding" (CW8, par. 543) of human experience to maintain intellectual objectivity even while responding emotionally. This objectivity permits combatting what Jung called the tendency of the "heart . . . [to] give way to sentiment" (CW17, par. 198). Both in objectivity and emotional response, the more familiar the interpreter is with human experiences, the more understanding he or she can bring to the interpretation of dreams.

There is no contradiction between the latter statement and the admonition that the interpreter should not inflict personal amplifications and perspective on the dream. The wider the interpreter's acquaintance with human experiences, the greater is his or her capacity to empathize with a broad variety of emotions. An interpreter with a narrow, personal vision is more likely to try to restrict the interpretation of a dream, to assume that what the interpreter perceives or thinks is identical with what the dreamer perceives or thinks. Jung went so far as to say, "The greatest mistake an analyst can make is to assume that his patient has a psychology similar to his own" (CW8, par. 498). The interpreter must recognize that the dream is the psychic product of the dreamer, whose psychology—not the interpreter's—is the basis of the interpretation.[12]

Jung's concepts of attitude and function types are helpful in assessing the differences and similarities between dreamer and interpreter. A decision of which type best characterizes the dreamer is not necessary. It is enough to recognize that the dreamer may look at the world through very different "spectacles" from the interpreter: the one may be extraverted while the other is introverted, or the one may use the sensation function best while the other is highly intuitive.

The consideration of all these factors makes it possible and necessary for dream interpretation to be based on a "dialectical process" (CW18, par. 492) between the two personalities—dreamer and interpreter—rather than on a struggle for domination of one over the other; that is, the understanding of the dream must develop out of joint reflection and must not go beyond the meaning that is useful to the dreamer.

Notes

[1] Jung said also that an interpreter "should in every single case be ready to construct a totally new theory of dreams" (CW16, par. 317). This seems to be simply another way of saying that each dream carries a unique message.

[2] Jung used as the adjectival form of "sign," the word "semiotic," to mean both "symptomatic" and "emblematic."

[3] Jung conceded that "on the philosophical level the concept is always a symbol even though it is an expression for something known" (Let-1, p. 202).

[4] Jung has been accused of denying the importance of sexuality. Freud's preoccupation with phallic symbols, however, can be seen as a reflection of nineteenth century attitudes toward sexuality. Almost any dream image can be interpreted to have some sexual significance if that is what the analyst is seeking.

[5] Jung saw dreams as "*the commonest and universally accessible source for the investigation of man's symbolizing faculty*, apart from the contents of psychoses, neuroses, myths, and the products of the various arts" (CW18, par. 431), and the "symbol-producing function of our dreams [as] an attempt to bring our original mind back to consciousness" (CW18, par. 591). These are valuable concepts but they do not affect the actual interpretation of dreams.

[6] In one essay, Jung acknowledged the latent content, equating it with "the associative material brought up by analysis" (CW8, par. 503). However, by latent content, he was referring, apparently, to the amplifications rather than the meaning of the dream.

[7] Some Jungian analysts reject Jung's interpretation that the customs official represented Freud. Following Jung's own rubric that a dream figure is not a substitution, they prefer to take the image entirely as a facet of Jung's personality.

[8] Jung wrote also that dream images are more like works of art than like scientific data. This statement may have some poetic significance, but it is not applicable here.

[9] Jung said in an unpublished work, "A peculiarity or a disturbance of the image betrays the interference of a secret thought behind" (Z2, p. 82). Apart from a general warning to pay attention to details, however, little practical help can be derived from this statement.

[10] Reminiscent of Freud's concept of wish-fulfillment (see Ch. 11).

[11] Jung elaborated the compass analogy with the specification that a "conscious correction" (CW10, par. 34) must be made. It seems to me that the correction is subsumed by the individualized meaning of the image for the dreamer.

[12] Jung admitted the difficulty of fulfilling this admonition in a personal communication to J. B. Wheelwright: "A man cannot transcend himself. So the fact is that Freud's, [Alfred] Adler's and my psychology are all generalizations and abstractions of our own psychology."

Chapter 10

OBJECTIVE AND SUBJECTIVE CHARACTERIZATION OF DREAM IMAGES

The amplification of the dream images has been completed, and the dream context has been established. The next major step is to determine the objectivity or subjectivity of the dream images. Are the figures in the images real people, or facets of the dreamer's personality? When a figure is characterized as objective, the image is given an objective interpretation; when the figure is characterized as subjective, the image is given a subjective interpretation. In making the objective-subjective distinction, Jung consistently applied the word "interpretation." In my analysis of the interpretive process, the interpretation of the image necessarily follows the characterization of the dream figure as objective or subjective; hence, the characterization and the interpretation are both objective or both subjective.

A figure is characterized as *objective* when it appears in the dream as an actual person in an actual relationship with the dreamer. The figure is characterized as *subjective* when it appears in the dream as portraying part of the dreamer's personality.[1]

A similarity between Jung's objective interpretation and Freud's manner of dealing with dream images, arises from the fact that both begin with breaking down the dream content into elements of waking experience with and impulses toward other persons and outer objects. Unlike Freud, however, Jung specified criteria for subjective as well as objective interpretations.

Subjective interpretation "detaches the underlying complexes of memory from their external causes, regards them as tendencies or components of the subject (the dreamer), and reunites them with that subject" (CW7, par. 130). In this context, "subjective" does not carry the customary definitions of insubstantial, personal, or illusory. Rather, it means that "all the figures in the dream [are] personified features of the dreamer's own personality" (CW8, par. 509). Jung likened the dream to "a theater in which the dreamer is himself the scene, the player, the prompter, the producer, the author, the public, and the critic" (CW8, par. 509).[2] Thus, a dream image of a particular person, taken subjectively, means that the dreamer has some characteristic, at least potentially, of that dream person.

Although Jung stated that "one dreams in the first place and almost to the exclusion of all else, of oneself" (CW10, par. 321), that is, subjectively, he made ample allowance for objective interpretation, which conveys to the dreamer the view from the unconscious regarding a specific person or external situation. This view is likely to be at some variance with the dreamer's conscious perception and evaluation.

Jung seemed to stress subjective characterization because it helps in understanding dream figures as parts of the dreamer, whose personal responsibility thus is increased. Jung used irony to spell out the value of interpreting dreams subjectively:

> The consequences for our psychology . . . can scarcely be imagined: we would no longer have anybody to rail against, nobody whom we could make responsible, nobody to instruct, improve, and punish! On the contrary we would have to begin, in all things, with ourselves; we would have to demand of ourselves, and of no one else, all the things which we habitually demand of others. (CW8, par. 524)

Jung criticized Freud for interpreting some images objectively and others subjectively, presumably on the ground that Freud made the distinction arbitrarily. Although Jung used both categories, he differed from Freud in that he specified the criteria for each.

When Jung defined and illustrated his criteria for choosing the objective or subjective interpretation, he focused on human figures only. In examples presented for other purposes, however, he included also the dream figures of animals and inanimate objects. It seems to me that these non-human figures can be characterized according to the same criteria as human figures. A door mat, for example, could be interpreted objectively, as something to be trodden under foot, or subjectively, as a part of the dreamer that creates susceptibility to being "stepped on."

Jung did not state specifically whether a dream must be considered as entirely objective or entirely subjective. Because the elements (distinguishable images) in a given dream stand in varying relations to the dreamer, however, we can infer that each element should be considered separately. Thus, a dream may contain some objective and some subjective elements.

The objective approach is indicated if the dream figure is a person important to the dreamer, such as a member of his immediate family or a very close friend; the "object" (the person represented) is important. But if the dream figure is not highly significant to the dreamer, a subjective interpretation probably is more applicable. The human figures who generally meet this latter criterion are remote relatives; someone the dreamer has not seen for a long time; a person who is known to the dreamer's family, perhaps, but plays little role in the dreamer's life; historical personages; and imaginary figures, including figures designated as unknown.

Jung used the example of a man's dream in which a male friend appears as a black sheep. If the friend is someone whom the dreamer has not seen for a long time, the figure should be taken subjectively: The dreamer has a "black sheep" in his psyche. But if the friend is someone currently important in the dreamer's life, the interpretation should be objective: The friend is a dishonorable person or there is something dark between him and dreamer.

Another criterion for choosing the objective or subjective interpretation is the manner in which the dream figure is depicted. If it is someone well known to the dreamer and appears "photographically" (as in life), the dream figure is interpreted objectively. But if the dream picture is inaccurate, the misleading traits probably are attributes of the dreamer or effects of the dreamer's behavior. An example is a man's dream in which appeared

> a drunken, dishevelled, vulgar woman called his "wife" (though in reality his wife was totally different) . . . . Clearly, the dream is seeking to express the idea of a degenerate female who is closely connected with the dreamer. This idea is projected upon his wife, where the statement becomes untrue. What does it refer to, then? . . . His female side was not nice . . . . The dream-statement . . . says: you are behaving like a degenerate female. (CW18, pars. 426, 428–429)

There are dream images, however, that seem to present a distorted image of someone close to the dreamer, but should be taken objectively. For example,

> [A] patient, a young woman who clung to her mother in an extremely sentimental way, always had very sinister dreams about her. She appeared in the dreams as a witch, as a ghost, as a pursuing demon. The mother had spoilt her beyond all reason and had so blinded her by tenderness that the daughter had no conscious idea of her mother's harmful influence. (CW7, par. 280)

The interpretation, therefore, must take into account the dreamer's conscious situation and the interpreter's judgment of what is needed for the dreamer's psychological development at the time. An objective interpretation in the case of the young woman, for example, would serve to protect and enhance the development of her still-weak ego. The subjective interpretation of the man's dream, in contrast, would assume a developed ego which now must take increased responsibility for the dark side of his personality.

Inaccuracy in the dream's presentation of an actual person can take the form of depicting the person too positively, perhaps possessing magical qualities. In this case, subjective interpretation would be necessary because the value, inaccurately attributed to the dream figure, is in the dreamer.

The accuracy or inaccuracy of the description of a person is, of course, disputable. Sometimes it can be ascertained after gathering further information, as in the case of the young officer's dreams of *the scandalous behavior of his fiancée* (CW8, par. 542). In other instances, the dreamer's direct perceptions are the only available information.

Even if the negative qualities are attributed to the dream figure quite accurately, the amplifications may reveal that they place the responsibility for the qualities on the dreamer, who may have elicited them by his or her behavior. The characterization is objective (because the negative qualities actually are in the object) but, as in all dream interpretation, ultimately the focus is on the dream's message of what is needed to overcome the dreamer's psychic imbalance.

The number of the dreamer's associations to the dream figure is not a criterion for objective or subjective characterization, but the emotional charge on the associations is significant. If the associations are highly charged emotionally, the figure probably should be treated as at least partially subjective, on the ground that strong emotion toward a person suggests a heavy projection of an unconscious content of the dreamer. This rule holds true, especially, when the dreamer associates to an unimportant dream figure, a person to whom the dreamer is connected by a strong emotion. Such a substitution is not a disguise, according to Jung, but a means of separating the emotion from the person who seems to arouse it and of pointing out an erroneous or inadequate attitude or way of acting. For example, when a person important to the dreamer appears in a dream as a slave, the unconscious may be reminding the dreamer that the person is not so powerful as the dreamer consciously believes.

Jung applied a subjective interpretation to one of his own dreams, in which an autonomous complex appeared in personified form. After a personal conflict with a Mr. A., Jung dreamed:

I consulted a lawyer on a certain matter, and to my boundless

*astonishment he demanded a fee of no less than five thousand francs
for the consultation—which I strenuously resisted.* (CW8, par. 511)

He associated the lawyer with "an unimportant reminiscence" (CW8, par. 512)
of his student days, during which he got into many arguments; the lawyer's
brusque manner with that of Mr. A.; and the 5000 francs with the amount of
a loan requested of Jung by a poor student. An objective interpretation would
have been possible: Mr. A had made an unreasonable demand on Jung. But
such an interpretation ignores the association to the 5000 francs and the
hypothesis that dream images of persons unimportant in the dreamer's current
life are to be interpreted subjectively. The subjective interpretation Jung
adopted has much more to recommend it: The brusque, argumentative
(student) part of himself is making a heavy demand on him. The dispute with
Mr. A. could not die "because the self-righteous disputant in [Jung] would
still like to see it brought to a 'rightful' conclusion" (CW8, par. 513).

Jung did not specify how to choose between objective and subjective
interpretation when some of the rubrics he offered contradict each other. For
example, a figure important in the dreamer's life which, therefore, should
be interpreted objectively, is likely to be associated with strong emotion in
the dreamer and, consequently, should be interpreted subjectively. Although
warning against overusing the subjective approach, Jung leaned in the direction
of using it in doubtful instances, because he felt it enhanced the dreamer's psychological development in that it forced dealing with the inner problem.

The question of choosing between an objective and a subjective
interpretation is complicated, especially, when the dream figure is the analyst.
In this instance, even more than in others, the nature of the relationship
between the dreamer and the dream figure cannot be discovered on the basis
of the conscious material alone. Transference can cause falsifications of
judgment and it may affect even the nature of the dream images. A positive
transference can result in dreams that depict the analyst as all-powerful; a
negative transference may produce demonic dream images of the analyst.
Interpreting the dreams as reflecting the dreamer's perception of the analyst
constitutes an objective interpretation. If this interpretation proves unproductive, the figure of the analyst can be interpreted subjectively, as a
projected content that belongs to the dreamer.

In dealing with the patient's dreams about the analyst, the latter must consider
also whether self-understanding, often unfavorable, can be gained.[3] In the reverse
situation, in which the analyst dreams about the patient, an objective interpretation usually is appropriate; it may tell the analyst something not known consciously about the patient or about the analyst's attitude toward the patient.
However, a subjective interpretation may be useful, in addition to the objective
interpretation, if the patient touches the realm of the analyst's own complexes.

Regarding the choice between objective and subjective characterization, von Franz (1975) concluded, "Whether a dream should be taken on the objective or the subjective level is seldom unambiguously indicated by the dream itself. The decision is much more *a question of feeling* on the part of the dreamer or of his consultant. Hence dream interpretation is also an ethical matter, not simply an intellectual procedure" (p. 93).

Even when an objective characterization is made, Jung insisted that the dream image cannot be identified with the actual person of whom one dreams. Instead, he said, one must make a distinction between the person as a person and the person as dream object. The dream reflects the way the dreamer sees the person—the dreamer's projection onto the dream object. The quality seen by the dreamer, however, actually must be present in the other person to some degree in order for the projection to take place. Jung referred to the quality in the other person as a "hook" (CW8, par. 519) for the dreamer's projection. But whatever trace of that quality is present in the object is exaggerated by the dreamer, and the significance of the quality is a product of the dreamer's own psyche. If there is no acknowledgement of the dreamer's situation as depicted in the dream, failure to take responsibility for his or her own attitudes may result.

The subjective approach should not be overdone, however. It can lead to "exaggerations in one direction or another" (CW8, par. 524), and to the dreamer's becoming unconnected with reality and, hence, quite isolated.

Along with these warnings on overdoing the subjective approach, Jung defended subjective interpretations as having a legitimate place in psychology, nevertheless.

It has often been objected that interpretation on the subjective level is a philosophical problem and that the application of this principle verges on a *Weltanschauung* and therefore ceases to be scientific. It does not surprise me that psychology debouches into philosophy, for the thinking that underlies philosophy, is after all a psychic activity which, as such, is the proper study of psychology. I always think of psychology as encompassing the whole of the psyche, and that includes philosophy and theology and many other things besides. For underlying all philosophies and all religions are the facts of the human soul, which may ultimately be the arbiters of truth and error. (CW8, par. 525)

I have found it useful to test out both objective and subjective interpretations, usually the objective first. With some dreams, only one will yield a possible interpretation. With others, especially those in which the dream figure is someone close to the dreamer, there is something to be gained from both interpretations as each contributes in its own way to the dreamer's understanding of unconscious processes. The dream is likely, indeed, to deal objectively with the dream figure and the dreamer's relationship with the person represented. But that relationship may have a large component of projection, which needs close examination and calls for a subjective understanding.

An apt example is the young man's dream of *his fiancée* (CW8, par. 542). They gave him an "objective" picture of her. Yet it probably was worth considering whether there was a part of him that wanted to behave as she did in his dreams. Jung said he felt that such a consideration would have been hard for the man; hence, if it were introduced by the analyst, it should be only after the original interpretation had been accepted and assimilated.

Another view of the interrelation between the objective and subjective characterizations is as an interaction. When the dreamer is involved in an intense love relationship, for example, the dreams may reveal the trait in the object (the loved one) that offers a "hook" to the projection. At the same time, the dreams may indicate what aspect of the dreamer is so fascinated with the loved one.

The subjective interpretation of dreams is no longer so controversial as when Jung introduced it as the alternative to Freud's almost exclusively objective approach. Many of the current dream theorists, even some of those identified as "neo-Freudian," are using it increasingly. This fact tends to confirm my impression that the objective-subjective distinction is the most useful of Jung's hypotheses about dream interpretation. For me, it ranks above his other hypotheses because it provides clear alternatives and more specific guidelines are available for its application.

Notes

[1] Objective and subjective characterizations often are referred to as "levels." Because the term may connote a value judgment of height or depth, I avoid using it.

[2] Elsewhere, Jung mentioned "the actors, the libretto, the theatre, and the public rolled into one" (Let-1, p. 355). In neither instance did he mention the director, but von Franz (1975) stated that "the dreamer is . . . the director" (P. 92). However the functionaries are listed, the Self can be considered to be the director.

[3] A comment of Jung's, that is relevant here, borders on a specific symbol, which is outside the scope of this book: When a patient dreams of telling the analyst something, the dream is a message from the dreamer's unconscious to the analyst (DA1, p. 195).

Chapter 11

THE COMPENSATORY FUNCTION OF DREAMS

The keystone of Jung's theory of dream interpretation is usually considered to be the hypothesis that nearly all dreams are compensatory. That is, the actual dream interpretation, with relatively few exceptions (see Ch. 12), is an answer to the question: What is the *"actual situation in the unconscious"* (CW8, par. 505) that compensates the dreamer's conscious situation? Thus, use of the concept of compensation[1] brings the unconscious into relation with consciousness and provides what is needed for psychic equilibrium and, ultimately, wholeness.

Jung's concept of compensation can be seen as a broadening of Freud's concept of wish fulfillment. Both concepts reflect the observation that dreams provide contents that are missing in consciousness. The two concepts differ, however, in that compensation provides what is needed for the wholeness of the individual while wish fulfillment serves merely the id or the ego.

Notwithstanding his opposition to theoretical biases in approaching dream interpretation, Jung treated the concept of compensation as generally useful. He acknowledged his inconsistency, however, by stating that "It is ... [best] not to make any assumptions at all, not even that dreams must of necessity be compensatory" (CW17, par. 189). Nevertheless, he applied the concept of compensation to most dream interpretations because he had discovered empirically, in attempting to sum up the varied ways in which a dream behaves, that "the concept of *compensation* [seems] to be the only adequate [formula]" (CW8, par. 545). Dream behavior varies from "flagrant opposition to our conscious intentions" (CW8, par. 545) to slight deviation from or even concurrence with the conscious attitudes. A non-compensatory dream is unusual and should be interpreted as such only after the possibilities for compensation have been explored thoroughly. Usually, prospective, traumatic, extrasensory, and prophetic dreams are non-compensatory.

Compensation Distinguished from Complementation

In order to explain what he meant by *compensation* Jung distinguished the concept from complementation.[2] "Complement" comes from the Latin *complere*, which means "to supplement or complete." Complementation occurs when the elements omitted consciously or unconsciously from one's awareness of a waking experience appear in a dream. For Jung, complementation was too narrow to describe the function of dreams sufficiently because "it designates a relationship in which two things supplement one another more or less mechanically" (CW8, par. 545).

The word "compensate," on the other hand, is derived from the Latin *compensare*, which means "to equalize." The derivation suggests a "balancing and comparing [of] different data or points of view so as to produce an adjustment or rectification" (CW8, par. 545) by the unconscious of that which has been lost from consciousness. That is, compensation accounts for the appearance in a dream of the psychic material that is necessary to correct a one-sided attitude in the conscious mind. The compensatory function modifies consciousness in a purposeful manner; complementation acts automatically, without specific psychological purpose.

It is difficult to demonstrate that a dream is merely complementary and Jung gave no examples of such dreams. Foulkes (1966), however, discussed what may be a complementary dream when he recounted a dream that contributed to his impression that the Poetzl phenomenon is possible. One of his subjects had a dream in which *someone showed her a painting which was mostly blue, and had shoes in it* (p. 151). Several weeks later, she noted that a calendar picture in her office had blue shoes in it. The complementation is seen in the dream's presentation of a perception of which the dreamer had not been aware.[3] Thus the complementary dream completed the dreamer's recent experiences.

Compensation is more flexible and resourceful than complementation. Compensatory dreams provide material that is directed toward producing wholeness[4] in the personality, as distinguished from awareness of a specific event or situation only.

Compensation as a refinement of complementation is illustrated in the dream of the business man that *his hands and forearms were covered with black dirt* (CW10, par. 826). Complementation is accomplished by the dream's reflecting the perception, which the man did not admit during the day, that his apparently honorable business deal would involve him in fraud. Compensation enters the dream with the psychic intention that he heed the darker aspects of his action. Jung did not specify the darker aspects, but we can infer that the dreamer, although honest in consciousness, had an unconscious willingness to act dishonestly for the sake of monetary gain.

The Foundations of the Compensatory Function of Dreams

The source of psychic compensation, in Jung's view, is in the collective unconscious, the "universal human being in us [which corrects and compensates] the . . . one-sidedness of our conscious life" (CW8, par. 557) "to form a totality, which is the *self*" (CW7, par. 274). The compensatory function of dreams is one of the psyche's self-regulatory mechanisms. The psyche's self-regulation can be compared to the homeostatic functions of the body: Under normal circumstances, one is unaware of the organic and chemical systems that are kept working together naturally and automatically; however, when a gross deviation from the normal occurs in one of the systems, systemic signals, such as fever, suppuration, or pain, announce the presence of malfunction.

The psyche works in a similar fashion. Jung hypothesized that, "under ideal conditions, when life is still simple and unconscious enough to follow the serpentine path of instinct without hesitation or misgiving, . . . the compensation works" (CW9–II, par. 40) without recourse to dreams. But the stresses impinging on the individual[5] often result in the imbalance of a one-sided consciousness, hence, an inadequate adaptation—inwardly, outwardly, or both. The unconscious, out of its unlimited resources, responds, often through dreams, by supplying whatever is needed to restore psychic balance. The specific purpose of a given dream may become evident only after careful and exhaustive investigation, if ever.

The function of compensation can be elucidated also, according to Jung, by the metaphor of a release of energy from the unconscious. This energy is made available by a loss of energy from consciousness, which "raises the psychic potency of certain compensating contents in the unconscious" (CW16, par. 372) and thrusts them into consciousness.

Far from the fulfilled wish of Freudian theory, the material supplied from the unconscious, in Jung's view, may be unpleasant or even painful because it shows those aspects of the dreamer's life—emotions and behavior—that are going wrong, but which the dreamer has not admitted to awareness. Dreams express what the ego does not know or understand: inner reality, not as the dreamer would like it to be, but as it is. The dreams may relate to a momentary condition (even just a mood), a more general situation in the dreamer's experience, or even over the entire life span. (When a dream's message reflects primarily a future condition, the dream probably is not compensatory but, rather, prospective.) Sometimes, the dream calls attention to seeming trifles, sometimes, to very important matters.

Because the compensatory material is part of the dreamer's actuality, the effects cannot be avoided by repressing or ignoring the material. To use another biological analogy, repression of thirst does not end the need for water but makes the need more pressing. If repression is continued long enough, negative effects result as normally as the increased difficulties that may follow the ignoring of physical symptoms. If one is unaware of the occasional twinges of a molar nerve, for example, greater pain follows; if that pain is not acknowledged, an abscess may form and the resulting infection may spread to the entire jaw. By the same token, the ego's ignoring the signals of dreams may lead to the build-up of an "unconscious opposition ... [of] symptoms and situations which irresistibly thwart our conscious intentions" (CW7, par. 187). Even a build-up of "explosive materials" (CW16, par. 333) is possible in the unconscious, and the release of the unconscious opposition through behavior that damages the person. An example of such destructive consequences is the professor's dream of *a train going too fast around a curve and being derailed* (D14). By refusing to acknowledge the dream's message, the dreamer continued to move ahead too fast and, eventually, his career was "derailed."

Varying Modes of Compensation

The concept of compensation is generally useful because it acts in various ways; that is, a dream can compensate the conscious situation in any mode from confirmation to opposition. The degree of disparity between the conscious situation and the message of the dream depends on the amount and nature of the psychic imbalance.

An example of a dream confirming the conscious attitude was reported by a middle-aged woman who had undertaken the direction of some organizational activities. Although she tried to give democratic leadership, she was concerned about being too domineering. She dreamed that *the Kennedys were having a sale to raise money for political campaigns. The congressman from her district and his wife were there, buying some things. The dreamer was interested in the jewelry, but bought none, even though it was inexpensive* (MAM Files). The dreamer associated the Kennedys with dominance and power, and the local congressman with firm leadership and concern for the rights and feelings of others. (Lest the reader suspect partisanship, I hasten to add that the congressman, like the Kennedys, was a Democrat.) In the dream, the valuables were going from the Kennedys, a power-oriented group, to the congressman, a person who exercised the kind of leadership the dreamer wished to give. Although some money (energy) went to the Kennedys, the valuables (worth more than the money paid for them) went to the congressman. The major meaning of the dream seemed to be confirmation that the dreamer was expending less of her energy on domination than on democratic leadership; her efforts were primarily in the hands of the humane, democratic animus. (The fact that the dreamer bought no jewelry might add to the interpretation, or it could be a reflection of the fact that, in waking life, she would not be likely to purchase such items.)

When a dream does not comment on a conscious attitude—especially a decision—it is possible for the attitude to be considered confirmed by the psyche. Also, dreams are not likely to comment on a situation until after the conscious mind has reached a decision.

Some dreams compensate the dreamer's conscious attitude by presenting it in exaggerated form. Jung characterized this kind of dream as "like curing like" (CW8, par. 489). An example is the dream of a young man in which *he met his former boss, Mr. T., who told the dreamer about his ailments. The dreamer comforted him, then reflected that Mr. T.'s ailments were due to smoking, and that he had hollow bones* (MAM Files). The young man associated the hollow bones with cancer of the bone, from which an acquaintance of his had died. He was angry with Mr. T. because of a controversy that had arisen between them. The dream compensated the dreamer's conscious situation of anger toward Mr. T. by presenting the anger in the exaggerated form of "wishing" Mr. T. to have cancer. Thus, the exaggeration occurred when the dreamer was not aware of the full emotional impact of a conscious experience, and was in danger of ignoring his feelings. Many anxiety-producing dreams also function in this way. The dreamer feels anxious but the dream reflects more anxiety than the dreamer realizes.

Some dreams deviate only a little from the conscious situation, and thus modify it but slightly. Such dreams occur when the conscious attitude is adequate for coping with reality and comes close to fulfilling the nature of the individual. A man dreamed: *I was in the woods with my wife. She had a shotgun in her hands. A wolf ran across in front of us. I took the gun from her, shot at the animal and missed* (MAM Files). The "wolf," in popular terms a pursuer of women, represented the dreamer's urge to flirt more with women. By taking the gun from his wife and aiming at the wolf, he was accepting her attitude that the wolf must be eliminated. When he shot at the animal, however, he missed—perhaps deliberately. Thus, by depicting him as threatening the animal, but not killing it, the dream modified the dreamer's conscious attitude of wanting the wolf side of his personality to live.

The dream takes a view that is generally opposite to consciousness when the conscious attitude is inadequate or even wrong, or when it threatens the dreamer's unperceived needs. Jung recounted one of his own dreams that provided this kind of striking contrast:

> *I was walking along a country road through a valley lit by the evening sun. To my right, standing on a steep hill, was a castle, and on the topmost tower, on a kind of balustrade, sat a woman. In order to see her properly I had to bend my head back so far that I got a crick in the neck. Even in my dream I recognized the woman as my patient.* (CW7, par. 189)

The patient in the dream was one whom he had considered a "rum customer . . .; [his] interpretation of her dreams [had not been] hitting the mark" (CW7, par. 189), and their sessions had become increasingly dull. Since he had to look up so far to see her in the dream, his attention was drawn to the fact that he had been looking down on her in waking life.

When the contrast between the conscious situation and the dream compensation is sharp, the conflict between the two may stimulate the dreamer to reconsider an attitude. The issue around which the conflict revolves, for example, may be the dreamer's self-perception. If this self-estimation is too low, the dream is likely to correct it upward; if the self-valuation is too high, the dream probably will remind the dreamer that some qualities need improvement.

Typical of the first category is the young man's dream of *jumping his horse over a ditch full of water, while the rest of the party fell into the ditch* (CW18, par. 519). The dream suggested that the young man was capable of more than he had attempted. The second category is exemplified in another dream of the ambitious professor in which *he returned to his home village and heard his former classmates, peasants, remark that he did not visit there often* (CW18, par. 163). The dreamer in the first example was encouraged by a superior performance; in the second, the dreamer was humbled by a reminder of his lowly origins.

Compensation may take more than one form in the same dream. Jung told of a modest and self-effacing man who frequently had dream encounters with great figures from history, such as Napoleon and Alexander the Great (CW18, par. 509). On the one hand, the dreamer's feelings of inferiority were reflected in his unimportance compared to such great and famous men; on the other, the dreams were establishing an exaggerated view of his importance by the reflected glory of his meetings with illustrious persons.

Jung mentioned some specific kinds of messages that are conveyed by dream compensation. One is a critical portrayal of the dreamer's personality traits which are exaggeratedly and offensively one-sided. The dream of the woman *who was ushered into a cowshed to meet her "friends"* (CW18, par. 469) is an example. It criticized her prejudiced and unreasoning approach to controversial issues.

Another form that compensation may take is to answer a question. The woman who dreamed of the *congressman buying jewelry at the Kennedys' sale* (MAM Files) had been asking herself consciously whether her leadership was too dominant. If the question has not been asked consciously, the compensation can inform the dreamer of the question, by implication, as well as of the answer. For example, the man who dreamed that *"his hands and forearms were covered with black dirt"* (CW10, par. 826) may have been asking himself, unconsciously, the question, "Is there anything wrong with that offer?"

Negative and Positive Compensation

Although virtually all dreams are compensatory, some compensate negatively, that is, reductively; others, positively, that is, constructively. Both kinds of compensation are purposive[6] or goal oriented in that they offer something the dreamer needs for psychic balance.

Reductive Interpretation

For some years after his break with Freud, Jung continued to define "reductive" interpretation in the literal (and Freudian) sense of "leading back," that is, tracing the dream images back to their "elementary processes of wishing or striving" (CW6, par. 788). "Reductive" was equated with "causal," but not in the popular sense of believing that a dream image is caused by a waking experience, such as witnessing an automobile accident or thinking of an old friend. (Jung referred to such experiences as marks of the "continuity *backwards*" [CW8, par. 444] of dream images.) Rather, "causal" refers to discovering the unpleasant events or repressed impulses out of which the images have arisen. To Freud, the impulses were always sexual, usually of an infantile nature. To Jung, they were not always sexual; the dream's effect was to pull the dreamer's consciousness backward to an awareness of whatever inner parts he or she had rejected—infantile and destructive motives, perhaps— but not necessarily sexual impulses.

Later, Jung came to see reductive interpretation as dangerous in that it devalues and even destroys conscious attitudes. He found the risk of using such interpretations unnecessary, evidently because the reductive interpretation is often invalid, and undesirable because it is almost certainly threatening to the already shaky ego of a person in psychotherapy.

In addition, Jung found that reductive interpretation, in leading back from the individual case to facts or commonly held attitudes, tends to encourage dealing with symbols as if they were fixed. A reductive interpretation may lose much of the value of a given image, therefore, by limiting its meaning to that of a class of images, such as phallic "symbols."

At the same time, Jung saw the importance of restoring to consciousness material which had been repressed because of its unpleasant nature, including tracing the roots of dream images to the emotions of childhood that are still alive in the adult dreamer. He achieved this aim by modifying the term "reductive" to mean "negatively compensatory." Thus, a reductive interpretation serves to help the dreamer to become conscious of "illusions, fictions and exaggerated attitudes" (CW17, par. 195) when the inner development has not kept pace with the outer adaptation and achievement. Although care must be taken to use it only to modify the dreamer's immediate attitude and not the entire personality, negative compensation is a necessary "retarding operation" (CW9-I, par. 277)[7] because it connects the dreamer with a natural and childlike side.

A reductive interpretation was required by a dream that was presented by the ambitious professor:

> [He] finds himself in a small village in Switzerland. He is a very solemn black figure in a long coat; under his arm he carries several thick books. There is a group of young boys whom he recognizes as having been his classmates. They are looking at him and they say: "That fellow does not often make his appearance here." (CW18, par. 163)

The dreamer had come to Jung because he suffered from vertigo, palpitation, nausea, and exhaustion. When Jung pointed out that these were symptoms of mountain sickness, often suffered by climbers, the man recognized them as such. The dreamer had risen rapidly from a poor peasant background and hoped to climb still higher to a prestigious appointment. The dream confronted him with the unwelcome repressed fact that he seldom recalled his origins and that he must recognize his limitations. The interpretation was no doubt painful for the professor to hear and seemingly destructive in its threat to his successful career. But it was negatively compensatory rather than merely reductive, in that it drew his attention to a part of his past experience which he had to take into account as he sought to achieve his conscious ends.

Constructive Interpretation

The primary alternative to the reductive interpretation is the constructive, or synthetic. It also answers the question, "Why?" but in the sense of "to what purpose?" or "what for?" Constructive interpretation adds something to the dreamer's conscious attitude, strengthening and protecting what is healthy and worth preserving in the dreamer, "so as to deprive the morbidities of any foothold" (CW17, par. 195). It is meant to be used when the conscious attitude is more or less normal but capable of greater development and refinement, or when the unconscious tendencies, which also are capable of being developed, are misunderstood and are being depreciated by the conscious mind. Thus, a constructive interpretation opens the way for "the realization of a part of the personality which . . . is still in the process of becoming" (CW8, par. 558). This realization can occur as the dreamer becomes more receptive to unconscious resources. That is, constructive interpretation prepares the way for reconciling contradictory values.

To illustrate the constructive approach, Jung applied it to the dream of the old general whom he had met on a train:

> *I was on parade with a number of young officers, and our commander-in-chief was inspecting us. Eventually he came to me, but instead of asking a technical question he demanded a definition of the beautiful. I tried in vain to find a satisfactory answer, and felt most dreadfully ashamed when he passed on to the next man, a very young major, and asked him the same question. This fellow came out with a damned good answer, just the one I would have given if only I could have found it.* This gave me such a shock that I woke up (CW17, par. 187).

Jung saw the purpose of the dream as that of adding to the general's conscious attitude the aesthetic interests which had been neglected rather than repressed. Thus, the dream is positively compensatory in encouraging the development of an underemphasized side of the dreamer's personality; it was pointing a way out of a narrow existence, "a possible line of advance [the dreamer] would never have thought of [himself] " (CW8, par. 847).

The danger in this approach is that if it is used incorrectly, it can exaggerate illusions. If it is used appropriately, however, it is more individual than the reductive because it captures more fully the significance of the particular image. Also, it enlarges the dreamer's view of creative possibilities, and it even may prepare the way, according to Jung, for the transcendent function.[8]

The choice of the reductive or constructive interpretation of a particular dream image depends on the nature of the material, the state of the dreamer's psychic development, and the interpreter's judgment on what is needed for the dreamer's development at the time. A decision on the basis of the nature of the material suggests that only a reductive *or* a constructive interpretation is possible for a given dream. Often, however, both are possible and the decision regarding which to use must be made on the basis of the dreamer's psychic situation. With some dreamers, the emphasis is on reductive interpretation, at least for a time, because the analysis and, consequently, the interpretations of dreams must start with "a careful study of infantile events and fantasies" (CW18, par. 518). With other dreamers, it is possible to start with constructive interpretations or, as Jung stated, to begin "at the top, even if this [means] soaring into a mist of most unlikely metaphysical speculations" (CW18, par. 518). Although recognizing the dangers, Jung found that such speculations may be required in "follow[ing] the gropings of [the individual dreamer's] unconscious towards the light" (CW18, par. 518). In any case, the choice between a reductive and a constructive interpretation "depends largely on the individual disposition of the dreamer" (CW18, par. 520).

In other instances, the interpreter must make a judgment on what is needed for the dreamer's development at the time. "If [the dreamer] is obviously convinced of his greatness . . . it will be easy to show from the associative material how inappropriate and childish his intentions are, and how much they emanate from infantile wishes to be equal or superior to his parents. But . . . where an all-prevading feeling of worthlessness has already devalued every positive aspect [of his personality], to show the dreamer . . . how infantile, ridiculous, or even perverse he is would be quite unfitting" (CW18, par. 514).

An example is the dream of the young man that *his father was driving while drunk* (CW16, par. 335). Jung saw two possibilities for a reductive interpretation: that the young man was projecting his own behavior onto his father, and that his positive conscious relationship with his father was based on unconscious "over-compensated resistances" (CW16, par. 335). Jung saw no ground for either of these interpretations. Rather, he chose a constructive interpretation: the dreamer's "unconscious is . . . trying to take the father down a peg [forcing] the son to contrast himself with his father, which is the only way he could become conscious of himself" (CW16, par. 336). This interpretation "was apparently the correct one, for it . . . won the spontaneous assent of the dreamer, and no real values were damaged, either for the father or for the son" (CW16, par. 337).

Archetypal dreams cannot be interpreted reductively, wrote Jung, because they "are spiritual experiences that defy any attempt at rationalization" (CW17, par. 208). When he made the statement he was referring, apparently, to the archetypal dreams which he saw as characteristic of the advanced stages of the individuation process, such as those he included in "A Study in the Process of Individuation" (CW9-I). He applied a reductive interpretation, however, to some archetypal dreams. The dream of the young man that *he was bitten in the heel by a snake* (CW8, par. 305), is an example. Jung's amplifications were archetypal, yet his interpretation was one of reducing the man's immediate problem—his inability to accept his feelings about being jilted by a young woman—to that of his attachment to his mother.

As Jung demonstrated, some dreams can be interpreted both reductively and constructively, without contradiction. With regard to one of his examples, Jung offered both interpretations, implying that the constructive was preferable: An unmarried woman dreamed that *someone gave her a wonderful, richly ornamented, antique sword dug up out of a tumulus* (CW8, par. 149).

Her associations were:

> Her *father's* dagger, which he once flashed in the sun in front of her. It made a great impression on her. Her father was in every respect an energetic, strong-willed man, with an impetuous temperament, and adventurous in love affairs. A *Celtic* bronze sword: Patient is proud of her Celtic ancestry. The Celts are full of temperament, impetuous, passionate. The ornamentation has a mysterious look about it, ancient tradition, runes, signs of ancient wisdom, ancient civilizations, heritage of mankind, brought to light again out of the grave.

Jung described the dreamer:

> [The] patient has a . . . rich tissue of sexual fantasies about her father, whom she lost early. She always put herself in her mother's place, although with strong resistances towards her father. She has never been able to accept a man like her father and has therefore chosen weakly, neurotic men against her will. . . . Up till now the patient has been the opposite [of her father] in every respect. She is just on the point of realizing that a person can also will something and need not merely be driven as she had always believed. . . . her character has been that of a perpetually whining, pampered, spoilt child . . . extremely passive.

The reductive interpretation is:

> . . . The dream digs up her wish for her father's "weapon," . . . point[ing] to a phallic fantasy.

The constructive interpretation is:

> It is as if the patient needed such a weapon. Her father had the weapon. He was energetic, lived accordingly, and also took upon himself the difficulties inherent in his temperament . . . . This weapon is a very ancient heritage of mankind, which lay buried in the patient and was brought to light through excavation (analysis). The weapon has to do with insight, with wisdom. It is a means of attack and defense. Her father's weapon was a passionate, unbending will, with which he made his way through life . . . . The will based on a knowledge of life and on insight is an ancient heritage of the human race, which also is in her, but till now lay buried. (CW8, par. 151)

If a choice had to be made, I would opt with Jung for the constructive interpretation. But reductive and constructive interpretations seem not to be mutually exclusive in this instance. It is entirely possible for a woman to have sexual fantasies (which Jung considered "instinctual impulses") about her father and, at the same time, to need his positive attitude toward life. Moreover, if the sexual fantasies are taken symbolically and not as signs, as Jung strongly recommended, her "sexual" desire for her father may be understood as a desire to incorporate his vigorous, passionate way of living. The dream indicated that such an attitude toward life was potential in her.

Evaluation of Reductive-Constructive Distinction

Some of the problems with the reductive-constructive distinction may be inferred from the discussion of the woman's dream of *an antique sword* (CW8, par. 149). Jung treated the reductive approach as essentially negative. Yet it is difficult to see how instinctual impulses can be considered entirely negative, however inconvenient they may be. They are necessary for wholeness, especially for overly intellectual people. That is, if instinctual impulses have been repressed, it is important that they be restored to consciousness. Looking at the reductive approach from this perspective makes it blur into the constructive. Thus, a useful message for the interpreter of dreams is to be careful neither to "fly with archetypes" (and hence "spiritual" interpretations) nor to reduce the psyche to biological urges alone.

Since the reductive and constructive interpretations are both compensatory, thoroughness requires an examination of whether the two directions (major modes) of the compensatory function, confirmation and opposition, apply to both reductive and constructive interpretations. It seems evident that they do. Among the examples given in the discussion of compensation, some dreams are interpreted in each direction and reductively, others in each direction and constructively. For example, the woman's dream of *the Kennedys' sale* (MAM Files) was confirming and constructive, while the young man's dream of *jumping his horse* (CW18, par. 519) was opposing and constructive. The man's dream that *he shot at a wolf and missed* (MAM Files) was confirming and reductive; the professor's dream of *hearing his former classmates saying that he did not visit his home village often* (CW18, par. 163) required an opposing and reductive interpretation. Thus, both contrasting directions (confirmation and opposition) of compensation apply to both reductive and constructive interpretations, and support is given to Jung's statement that both interpretations must be available to gain a "complete conception of the nature of dreams" (CW8, par. 473).

*Pairing Subjective and Objective with Reductive and
Constructive Alternatives*

Jung used the term "analytic" as synonymous with "reductive," but also to describe objective characterization. Similarly, he used "synthetic" to mean "constructive," and to describe subjective characterization. The implication seems to be that an objectively understood image can be interpreted only reductively, and a subjectively understood image requires a constructive interpretation. Some of Jung's examples demonstrate, however, that such a generalization does not hold. One rather clear-cut instance of a reductive interpretation for a subjectively understood image is the dream of the professor *hearing his former classmates saying that he did not visit his home village often* (CW18, par. 163). The former classmates portrayed—subjectively—the part of him that still lived in the village of his childhood. Yet the interpretation was reductive, also, in reminding him of the unwelcome fact of his humble origin.

The objective-constructive combination is exemplified by the dream of the young man that *his father was driving while drunk* (CW16, par. 335). The dream was objective in that it commented on the dreamer's relationship with his actual father; it was constructive in urging the young man to become aware of his own assets.

This modification of Jung's theory (that both objective and subjective interpretations can be linked to both reductive and constructive interpretations) does not detract, in my view, from the value of either the reductive-constructive or the objective-subjective alternatives. Rather, it renders them more useful by recognizing them as independent factors. That is, it gives four possible approaches, hence greater flexibility, where only two existed according to Jung's grouping.

Possible Therapeutic Effects of Compensation

Discovering the compensation in a dream is not just an intellectual exercise; it stimulates self-reflection that leads the dreamer beyond the concerns of the ego into communication with split-off parts of the psyche, including the "thoughts that were not thought and the feelings that were not felt by day" (CW8, par. 300). The assimilation of the psychic facts revealed in the dream often results in healing; that is, the dreamer undergoes a change in attitude, such as coming to understand the reason for a particular emotion, or accepting the darkness within. Although the effect of any one dream may not be dramatic, the cumulative effect of compensatory dreams is "a new level of consciousness" (CW11, par. 779). Categories and examples of some of the possible therapeutic effects of dream compensation follow.

Understanding the Basis for Emotions

A young married woman came to understand the reason for a particular emotion as a result of the interpretation of the following dream: "*I was married to D. in a wedding ceremony. Afterwards he wouldn't be my husband. He wouldn't live with me*" (MAM Files). D. was a younger man about whom the dreamer had had sexual fantasies which, she felt, were inappropriate, and she had pushed them out of her mind. D. never had paid much attention to her. She had spent the evening before the dream with a group of friends, including D., and he had ignored her. She found herself in an angry mood the day after the dream. The dream could be seen as an explanation of her anger, as a reaction to D.'s ignoring her, and as a projection of her rejection of the sexual fantasies she had entertained about him. For this dreamer, who had strong and frequent negative emotions—some were unaccountable to her and others she attributed to her husband's or children's actions—it was therapeutic to be confronted with the part played by her own expectations.

Change in Attitude

A change in attitude on two levels was the effect of another young woman's dream:

> Driving a tractor or bulldozer, H. comes over to me. He asks if I know about the Number 7 gear. I say yes, it's reverse. He goes into a lengthy technical explanation about it. I'm not interested in his explanation. It is sufficient for me to know what Number 7 gear is and how it acts. (MAM Files)

Both the dreamer and H., a colleague, worked with technical matters. The dream made the young woman realize that she had been uninterested in the technology behind her work. After discussing the dream in her analytic sessions, she became more interested in technical explanations and also in her motivations, which could be understood as the "technology" behind actions.

Accepting the "Other" in Oneself

The need for psychotherapy often is experienced as depression, which may come, go, and come again unaccountably. Many Jungian analysts find that depression is often due to denial of the unacceptable aspects of the dreamer's personality. When these are faced consciously, as can happen through dream analysis, there is pain at the time but the chronic depression is likely to lift.

The less acceptable part of oneself may appear as an "other," perhaps unknown, among the dream figures. One highly intellectual, thinking-type young woman dreamed that *her friend found a feeble-minded young woman in the woods, and hacked her with an axe* (MAM Files). The friend was a feeling type. The dream indicated that the dreamer's inferior function was violently destructive to the undeveloped part of her intellect. As her analysis proceeded, the dreamer came increasingly to accept both her feeling side and her own lack of development in certain intellectual areas.

The purpose of the dream compensation is not always a "moral" one; that is, it does not always encourage the dreamer to behave better. Sometimes it makes the dreamer aware of an "immoral" tendency. Such a person was the man whose wife bored him and who was having difficulty recognizing his erotic impulses (D8). Such awareness may result in a highly moral person's taking actions which he or she had rejected previously.

In other instances, a repressed moral side comes to consciousness, as in the case of the young man who dreamed of *picking an apple* (D4); he became aware of the guilt he felt over his affair with a housemaid.

Effectiveness of Compensation without Dream Interpretation

The compensation can be effective, sometimes, even if the dream is not understood. An example of a dream that served a compensatory function before being interpreted was that of Barbara, a 40-year-old woman:

I was watching a sheriff shoot a pistol. I looked up into the trees and there were many dead squirrels. They had holes in their abdomens and I could see sunflower seeds sticking out. I wondered if they had burst and died from being too full of sunflower seeds. I felt really bad about their being dead; I loved the squirrels. I got the horrible feeling that the sheriff had shot and killed the squirrels. I was repulsed by the whole thing, and thought they hadn't burst their bellies from too many sunflower seeds after all. He was very cold and matter of fact about the whole thing. (MAM Files)

Barbara's mother had been visiting her. The mother tended to be unenthusiastic about or even critical of Barbara's varied educational activities: a class in Spanish, piano lessons, and Yoga instruction. Before the dream, Barbara responded to her mother's attitudes with a coldness she did not like in herself. After the dream, she began to find that she was less angry with her mother's criticism, and she was able even to express some warmth toward her.

A few days later the dream was interpreted in an analytic session. Barbara associated the squirrels with those she was accustomed to seeing daily in the trees outside her kitchen window. She saw them as playful, full of life, "enjoying being squirrels." She recounted their running to the end of a limb and squealing when it bent, appearing to be playing tag. She associated the sheriff in the dream with the local sheriff whom she saw as cold, condemnatory, and sarcastic, especially in his dealings with young people. Sunflower seeds, when toasted and salted, were enjoyed as snacks by her children. The dream was interpreted as indicating that her playful side was not killing itself with overindulgence in tasty morsels but, rather, that the coldness in her was killing the playful side. The emotional impact of the dream, perhaps by a kind of subliminal realization of this message even before the dream was interpreted, made it possible for her to change her attitude toward her mother. Despite the possibility of a dream's compensating without being interpreted. Jung saw the compensation as even more effective when the dream is understood through a valid interpretation.

Individuation Process

The individuation process, according to Jung, depends on the assimilation of unconscious contents that are made accessible through dreams. By attending to the dream images, which give expression to the deepest levels of the psyche, the dreamer "can be led back to the natural law of his own being" (CW16, par. 351). Thus, the day-to-day therapeutic importance of dreams, with their successive acts of compensation, gives way to a developmental process in the personality. The therapist can observe "in long and difficult treatments [including] a series of dreams often running into hundreds, . . . [that what seem to be momentary adjustments of one-sidedness] seem to hang together and . . . be subordinated to a common goal, . . . this unconscious process spontaneously expressing itself in the symbolism of a long dream-series [is] the individuation process" (CW8, par. 550). A series of dream reflecting such a developmental process is found in *Psychology and Alchemy* (CW12).

Each step of the individuation process begins with a psychic conflict that, usually, is based on the resistance of the conscious attitude to the intrusion of incompatible thoughts and feelings from the unconscious. The psyche is stimulated by the conflict to create a satisfactory solution in the form of a new attitude that can deal with opposites, such as light and darkness. Eventually, a subsequent life-situation is reached wherein the solution thus produced is inadequate, and a new conflict develops, eliciting a new compensatory response from the unconscious, thus initiating the next step in the individuation process.

Problems with Compensation

Although the compensatory function of dreams works in general toward greater psychic wholeness, it is not always benevolent. For example, when a person seems headed for a decision or action that threatens to have destructive results, even suicide, the dream may not restrain the dreamer; it may even lead further in the destructive direction. Jung believed that this eventuality is compensatory in that it shows the dreamer all aspects of the psyche; he based his belief on the ground that "it is apparently more important to nature that one should have consciousness, understanding, than to avoid suffering" (Z10, p. 71).

It is advisable, at the same time, to look twice at what is being threatened with destruction. It may be something which is "hopelessly inefficient or evil" (CW14, par. 149); its destruction is a compensatory response. The dream of *the murder of Alice* (MAM Files) could have been interpreted either as revealing the dreamer's murderous anger, or as a healthy impulse to eliminate something that had been destructive to her throughout her life. The latter interpretation was obviously preferable. Some seemingly destructive dreams lose their dangerous aspect, moreover, when the dreamer takes a receptive attitude to the unconscious.

The value of the compensatory function of dreams may be lost when the conscious attitude is "negative, critical, hostile, or disparaging" (CW10, par. 33). The loss may occur through the incomprehensibility of dream images or a person's inability to remember dreams. It may occur through nightmares, which the dreamer avoids remembering or reflecting on, or through the dreamer's experiencing dreams as menacing, to the point of sleeplessness. Moreover, even "the most beautiful and impressive dreams often have no lasting or transformative effect on the dreamer" (CW9-I, par. 211), for unknown reasons.

Sometimes a dream fails to function in a compensatory way; this failure is a danger signal. The mountain climber's dream that *he experienced ecstasy as he climbed higher and higher until he stepped into empty air* (D1) is an example of a dream without a compensatory function. (This dream was anticipatory; see Ch. 12.)[9] His feeling of ecstasy in the dream did not give a true picture of the catastrophe that could follow the action and left him subject to the subsequent acting out of his own self-destruction.

Such extreme examples occur only rarely, probably, but Jung found that he had many cases of dreams which "showed signs of a tendency to self-injury weeks beforehand" (CW7, par. 194). He found that "If the warning of the dream is not heeded, real accidents may take its place" (CW18, par. 471).

In other dreams, absence of a solution to an obvious catastrophe may indicate a failure of compensation. An example is the reported childhood dream of *the child's father standing in a crater and calling for help* (CD38, p. 80).

The compensatory action of dreams can be lost, also, when the conscious mind is overemphasizing the importance of the unconscious. Jung warned that "The recognition of the unconscious is not a Bolshevist experiment which puts the lowest on top and thus re-establishes the very situation it intended to correct" (CW16, par. 338). In such a "Bolshevist experiment," the newly repressed content would reappear as an unconscious compensation. Even worse, if the unconscious is treated as superior to consciousness, "we should then be degraded to the mental level of fortune-tellers and would be obliged to accept all the futility of superstition, or else, following vulgar opinion, to deny any value at all to dreams" (CW7, par. 489).

Thus the values of the conscious personality must remain intact if unconscious compensation is to be effective. "Assimilation is never a question of 'this *or* that', but always of 'this *and* that' " (CW16, par. 338), wrote Jung. The conscious values must be maintained, especially when dream compensation is considered in making decisions. If the conscious mind does not "[fulfil] its tasks to the very limit" (CW8, par. 568), the unconscious will be overrated and the power of conscious decision impaired.

Testing the Theory of Compensation

Experimental data supporting the compensatory function of dreams were gathered by Bash (1952). In his study, Plate IX of the Rorschach ink-blot test was exposed 200 times to each subject. In a dark room, the plate was illuminated for five seconds, after which a response was requested. "Certain subjects gave responses rich in fantasy, connected and of a dream-like character, which they themselves often spontaneously compared with dreams." When these responses were compared with the Rorschach responses of the same subjects after they were given the test under ordinary conditions, "in the great majority of the cases a reversal of the experience type had occurred during the dream-like episode" (p. 295); that is, extraverts gave introverted responses and vice versa. Bash saw these findings as a confirmation of Jung's thesis that the attitude of the unconscious is compensatory to that of the conscious mind.

Dallett (1973) examined the degree to which dreams compensate the inability of a person to meet an important psychological need, such as sensory stimulation or social interaction. Her results were clearly positive only in selected cases, and she concluded that "what is compensated may be in part the dreamer's weakness in relation to a particular environment, if that environment is salient for him" (p. 4).

Since the theory of compensation is thought by many to be the heart of Jung's approach to dream interpretation, it seems to me that it should receive maximal attention in explanation, illustration, clinical demonstration, and testing by further empirical studies. Indeed, relevant work has been done by dream investigators outside the Jungian school. Some of the most careful quantitative work on dreams has been done by Hall and his co-workers, using the method of content analysis. Their research led them to believe that dreams reflect the waking personality. For example,

If a person has a lot of dreams in which he is quarreling or fighting with other characters one would conclude that he is an aggressive person in waking life. Usually this is the case. Aggression in dreams tends to mirror aggression in waking life. Sometimes, however, aggressiveness in waking life does not manifest itself in overt behavior but expresses itself in private fantasy and thought . . . . In such cases, it might be concluded that dreams were compensating for what a person lacked in waking life. Actually, however, this apparent lack of correlation or inverse correlation between how a person acts in his dreams and how he acts in waking life is rare. (Bell & Hall, 1971, p. 122)

The authors' conclusion that dreams rarely "compensate for what a person lack[s] in waking life," could be considered a disconfirmation of the theory of compensation. It seems to me, however, that Bell and Hall were not challenging the total concept of the compensatory function of dreams so much as they were limiting it to one aspect. It is entirely congenial to Jung's theory to hypothesize that many dreams reflect the dreamer's waking behavior. Indeed, early in his career he wrote that "the dream is . . . a subliminal picture of the actual psychological situation of the individual in his waking state" (CW4, par. 552). Although his later statements, quoted at the beginning of this chapter, stress the dream's function in reflecting unconscious contents, the distinction may be less sharp than it would seem. Waking behavior is not always conscious. A person may act very aggressively, for example, but experience such behavior subjectively as necessary defense against unwarranted attacks. In addition, a person may be aware of certain behaviors but be unaware of the motivations for such behaviors. For instance, activity in a political cause may be, as far as one knows, entirely to help suffering humanity. However, mixed with that motivation may be a strong desire for power. Dreams could compensate consciousness by pointing out the unconscious motivation of the behavior.

It is evident that the theory of compensation is a very difficult one to test. Hall and his co-workers, as well as Bash, have made a beginning, but to test Jung's hypotheses thoroughly will require the refinement of research methodology and, perhaps, of the theory.

Notes

[1] Strictly speaking, the correct term is "the compensatory function of dreams." Like Jung, however, I follow the practice of using the briefer and more manageable term, "compensation."

[2] Sometimes Jung used the two terms synonymously, although usually he differentiated between them. In addition, he defined compensation as a "psychological refinement" (CW8, par. 545n) or broadening of complementation. Thus, on one occasion he used "complementary" to mean opposed to the conscious attitude: "The more one-sided the conscious situation is, the more the compensation takes on a *complementary* character. Obvious examples of this can be found in people who naively deceive themselves or who hold to some fanatical belief. As we know, the most lurid scenes of temptation are depicted in the dreams of ascetics" (CW18, par. 1487).

[3] A compensatory interpretation of the dream might be possible, also, were we able to examine the entire dream content.

[4] Jung sometimes used the term "psychic balance" and sometimes "wholeness" to characterize the result of dream compensation. He seemed to assume that each successive compensatory dream redressed the dreamer's psychic balance a little more and brought him or her closer to wholeness.

[5] Jung attributed the stresses and resulting psychic imbalance to the influence of civilization (CW9-II, par. 40), but anthropological studies postdating Jung's work show that preliterate people also suffer from psychic imbalances.

[6] Jung sometimes used "finally oriented" synonymously with "purposive," but he distinguished "final" from philosophical teleology, which had been rejected by the natural science of his time, adding, "By finality, I mean merely the immanent psychological striving for a goal" (CW8, par. 456). The question with which Jung struggled, as reflected in this statement, is no longer such a problem. Although Aristotle's "final cause" probably is still unacceptable to most scientists, purposeful behavior of human beings, lower animals, and even machines is a generally accepted fact. For example, as A. Rapaport (1959) explained, the very existence of servomechanisms corroborates the claim that the behavior, including purposeful behavior, of organisms, "can be explained in terms of known physical laws" (p. 1744).

[7] Jung did not label the "retarding operation" passage as applying to reductive interpretation, but the content makes the connection clear.

[8] In his essay, "The Transcendent Function" (CW8, pars. 131–193), Jung stated a preference for non-dream sources of unconscious material because he found them more useful than dreams in developing the transcendent function: "ideas 'out of the blue,' slips, deceptions and lapses of memory, symptomatic actions, [and] spontaneous fantasies" (CW8, pars. 154–155), as well as the process he later called "active imagination." When this essay was written in 1916, he found dreams "unsuitable or difficult to make use of in developing the transcendent function, because they make too great demands on the subject" (CW8, par. 153). Nevertheless, Jung later found increasingly that the transcendent function is active in dreams. He discussed it specifically, however, only in relation to constructive dream interpretations. In my view, a reductive interpretation also could prepare the way for the transcendent function by making conscious the conflict between the repressed shadow and the conscious values.

[9] An anticipatory (prospective) interpretation is commonly assumed to be "better" than a compensatory interpretation. This dream refutes that assumption: It falls short of serving a compensatory function and has a negative import, yet serves a prospective function.

Chapter 12
NON-COMPENSATORY DREAMS

Although the preponderance of dreams are compensatory, some are not. Non-compensatory dreams can be classified as prospective, traumatic, extrasensory, or prophetic.[1]

Prospective Dreams

The most numerous, probably, of the non-compensatory dreams are the prospective,[2] or anticipatory. They can be distinguished from compensatory dreams by the situation in which they occur, and by their psychic function. A compensatory dream occurs when "the conscious attitude is more or less adequate" (CW8, par. 494); it indicates what is needed for wholeness. A prospective dream occurs when the conscious attitude is "obviously unsatisfactory" (CW8, par. 494); it shows how the needed development might come about[3] or the consequences of proceeding on the present course.

A prospective interpretation is appropriate when the conscious attitude is highly unsatisfactory and the unconscious produces a dream that is more than compensatory. Such a dream prompts the dreamer toward an adaptation, inwardly and outwardly, on his or her "true level" (CW8, par. 495). Jung found such dreams to be relatively rare but, when they occurred, they were nearly always effective in changing the dreamer's attitude.

A prospective dream can be likened to a preliminary exercise, sketch, or plan that is roughed out in advance.[4] It may outline the solution of an unusually difficult conflict or it may prepare the dreamer for a future attitude that may not be recognized as needed until weeks or even months after the dream. The dream can be either positive or negative in its import and, occasionally, it may foreshadow specific good fortune or catastrophe. The prospective function of dreams "meets with the approval of the *consensus gentium*, since in the superstitions of all times and races the dream has been regarded as a truth-telling oracle" (CW8, par. 491).

Natural phenomena, however, provide the basis for the prospective or anticipatory function of dreams. Jung found that "Dreams prepare, announce, or warn about certain situations often long before they actually happen. This is not necessarily a miracle or a precognition. Most crises . . . have a long incubation [in the unconscious]" (CW18, par. 473). Thus, a prospective dream "results from the fusion of subliminal . . . perceptions, thoughts, and feelings" (CW8, par. 493).

As examples of the prospective function of dreams, Jung cited three dreams of a young woman who came to him after she had attempted treatment with two other analysts. At the beginning of treatment with each analyst she had a dream. Jung reported the three dreams as follows:

> *I have to cross the frontier into another country, but cannot find the customs house where I should go to declare what I carry with me, and nobody can tell me where it is.* (That dream gave her the feeling that she would never be able to find the proper relation to her analyst; but because she had feelings of inferiority and did not trust her judgment, she remained with him . . . for two months although the treatment proved unsuccessful, and then she left. She then went to another analyst. Again she dreamed: *I have to cross the frontier, but the night is pitch-black and I cannot find the customs house. After a long search I see a tiny light far off in the distance. Somebody says that the customs house is over there. But in order to get there, I have to pass through a valley and a dark wood in which I lose my way. I am afraid to go on, but nevertheless I go through it, and then I notice that someone is near me. Suddenly he clings to me in the darkness like a madman. I try to shake myself free, but that somebody clings to me still more, and I suddenly discover that it is my analyst.*
>
> This treatment, too, was broken off after a few weeks because the analyst unconsciously identified himself with the patient and the result was complete loss of orientation on both sides.
>
> The third dream took place under my treatment: *I have to cross the Swiss frontier. It is day and I see the customs house. I cross the frontier*

and go into the customs house, and there stands a Swiss customs official. A woman goes in front of me and he lets that woman pass, and then my turn comes. I have only a handbag with me and think I have nothing to declare. But the official looks at me and says, "What have you got in your bag?" I say, "Oh, nothing at all," and open it. He puts his hand in and, to my astonishment, pulls out something that grows bigger and bigger, until it is two complete beds. Her problem was that she had a resistance against marriage; she was engaged and would not marry for certain reasons, and those beds were the marriage-beds. I pulled that complex out of her and made her realize the problem, and soon after she married. (Edited composite of accounts in CW16, pars. 307–312, and CW18, pars. 346–348.)

The first two dreams were "anticipations of the difficulties she is to have with the doctors concerned" (CW16, par. 311), based on her subliminal perceptions of the therapists; the third anticipated both a more fruitful treatment and the specific problem with which she would have to deal.[5]

The situation anticipated by the dream is more likely to relate to an inner state of the dreamer than to an outer event. Jung used the example of approaching death. The dream is unlikely to forecast the death, but it may comment on the dreamer's potential attitude toward death and related matters, such as the possibility of immortality.

Whatever the specific content, Jung found that prospective dreams embody the fact that "everything that will be happens on the basis of what has been" (CW9-1, par. 499). "The unconscious is capable . . . of manifesting an intelligence and purposiveness superior to the actual conscious insight . . . this is a basic religious phenomenon, [sometimes] observed . . . in a person whose conscious mental attitude [seems] most unlikely to produce religious phenomena." (CW11, par. 63).

Prospective dreams may seem prophetic, as many people assume all dreams to be, in the sense of foretelling specific future events, but the dreams are not prophetic any more than "a medical diagnosis or a weather forecast. They are merely an anticipatory combination of probabilities which may coincide with the actual behavior of things but need not . . . agree in every detail" (CW8, par. 493). (Such dreams, like that of the mountain climber who acted out his dream, are classified by Jung as anticipatory rather than prophetic, evidently because the action results from the same psychic state that produced the dream.)

The prospective function of dreams is a very appealing concept, but it carries corresponding dangers. Jung linked the function with creativity as well as individuation, and sometimes he implied that a prospective dream anticipates only positive developments. The examples he gave, however, such as the first two dreams of *crossing the frontier* (CW16, pars. 307–308; CW18, pars. 346–347), demonstrate the incompleteness of this view. Although some prospective dreams provide solutions, others anticipate negative, even catastrophic developments.

Jung did not provide adequate criteria for choosing a prospective rather than a compensatory interpretation of a dream. From the choices he made, however, one can infer that a prospective interpretation is allowable only when a compensatory one does not seem valid. Even then, the interpreter must be open to the possibility that he or she simply has not found the compensatory interpretation. Thus, Jung warned against overuse of prospective interpretations, "for one might easily be led to suppose that the dream is a kind of psychopomp which, because of its superior knowledge, infallibly guides life in the right direction" (CW8, par. 494). I have found, moreover, that a prospective interpretation can lead to an inflated notion of the dreamer's possibilities, either positively or negatively. Hence, I tend to move cautiously into such interpretations. Nevertheless, the occurrence of a prospective dream is unpredictable. Whatever the dream, it must be interpreted correctly, or the individuation process may be frustrated.

Traumatic Dreams

A reactive or traumatic dream is one that recalls a life-threatening situation, such as war or natural catastrophe, or reflects pathological physical conditions, such as severe pain. It is always a recurring dream. It is not compensatory because it is unrelated to the conscious situation of the dreamer (except for the preoccupation with the traumatic experience), and "conscious assimilation of the fragment [of the psyche] reproduced by the dream does not . . . put an end to the disturbance which determined the dream" (CW8, par. 500).

Not all recurring dreams that rehearse experiences charged with affect are traumatic. In order for a dream to qualify as traumatic, its significance must lie solely in the reliving of an actual experience. Whether a dream so qualifies is determined by events subsequent to interpretation. Non-traumatic dreams cease to recur once they are interpreted correctly. True traumatic dreams are undisturbed by analysis; they continue to recur until the emotional impact of the trauma has diminished sufficiently.

Military psychiatrists in World War I had, according to Jung, an intuitive awareness of the non-compensatory nature of dreams of war scenes. They noted that, ordinarily, "Soldiers in the field dreamt far less of the war than of their homes. Military psychiatrists considered it a basic principle that a man should be pulled out of the front lines when he started dreaming too much of war scenes, for that meant he no longer possessed any psychic defenses against the impressions from outside" (MDR, p. 273).

Extrasensory Dreams

A third type of non-compensatory dream reflects extrasensory perceptions. Jung mentioned two kinds: telepathic and precognitive. A telepathic dream often has compensatory meaning also, and the telepathic significance may not be recognized at the time the dream is analyzed. It can be discerned only when the event reflected by the dream becomes known to the dreamer. Moreover, the telepathic significance is found solely in the manifest content, that is, the context is disregarded. Although a telepathic dream often deals with an event as important as a death, it can foretell something as unimportant as the arrival of an inconsequential letter. Jung saw telepathic dreams not as supernatural but as based on something inaccessible to our present level of knowledge.[6]

He cited the example of a dream in which the dreamer

> *saw and experienced . . . the sudden death of a friend, with all the characteristic details.* The dreamer was in Europe at the time and the friend in America. The death was verified next morning by telegram, and ten days later a letter confirmed the details. Comparison of European time with American time showed that the death occurred at least an hour before the dream. Experiences of this kind frequently take place a little before or after the critical event. (CW8, par. 852)

Jung, however, did not take apparently telepathic dreams at their face value of "action at a distance" (CW8, par. 503); he insisted that they be explored for other possible explanations. He mentioned the possibilities of cryptomnesia (hidden memory, which was defined by Masserman [1946, p. 271] as the "recall of events not recognized by the subject as part of his actual experience"), "parallel psychic processes" or "concordance of associations" (CW8, par. 503). Evidently Jung considered the latter two terms synonymous, designating either a tendency among persons with close psychic connection, such as a family, to produce similar images and other mental contents, or paramnesia (defined in Random House Dictionary as "a distortion of memory in which fact and fantasy are confused"). The rather common experience of "déjà vu" may be based on an earlier dream image, perhaps with a telepathic source.

There is some experimental support for Jung's hypothesis of telepathic influence on dreams. Ullman, Krippner, and Vaughan (1973) cited numerous experiments in which dream images were influenced through telepathy, as indicated by a statistical level far above chance. For example, "the target concentrated on by [the experimenter] was a picture of a colored mosaic. The color violet, prominent in the picture, came through in a couple of [images] " (p. 88).[7] The experimental dreams were less clearly influenced by telepathy, however, than those mentioned by Jung as telepathic, such as the dream of the friend's death.

Prophetic Dreams

Precognition, another form of extrasensory perception, is the basis for "prophetic" dreams, the fourth kind of non-compensatory dream. They foretell in accurate detail specific future events (beyond the next day) that are of importance to more people than just the dreamer. Although popular opinion would have it that many dreams are prophetic, Jung found them to be rare and cited only one example that he labeled as prophetic, that is, precognitive.[8] The dream cannot be considered telepathic because it clearly meets his specifications for prophecy, except that he did not specify whether and how it was of more than personal importance.

> I remember the story of a student friend whose father had promised him a trip to Spain if he passed his final examinations satisfactorily. My friend thereupon dreamed that *he was walking through a Spanish city. The street led to a square, where there was a Gothic cathedral. He then turned right, around a corner, into another street. There he was met by an elegant carriage drawn by two cream-coloured horses.* Then he woke up. He told us about the dream as we were sitting round a table drinking beer. Shortly afterward, having successfully passed his examinations, he went to Spain, and there, in one of the streets he recognized the city of his dream. He found the square and the cathedral, which exactly corresponded to the dream-image. He wanted to go straight to the cathedral, but then remembered that in the dream he had turned right, at the corner, into another street. He was curious to find out whether his dream would be corroborated further. Hardly had he turned the corner when he saw in reality the carriage with the two cream-coloured horses. (CW8, par. 973)

Jung saw the dream as demonstrating an "existing foreknowledge" (CW8, par. 973); nevertheless he reminded his readers that little or nothing is known about the source of such precognition.

Another example of a prophetic dream, although not so identified by Jung, was

> the dream of an old chief, in which *he learnt that one of his cows had calved, and was now standing with her calf down by the river, in a particular clearing.* He was too old to keep track of his many cattle that pastured in the various open places in the forest, so he naturally didn't know this cow was going to calve, let alone where. But the cow and the calf were found just where he had dreamt they would be. (CW18, par. 1291)

The dream fulfills the requirement (for a prophetic interpretation) of matching the outer situation. Although the old chief presumably was in communication with the herders who probably knew that the cow was pregnant and when she was due to calve, his dream image of the actual spot where the animals could be found was prophetic; furthermore, finding the animals probably had some importance for a tribe that lived at the subsistence level.

Occasionally, a dream appears to prophesy a significant event in the lives of many people or, even, for one or more nation states. Such an event was the assassination of President Kennedy; many people claimed to have dreamed about it beforehand. Dreams of this kind seem to be rare. A study to determine their frequency would require records of the entire remembered dream production of a large number of persons.

Jung's scepticism about prophetic dreams suggests that he entertained the possibility of such unlikely events only because he had found instances of them. Moreover, he insisted that each precognitive dream can be verified as such "only when the precognized event has actually happened" (Let-1, p. 460), usually long after the dream's occurrence; hence, such dreams are of little use in foretelling the future. It is apparent, therefore, that Jung approached dreams with empiricism, rather than with the mysticism of which he is accused.

Notes

[1] Frey-Rohn (1974) stated that only traumatic dreams are non-compensatory. However, in acknowledging the dream as "*a spontaneous expression of unconscious processes* [as well as] a meaningfully compensating response to conscious convictions and tendencies" (p. 241; italics added), she implicitly recognized the prospective function as one that is not subsumed in the compensatory function.

[2] Jung (CW6, par. 701) gave credit to Alphonse Maeder (1916) for the concept of the prospective function of dreams. Maeder was a German neurologist and psychiatrist and, for a time, a disciple of Freud's. He was president of the Zurich Psychoanalytical Association in 1912, when the break between Freud and Jung was nearing its culmination, and afterward he allied himself with Jung. Maeder was younger than Jung and, like him, was on the staff of the Burghölzli Hospital. There, he later developed a method of brief psychotherapy based on the principles of the self-regulation of the psyche and self-healing.

[3] In his earlier works, Jung sometimes used "prospective" interchangeably with "constructive." In some passages (e.g., CW3, par. 391; CW8, par. 496), he defined "prospective" as I have defined "constructive"; in other passages (e.g., CW8, par. 493), he used "prospective" as I have defined it here. Since the latter usage is maintained in Jung's last published statement on dream interpretation (CW18, par. 545), I am adopting it as representative of his refined thought.

[4] This idea is an expansion of a statement in Jung's 1912 work, *Psychology of the Unconscious* (CW5, *Symbols of Transformation*), in which he asserted, "The dream . . . prepares the dreamer for the events of the following day" (CW5, par. 5).

[5] Jung commented that his "interpretation of the third dream was a disappointment to her, but the fact that the dream showed the frontier as already crossed encouraged her to go on in spite of all difficulties" (CW16, par. 312).

[6] Toward the end of his life, Jung posited ESP or "Psi phenomena" as synchronistic rather than "due to any supranormal (psychic) faculties," on the

ground that "they are *bound to occur* under certain conditions if space, time, and causality are not axiomatic but merely statistical truths" (Let-2, p. 541). That is, "the archetype can by its very nature manifest itself not only in the individual directly concerned but in another person or even in several people at once—for instance in parallel dreams, the 'transmission' of which should be regarded more as a Psi-phenomenon than anything else" (Let-2, p. 542).

[7] Faraday (1974) criticized Ullman's conclusions on the ground that "we can never know whether ESP takes place in the dream itself or entered the mind in waking life too quickly to be consciously registered; like any other stimulus picked up during the course of the day, it could remain dormant until the dreaming brain replays the day's events in depth" (p. 258). Thus, she seemed to refer to the phenomenon Jung called "cryptomnesia."

[8] Jung presented the dream as an example of synchronicity, but stated that "it is sometimes difficult to avoid the impression that there is a sort of foreknowledge of the coming series of events" (CW8, par. 972). J. W. Dunne (1938) cited many dreams that he considered truly prophetic.

Chapter 13
DREAMS AND THE
THERAPEUTIC PROCESS

In Jungian therapy, dream analysis is taken for granted, "if there are no counter-indications" (CW18, par. 476). It is considered to be the most direct and efficacious way of discovering the unconscious contents that the dreamer needs to assimilate, of bringing consciousness and the unconscious into relation with each other, a relation that is necessary for wholeness, and of effecting the assimilation of unconscious contents. Jung found that therapy requires "a change in and through the unconscious [and that] in the light of our present knowledge this can be achieved only by the . . . assimilation of unconscious contents" (CW16, par. 326). Without such assimilation, the unconscious components of the personality "appear merely as neurotic symptoms" (CW16, par. 326).

A person seeking psychotherapeutic help is acknowledging inability to solve problems without aid. The therapist, who can offer help only on a time-limited basis, uses any available resource to move the patient quickly into the healing process. The patient's dreams are such a resource.

The therapist must make a judgment, of course, on whether and when to undertake dream analysis with a particular patient. Jung advised, "So long as other methods of education are efficacious and useful, we do not need the assistance of the unconscious. Indeed, it would be a more reprehensible blunder if we tried to substitute analysis of the unconscious for well-tried conscious methods. The analytical method should be strictly reserved for those cases where other methods have failed" (CW17, par. 282). In this statement he virtually equated the analytic method with dream analysis, underscoring the centrality of work with dreams in analysis but not in all psychotherapy. Nevertheless, many patients who gravitate to Jungian therapists have found that therapy is inadequate if it does not make use of dreams. (Although Jungians make no precise distinction between therapy and analysis, the term "analysis" is usually reserved for a deeper, more prolonged process.)

Dream analysis can be useful outside the therapeutic process; this use is discussed later in this chapter. Most dream interpretation, however, takes place within the context of therapy. The use of dream interpretation in therapy has important ramifications: Dreams both influence and are influenced by the therapeutic situation and process. That is, in dream-oriented therapy, many dreams probably are determined by the patient's relationship with the therapist. Indeed, the therapist appears as a figure in some dreams. Moreover, the interpretation of dreams influences subsequent dreams. And Jung found that it was a "daily occurrence in analysis [that he would say to a patient] 'I don't know what the answer is, but we shall see what the unconscious has to say about it' and then the next dream [would bring] a most amazing solution, as if [we] had submitted the whole thing to a higher supreme authority" (DA2, p. 123). The interpretations heighten the significance of all dreams in the patient's life, furthermore, and often affect the frequency of remembered dreams.

Frequency of Dreams

Patients differ widely in the number of dreams remembered and brought into the sessions. The question often arises of what factors make the difference, especially when few or no dreams are reported. Studies (e.g., Rechtschaffen & Verdone, 1964) have shown reliable individual differences in the amount of REM sleep, and the amount of REM sleep is correlated with the number of dreams remembered on waking (Antrobus, Dement & Fisher, 1964; Goodenough, Shapiro, Holden, & Steinschriber, 1959). Thus some dreamers may have more dreams potentially available to recall.

Nevertheless, everyone dreams, and in my experience, as in Jung's, patients usually begin to remember their dreams when they go into treatment with therapists who value dreams and, consequently, the patients pay more attention to their dreams. Some patients bring accounts of vivid dreams at the beginning of therapy and subsequently report none. (Although Jung sometimes said that such patients did not dream, he said on other occasions that they did not remember their dreams. The latter explanation is clearly preferable in the light of the psychophysiological evidence that everyone dreams.) Situational factors, such as being wakened by an alarm clock or immediate responsibilities upon waking, may appear to reduce the number of remembered dreams. These factors, however, often can be mitigated by an earlier awakening.

When a patient could not remember dreams, Jung found frequently that the patient was holding back some conscious material from the analysis, or wished to remain passive and let the therapist do the work. A patient who may be unable to admit to the therapist a disliked personal quality consequently may project the "defect" onto the therapist, "calmly assuming that since [the therapist] is more or less deficient morally, certain unpleasant things [cannot be communicated] to him" (CW4, par. 535).[1] By "deficient morally" Jung seemed to mean lacking in the courage to face the offensive realities of life. Probably the most common hindrance to remembering dreams is the patient's fear that the dreams will reveal something that he or she will not like knowing.

There are other reasons for a paucity of reported dreams. Sometimes a patient neglects to record or report a dream that does not make a coherent story or seems too small a fragment even to be described. Sometimes, it appears to me that, if the dreams brought to one session have not been interpreted adequately, the patient's remembering of subsequent dreams is inhibited. An inadequate interpretation may be due to insufficient discussion or incorrect interpretations of the dreams brought in.

At times, the patient focuses so intensely on dreams as to pay too little attention to other aspects of life. The unconscious then may seem to retaliate by blocking out the memory of dreams, as if the patient must face those aspects of life before becoming able to remember dreams. Indeed, Witkin and his co-workers (cited by Ullman et al., 1973) found empirically that people who do not remember dreams may be "less differentiated," that is, they may "rely more on the outside world for their sense of identity" (pp. 75–76). When the barriers have been overcome, the patient is likely to begin or to resume remembering dreams. (For practical helps in remembering dreams, see Reed, 1976.)[2]

Decreased frequency of dreams may be found also, according to Jung, in the later stages of analysis when "the objectivation of images replaces the dreams" (CW18, par. 399). Jung referred here to the use of his technique of "active imagination," that is, the active effort by the analysand to observe and interact with dream images and waking images. He believed that this procedure tends to quicken the individuation process. In my experience, individuation indeed is quickened by active imagination, but there is not necessarily a decrease in dream frequency.

At the other end of the frequency scale is the dreamer who recalls a great many dreams. Such high frequency itself is not abnormal but may be due to "an overloading of the unconscious . . ., usually because there is a problematical situation which the dreamer has tended to overlook or has not mastered" (Let-1, p. 182). The dreamer may become emotionally upset by the quantity and content of the remembered dreams, but the upset usually is temporary and not a cause for alarm.

A less demonstrable basis for an unusually high frequency of dreams is that of "unrealized, unconscious fantasies" (CW9-I, par. 101), a Freudian-sounding hypothesis posited by Jung as late as 1936. When these fantasies, based on "[repressed instincts] , . . . are made conscious, the dreams change their character and become weaker and less frequent" (CW9-I, par. 101). Again, my experience is not entirely consonant with Jung's. I find that patients in all stages of development and any momentary state may remember numbers of dreams far above or below the average for themselves or for patients in general.

Diagnosis and Prognosis by Dream Interpretation

Although Jung warned against using dreams solely to discover the origin of the dreamer's neurosis, he considered some dreams to provide valuable facts for the assessment of the dreamer's problems to a degree at least equivalent to the Word Association Test. In some instances, the dream facts provide the key to the dreamer's psychology—reveal complexes. Such a key could be used to test other clues to the complexes, or in the absence of such clues.

Sometimes the interpretation of a dream provides a diagnosis in the form of a psychiatric category, perhaps accompanied by the corresponding prognosis. An example of such a dream was given by Jung in the case of the 16-year-old male patient who

> had as the initial symptom of a severe compulsion neurosis the following dream: *He is walking along an unfamiliar street. It is dark, and he hears steps coming behind him. With a feeling of fear he quickens his pace. The footsteps come nearer, and his fear increases. He begins to run. But the footsteps seem to be overtaking him. Finally he turns around, and there he sees the devil. In deathly terror, he leaps into the air, and hangs there suspended.* This dream was reported twice, a sign of its special urgency . . . .
> After this dream the neurosis started, and its essential feature was that the patient had, as he put it, to keep himself in a "provisional" or "uncontaminated" state of purity . . . . Even before the patient had any suspicion of the hellish existence that lay before him, the dream showed him that if he wanted to come down to earth again there would have to be a pact with evil. (CW7, par. 285–286)

Thus the dream, in addition to acting as a symptom of the neurosis, suggested the diagnosis and hinted at the means of healing.

Dreams are diagnostic also when they reveal the aetiology of the specific symptoms. An example is one of the dreams of the professor who came to Jung suffering from the symptoms of "mountain-sickness," which afflicts mountain climbers who climb too fast. The dream was that *he visited his home village and heard his peasant boy former classmates remark that he seldom came there* (CW18, par. 163). Jung interpreted the dream as meaning that the professor had lost touch with his humble origins in climbing—professionally—too fast.

The professor's second dream was prognostic. It was the dream in which *he saw the train he had intended to take, going too fast around a curve and being derailed* (D14). The prognosis was that his present way of living would result in psychic destruction but it was still possible for him to avoid the catastrophe.

Diagnosis and prognosis converge when a dream warns of a latent psychosis.[3] Jung was presented with such a dream by a physician who said he wanted to become an analyst. The man was sure he had no problems, and in the first sessions he seemed to be normal in every respect. He recounted as few dreams as problems, however, and Jung began to be uneasy about him. After about two weeks the patient brought a dream from which he had awakened in a panic: *He was in a building empty of other people, and eventually made his way to a gigantic room. In the center of it was an idiot child of about two years, sitting on a chamber pot, smearing himself with feces* (D15). Jung did not interpret the dream to the patient; he saw it as indicating a latent psychosis for which the dreamer's apparent supernormality was compensating. The sessions were continued, but only until Jung could find an acceptable pretext for ending the analysis. The man had no subsequent severe difficulties but Jung was convinced that if the analysis had continued, the psychosis would have surfaced.

The absence of lysis in a dream also may indicate an unfortunate prognosis, although not necessarily. In fact, no particular psychological diagnostic category has any certain signs in dreams. For example, although Jung sometimes diagnosed a latent psychosis, he warned that such a disturbance is not easy to detect. Even the strangest dreams and visions do not necessarily indicate the current presence of a psychosis; the same strange unconscious material is found in the dreams of neurotics and normal people as in the dreams of psychotics, and in the work of poets and other artists.

Experimental evidence seems not to support Jung's hypothesis that the dreams of psychotics are indistinguishable from those of normals. Although some studies (Bolgar, 1954; and Kant, 1942) failed to find significant differences in dream content between the two groups, others (Sheppard, 1963; and Sheppard & Saul, 1958) discovered that by using an ego-rating system for the dream content, they could distinguish clearly between the dreams of a group of psychotic patients and those of a group of industrial employees.

A dream can be prognostic in organic as well as psychic illnesses. Two dreams, one from antiquity and one modern, used similar images with the same apparent meaning. The first was quoted by Artemidorous of Daldis[4] in the second century A.D.:

> A man dreamt that *he saw his father die in the flames of a house on fire.* Not long afterward, he himself died of a *phlegmone* (fire, high fever), presumably pneumonia. (CW18, par. 544)

A modern parallel was cited by Jung:

> A colleague of mine was suffering from a deadly gangrenous fever—in fact, a *phlegmone.* A former patient of his, who had no knowledge of the nature of the doctor's illness, dreamed that *the doctor was perishing in a great fire.* The dream occurred . . . when [the doctor] had just entered the hospital and the disease was only . . . beginning. The dreamer knew nothing but the bare fact that the doctor was ill and had entered hospital. [Three weeks later, the doctor died.] (CW18, par. 544)

In metaphorical terms, such as presenting "the diseased body as a man's earthly house, and the fever as the heat of a conflagration that is destroying the house and its inhabitant" (CW18, par. 545), both dreams gave an accurate and graphic prognosis of death by "burning up."

As an example of a dream that identified an organic illness in a specific part of the body, Jung mentioned a dream that had been reported by a patient of Dr. T. M. Davie (1935):

> *Someone beside me kept on asking me something about oiling some machinery. Milk was suggested as the best lubricant. Apparently I thought that oozy slime was preferable. Then a pond was drained, and amid the slime there were two extinct animals. One was a minute mastodon.* I forgot what the other one was.
>
> Davie's comment: "I thought it would be of interest to submit this dream to Jung to ask what his interpretation would be. He had no hesitation in saying that it indicated some organic disturbance, and that the illness was not primarily a psychological one, although there were numerous psychological derivatives in the dream. The . . . pond [which was drained] he interpreted as the damming-up of the cerebrospinal fluid circulation." (CW18, par. 135n)

Jung's interpretation was an apt description of the disease that was diagnosed later: periventricular epilepsy.

The young woman's dreams in which *her mother committed suicide by hanging* and *a horse jumped out a window to his death* (D11) seemed to predict the death of the body. The mother can be understood as the origin, that is, the necessary basis, of the young woman's life. The horse can be construed as the animal, or biological, life. The death of either figure is an image of bodily death.

Jung's finding that dreams can diagnose organic illness has been supported by other dream theorists. Medard Boss (1957), for example, also gave examples of such dreams. (He maintained that they reflected a state of the dreamer's "whole essence" [p. 160], one aspect of which is the physical disease.) For example, one patient had a dream recurring more than once on each of two successive nights in which

> *a Balinese demon of disease would appear to her and force her to sit on an overheated central-heating pipe.* She experienced an insupportable burning pain between her legs . . . which always woke her. However, after waking she no longer felt the slightest bit of pain. On the third night the pain persisted after waking [from the dream]. At the same time she was suffering from ague. The doctor (who had previously omitted to test the patient's urine), could now diagnose acute cystitis. (p. 160)

The examples demonstrate that when an organic diagnosis is indicated, the personal associations of the dreamer to the dream images are not adequate to establish the dream context because in such dreams the images are relatively fixed. The necessary amplification is the analogous dysfunction, a knowledge of which is transmitted to the dreamer by means of subliminal perceptions.

That subliminal perceptions can be internal is posited also by a dream investigator cited anonymously by Diamond (1962). "When we don't have to attend to the bustle of external events, we may become aware of faint aches and pains which had previously gone unnoticed" (p. 209). Evidence for such phenomena is found in sensory-deprivation experiments. In one such experiment,

> Among . . . 12 subjects were three physicians who remained in [a] tank up to six hours, floating in the tepid water with latex masks covering their faces. One physician reported how startled he was to hear his own heart sounds with "ear-filling intensity". Another said he heard "the repeated snapping sound" of his own aortic cusps closing at the end of each systole, or contraction, of the heart. A third reported in awe that for the first and only time in his life he heard "the gliding sound" made by the moving of his large joints. (Shurley, 1960, p. 210)

Initial Dreams

To one of the first therapy sessions, the patient may bring an "initial dream" of far-reaching importance. The content of such dreams varies greatly, of course, since each reflects the particular situation and need of the dreamer, but it is possible for an initial dream to "reveal to the doctor . . . the whole programme of the unconscious" (CW16, par. 343). (If it does, it is a prospective dream.) An initial dream may recall forgotten experiences from the past, in which the major possibilities for development as well as severe wounds, may lie buried; or it may point to present facts, such as the dreamer's marriage or social position, a problematical aspect of which has not been acknowledged by the conscious mind.

When the patient's problems are very serious, the initial dream may be of a visionary nature in its clarity and impressiveness. Initial dreams in general, according to Jung, tend to be more transparent than dreams brought later in analysis. This transparency may be due to the patient's naivete.

Identification of an initial dream is based on no clear criterion. It may be the first remembered dream after the first analytic session, or one just preceding the first session; sometimes the dream occurs shortly before or after the prospective patient makes the appointment for the first session; in other cases, the dream brought in may be actually the second or third which occurred after one of these events. Then, of course, it is "initial" only in a general sense of "early," not literally "first."

Initial dreams are among those most likely to provide a diagnosis and, perhaps, a prognosis of the dreamer's psychological condition. The professor's dream of *visiting his home village and hearing his peasant-boy former classmates remark that he seldom came there* (CW18, par. 163) was diagnostic. The same man's dream of *the train going too fast around the curve and being derailed* (D14) was prognostic. Both can be considered initial dreams because both were from the night before the dreamer's first consultation with Jung.

A few initial dreams indicate a prognosis for the therapy rather than for the "disease." One such was the dream of the young woman who came to Jung after seeing two therapists previously. Her initial dream in the treatment with the second doctor portrayed her as *losing her way and finding someone clinging to her like a madman* (CW16, par. 308). The dream anticipated correctly the therapist's unconscious identification with the patient.

Alternatively, the initial dream may reflect the patient's attitude toward the therapist, even before the two have met, and toward the therapy being undertaken. Another young woman, who also had been in analysis with two previous analysts, dreamed, after her initial session with the third, that

> she told her husband she could not go on with analysis. She was feeling completely drained and depressed. Her husband asked why the doctors had let things come to this point with her. Finally, as she sat saying nothing, her husband talked to the head man. Somehow it was agreed that she would see him at a cost of $X. (MAM Files)

The dreamer tended to depreciate all her analysts; she was depressed about the difficulty of becoming psychically healthier through therapy, and she was passive in the therapy sessions. Furthermore, $X was more than her previous analytic sessions had cost. The dream seems to reflect her passive and negative attitudes toward the therapy. Thus, it indicated her attitude at the time. It anticipated, also, her attitude throughout the therapy (which was terminated after a year because she moved to a distant state).

Other initial dreams give an idea of the course of treatment the dreamer needs. Such a dream was another of those of the young woman who came to Jung after having seen two other analysts. In her initial dream of the analysis with Jung, *a customs official pulled a pair of twin beds out of her bag* (CW16, par. 310). Jung saw the twin beds hidden in her bag as indicating a resistance to marriage. Thus the dream "prescribed" the treatment: She must be helped to recognize her resistance.

A difficulty in making maximum use of the initial dream is that the new patient may be so preoccupied with the crisis which made therapy necessary that the first few sessions are spent in a description of the situation and assimilating the heightened emotions which have been aroused. By the time any attention can be paid to dreams, the conscious situation of the initial dream cannot be ascertained. If it is not sufficient to take the beginning of the analysis as the conscious situation, little interpretation is possible.

Various Stages of Therapy and Dreams

The beginning stages of therapy are especially important for the observation of dreams, but a complete analysis of each dream may be less important, at this time, than the gathering of amplifications. When the dreamer has begun to be aware of problems through the associations, dream interpretation can begin to hypothesize what the unconscious is saying.

The early dreams in therapy, according to Jung, contain a great deal of dark material which the dreamer is reluctant to look at, including some that reveals the dreamer's ways of resisting self-knowledge and retaining wrong attitudes. These dreams, he found, are likely to be more complete and better composed than later ones.[5] However, in my experience, the early dreams are more likely than later ones to be diffuse, so that it is difficult to discover focused messages in them. In any case, the interpreter and dreamer do what they can with the available dreams.

As always, the dream context is of crucial importance for valid dream interpretation. At the beginning of therapy, more than later, the dreamer's subjective view of his or her problems and needs is likely to be distorted by complexes. Therefore, an accurate assessment of the dreamer's conscious situation is especially important.

After the initial dream with its probable clarity and far-reaching importance, and the early dreams which may be clear to the interpreter if not to the dreamer, there often come dreams which seem much more obscure. Jung warned that the interpreter cannot assume that such dreams reflect the dreamer's resistance to therapy. They may reflect, rather, the fact that the therapy has reached important layers of the personality.

Different stages of therapy require varying interpretations of some dream images, according to Jung, because of the changing requirements of the dreamer's psychological development. An explicit sexual image, such as the dreamer's having sexual intercourse with a loved one, for example, may be interpreted as a wish for that experience if the dream occurs early in the therapy, when the dreamer's sexual impulses may be still under repression. Later, when the dreamer's sexual impulses have been brought into consciousness, the same interpretation could result in arresting personality development. More appropriate then would be a symbolic interpretation of the sexual contact as a potential or actual union with an unconscious aspect of the dreamer's personality. In general terms, dreams that occur later in the therapy are more likely than early ones to require a subjective and a constructive interpretation.[6]

At any stage of therapy, consideration of dreams can enhance the therapeutic process even without interpretation. In addition to the therapeutic value of amplifications discussed earlier, I have found that a dream may be so obviously relevant to a particular problem that the dreamer knows as soon as the dream is recorded that the problematic topic or situation which has been avoided must be brought into an analytic session.

Transference and Dreams

The analysand's unconscious response to the analyst is known as transference. Jung defined transference as the "projections which act as a substitute for a real psychological relationship" (CW16, par. 284). It is not always, as Freud had it, a transference to the therapist of the patient's response to one or both parents; in the Jungian view, some transference from parents to therapist may be found, but projection is always present. For instance, the patient may perceive the therapist as the fount of all wisdom. The therapist, however wise, is human and the patient's perception is an obvious exaggeration. The patient evidently is projecting his or her own potential for wisdom onto the therapist.[7]

When Jung wrote that "The transference phenomenon is an inevitable feature of every thorough analysis" (CW16, par. 283),[8] he seemed to mean that the patient discovers some inner potential (e.g., the potential for wisdom) through the emotions that are aroused because of projecting that quality onto the therapist. These emotions are both positive and negative; for example, adulation of the "wise" therapist, and anger that the therapist does not always speak and act wisely.

Transference often is a help to dream analysis, especially for patients who experience dreams as little more than curious anecdotes. For them, transference to the analyst may be both a temporary substitute for and a way of achieving interest in their dreams. If the analyst is convinced of the importance of dreams, his or her patients are likely to begin to value them also.

An additional interaction between transference and dreams is that the first clues to the appearance of transference may be found in dreams. The following dream, reported by a woman in the early weeks of analysis, contains evidence of her not-yet-conscious feelings toward the analyst:

> *I was looking for a place that was supposed to help me get well. A woman who looked something like [my analyst] was helping me to look. I did not understand how a place could help me until it occurred to me that I could leave my burden there.* (MAM Files)

The subsequent course of analysis confirmed the impression that the "place" was the analyst's consulting room. The analyst's helping the dreamer to "find" it may mean helping her to realize its availability. The transference in this instance was the dreamer's seeing the analyst as helper.

In some situations, a dream interpretation can even contribute to the development of a positive transference, that is, when the interpretation impresses the dreamer with its aptness. Such was the case with the woman's dream that *her nephew had died* (MAM Files). The dreamer had responded positively to the analyst prior to the dream but she had not been able to comprehend the basis and implications of the analyst's attempts to make her aware of how she was clinging to traditional principles. The dream interpretation increased her confidence in the analyst's understanding of the unconscious so that she could become more open to changes in her own attitudes.

Other dreams reveal specific attitudes of the dreamer that reflect the transference, such as negative and critical feelings which the patient has not expressed in words. In one such dream, *the dreamer was riding in a car driven by his analyst. A giant black man appeared in front of them, and the dreamer wondered if the analyst would get away from him. He did* (MAM Files). With the impetus of the dream, the patient was able to say that he felt that the analyst was helping him to avoid confronting his dark side. Jung advised each therapist to take seriously the criticism brought by such dreams in order to gain insight. Only when the criticism has been given careful consideration and found not applicable should the analyst conclude that the dream image is subjective— reflecting the patient's projected unconscious contents. In my experience, whether the analyst image is treated objectively or subjectively, it nearly always reveals the patient's impression of the analyst's personality.

The influence of dreams on transference also is seen in the resolution of the transference. In an example of a very difficult transference, which had to be resolved in order for the patient to be cured of her neurosis, the patient dreamed that

> *Her father* (who in reality was the small stature) *was standing with her on a hill that was covered with wheat-fields. She was quite tiny beside him, and he seemed to her like a giant. He lifted her up from the ground and held her in his arms like a little child. The wind swept over the wheat-fields, and as the wheat swayed in the wind, he rocked her in his arms.* (D16)

At first, Jung thought the dream meant that in her fantasies the dreamer was seeing him as a semi-divine combination of father and lover. When this interpretation, and similar ones of other dreams, failed to achieve the objective of resolving the transference, he sought an alternative interpretation. It occurred to him that the dream might mean that the patient was trying to create a god as an answer to a deep longing that was stronger than the longing for the love of a human person. This hypothesis was not entirely acceptable to his "very critical patient . . . . Nevertheless . . . there now occurred . . . a kind of subterranean undermining of the transference. Her relations with a certain friend deepened perceptibly, . . . so that when the time came for leaving [Jung] it was no catastrophe, but a perfectly reasonable parting" (CW7, par. 217).

Assimilation and Individuation

The genuine understanding of a dream—at the emotional level as well as the intellectual level—contributes to the therapeutic process. The patient assimilates the unconscious contents presented by the dream, that is, attitudes and behavior are modified.[9]

The assimilation usually occurs slowly. The slowness is probably an asset because it may alleviate the fear of some dreamers that the conscious mind will be overwhelmed by emotion-laden unconscious contents. However, according to Jung, this danger is great only when the ego is very weak. The overwhelming of the conscious mind is more likely to occur when the unconscious is depreciated by exclusion from life or is falsely interpreted. With assimilation over time, the division between various parts of the personality, particularly between conscious and unconscious contents, is likely to be overcome. Sharing dreams with someone who respects but does not fear dreams, such as an analyst, seems one of the best ways to enhance gradual assimilation.

The successive assimilation of unconscious contents can be far more important than curing the symptom; it fulfills the purpose of analysis—psychological development—and may even lead to "the complete actualization of the whole human being, that is, individuation" (CW16, par. 352).

Dream Interpretation Outside the Therapeutic Situation

The interpretation of dreams outside the psychotherapeutic situation was a topic on which Jung had little to say. He seemed, in fact, to dub such attempts generally unproductive when he wrote that he did not understand his own dreams any better than someone with no knowledge of dream interpretation (CW18, par. 244). Nevertheless, he recorded having understood "in a flash" (CW18, par. 490), because of what he termed his "overwhelming" intuition, a dream that he recounted to Freud, and he apparently worked consistently at interpreting his own dreams. The difficulties he encountered are reflected in his statement that he had to "begin at the very beginning and come to the most painstaking analysis" (DA1, p. 185).

My own dreams seem neither so easy nor so difficult to understand as Jung estimated. Analysis of them is helped by the fact that my personal associations and conscious situation are more readily available to me than are those of another person. Given a comparable supply of amplifications, however, interpretation of one's own dreams carries difficulty because of the dreamer's psychological blind spots, which dream interpretation is designed to illumine.

Jung saw dreams as primarily a subject for analytic therapy, as evidenced by his statement that "it is chiefly the doctor who will have to concern himself with dreams, because their interpretation offers the key to the unconscious" (CW17, par. 191). (By "doctor" he seemed to mean specifically a medical analyst.) On the ground that dreams are normal, not pathological, phenomena, he acknowledged that "dream psychology is . . . the prerogative . . . of psychologists in general" (CW17, par. 191). Yet he did not foreclose on one's interpreting one's own dreams without the help of a therapist. Jung viewed dream interpretation as part of the education of normal people as well as a method of dealing with problems that are severe enough to require psychotherapy. (He used "education" in the sense of psychological development, not as an accumulation of cognitive material.)

Specific suggestions for dream interpretation outside the therapeutic situation were addressed by Jung mainly to persons in therapy who are about to terminate. He urged them

> to keep a careful record of their dreams and of the interpretations given. [He also showed] them how to work out their dreams . . . so that they can bring the dream and its context with them in writing to the consultation. At a later stage [he asked] them to work out the interpretation as well. In this way [he found] the patient learns how to deal correctly with his unconscious without the doctor's help. (CW16, par. 322)

Most Jungian analysts follow this practice of encouraging their analysands to continue to interpret their own dreams after termination of the analysis.

Jung advised dreamers who have not been in therapy to write down each dream immediately on waking, in one column, with additional columns for amplifications and attempts at interpretation.

Despite the paucity of specific suggestions from Jung on how to interpret one's dreams outside of the therapeutic situation, I believe that the methods and guidelines detailed in this book, if they are followed carefully, can help people to interpret their own dreams. For most people, dream interpretation is best undertaken initially in the company of one friend or a very small group of persons who know and trust each other enough to share the intimate experiences inherent in dreams. Jung warned, "Unintelligent and incompetent application of dream analysis and interpretation is indeed not advisable, and particularly not when there is a "dissociation between a very one-sided consciousness and a correspondingly irrational or 'crazy' unconscious" (CW18, par. 476). In any case, he found it essential to approach dreams with a humble attitude, because the most important dream messages are ahead of the dreamer's current knowledge and understanding. (For an additional discussion of dealing with one's own dreams with a Jungian approach, see Hillman, 1967, Ch. 11. Faraday, 1972, 1974 has an eclectic approach to dream interpretation but it incorporates much of Jungian theory and is essentially in harmony with it.)

Sometimes, dreams bring a person into therapy. That is, a dream may be so vivid, compelling, or frightening that the dreamer decides to consult someone who can help in understanding it. A session or two with a dream-oriented therapist may suffice, or the dreamer may want to undertake a more extensive process with a therapist.

Notes

[1] Although this statement was written in 1913, it seems to be consonant with Jung's most developed thought.

[2] Jung mentioned also the possibility of a "mental condition, in which dreams are redundant, inasmuch as compensations for the conscious attitude are not needed" (Let-2, p. 514). He seemed to mean a rare psychic state that is well enough balanced to obviate the necessity of dream compensation. Experimental evidence tends to disconfirm Jung's statement, however.

[3] By "latent psychosis" Jung meant "the possibility that an individual may become mentally deranged at some period of his life" (CW3, par. 520). Other psychiatrists have used the term "potential psychosis."

[4] A soothsayer of Ephesus. He said he wrote "upon Apollo's exhortation" the four books on the art of dream interpretation, Oneirocritica, which are mainly a compilation of the works of earlier authors. Much or all of his work on dreams has been preserved (Encyclopedia Britannica, 1965, Vol. 2, p. 507a).

[5] Jung wrote also that "The great majority of dreams, especially those in the early stages of analysis, are superficial . . ." (CW10, par. 99). He seemed to mean that they are nonarchetypal.

[6] Jung wrote also, "Discovery of the dream's prospective . . . meaning is

particularly important when the analysis is . . . far advanced" (CW4, par. 548). This sentence appeared, however, in a 1913 article, before he had differentiated "prospective" from "constructive." Considering that his examples of prospective dreams include a large proportion of initial dreams, it seems likely that he meant "constructive" rather than "prospective" in its refined definition in the quoted statement.

[7]Some people would argue that, because a child sees the parents as wise, projection of wisdom onto the analyst is a father- or mother-transference. Since not all parents are wise, the transference may be of the archetypal father or mother. When Freud wrote of the transference, he seemed to mean projection onto the therapist of actual qualities of the actual parent.

[8] Jung stated also that transference is not necessary for healing, if the analyst can interpret sufficient essential material in the patient's dreams. The seeming contradiction disappears in the light of Jung's repeated statement that he found it more comfortable not to be the object of a strong transference. My impression is that in the latter statement he used the term "transference" to mean emotional dependency, which may result from transference—for example, of the strong parent.

[9] Jung wrote, "Assimilation . . . means mutual penetration of conscious and unconscious, and not—as is commonly thought and practised—a one-sided evaluation, interpretation, and deformation of unconscious contents by the conscious mind" (CW16, par. 327). Since he did not explain how the conscious can affect the unconscious in a desirable way, the "penetration" of the unconscious by the conscious may be a seeking and activating, rather than an insertion of a new content.

Chapter 14

CHILDHOOD DREAMS

Jung's interest in childhood dreams was determined, in part at least, by his own early dreams that he remembered all his life. Many adults remember dreams from childhood; those recalled tend to have been frightening and recurring. Some childhood dreams are brought spontaneously into analysis; others are requested by the analyst. Nearly all the childhood dreams that Jung analyzed, including those recounted in the three volumes of his unpublished seminars on "Psychological Interpretation of Children's Dreams" (CD36, 38, 40), were told to him by adults. Although most of his statements about interpreting children's dreams were based on experience with childhood dreams reported by adults, they seem to apply equally well to the analysis of children's current dreams.

The frightening character of children's dreams may be due to their usually containing archetypal contents. Such contents are nearly always impressive and dreams remembered for a long time tend to be frightening ones. Children's archetypal dreams, according to Jung, "are the last vestiges of a dwindling collective psyche" (CW17, par. 94) which is dominant in the child at birth. Although Jung based his statements about children's dreams on clinical findings, further empirical confirmation was provided by Kluger (1975) and Van de Castle

(1970). Van de Castle stated (p. 39), "Animals are important [characters in children's dreams], possibly representing archetypal symbols in the Jungian sense." Kluger (1975) analyzed the contents of children's dreams and found that mythological parallels were present in 47% of the dreams up to age 6, and in 36%, up to age 9, as compared with 26% of adult dreams.

Although an adult has little access to the childhood associations to early dreams, he or she may have some memory of the relevant conscious situation. Current associations to a dream image may be useful in its analysis, however, especially if the childhood dream is recalled because of a current dream. The current dream and its associations contribute to the amplifying of the childhood dream, and vice versa. Nonpersonal amplifications are not dependent on current associations, of course, and can and should be applied when relevant.

When a child brings in a current dream, more specific questions can be asked. For example, if one of the dream images is a bridge, the interpreter might ask how the child feels about bridges, whether something had happened on that bridge, where home is in relation to it, and where he or she might be going when crossing that bridge.

Even when the child dreamer is available, it may be difficult to ascertain the personal associations and conscious situation, because of the contamination of the child's psyche by that of a parent. Jung found marked contamination to exist in the dreams of an 8-year-old boy, whose father was in analysis with Jung. The father did not remember any dreams for some time after he began his analysis. At Jung's request, the man recounted his son's dreams, which seemed to Jung not to belong to a child. Jung analyzed the dreams as if they were the father's, and they proved to spell out the man's erotic and religious problems. The boy's adult-style dreams stopped when his father began to remember dreams (CW17, par. 106).

Nearly all of the images in the children's dreams that Jung interpreted in his published and unpublished works were given objective characterization. A partial exception is the dream of a 13-year old girl:

> *I saw my mother slipping down the bath and I knew she was drowning, but I could not move. Then I grew terribly frightened and started to weep because I had let her drown.* I woke up crying. (CW17, par. 221)

Jung's objective characterization led to the interpretation that the dream referred to "[a wish for] the death of the mother, . . . the answer of the child's unconscious to the mother's blind ambition . . . [which 'killed'] her daughter's individuality . . ." (CW17, par. 223). He added a subjective interpretation, however, in a footnote: "For the daughter the mother signifies the feminine instinctual ground-layer which in this case is profoundly disturbed" CW17, par. 223n). Thus, Jung seemed to see the dream as signifying the death of the "mother" part of the dreamer.

The predominance of objective interpretations of children's dreams is due, in part, to the frequency with which parents' problems are reflected in them. For example, the father's problem was revealed in the dream of his 9-year-old daughter who was strongly attached to him. The parents were considering divorce, and the child was listless and unable to attend school, and had run a subnormal temperature for three months. She dreamed:

> *I went with Daddy to see Granny. Granny was in a big boat. She wanted me to kiss her and wanted to put her arms round me, but I was afraid of her. Daddy said, 'Well then, I'll kiss Granny!' I didn't want him to do it, as I was afraid something might happen to him. Then the boat moved off and I couldn't find anybody and I felt frightened.* (D17)

The dream reflects the father's erotic attachment to his mother (he said he would kiss her) and the girl's feeling that she was isolated by the attachment ("the boat moved off and I couldn't find anybody").

In another example, the dreams of three daughters reflected the potential psychosis of a

> *most* devoted mother. When [the girls] were approaching puberty they confessed shamefacedly to each other that for years they had suffered from horrible dreams about [their mother]. They dreamt of *her as a witch or a dangerous animal*, and they could not understand it at all, since their mother was so lovely and so utterly devoted to them. Years later the mother became insane, and her insanity would exhibit a sort of lycanthropy [imagining oneself to be an animal] in which she crawled about on all fours and imitated the grunting of pigs, the barking of dogs, and the growling of bears. (CW17, par. 107)

Later, Jung concluded that the "adult" tone of many children's dreams was partly a reflection of their archetypal character, but he continued to be alert to parents' problems as psychic determinants of children's dreams.

Many children's dreams are "simple, 'childish' dreams and . . . immediately understandable" (CW8, par. 98). That is, they depict the fulfillment of the child's known wishes. Other dreams of children are of quite a different quality; a child's dream is more likely than an adult's to have far-reaching significance in forecasting and shaping the person's destiny. By this statement Jung seemed to mean that a child's dream usually requires a constructive interpretation. However, he found that some children's dreams answered questions of causality. Such dreams, presumably require reductive interpretation. Still others, unlike adult dreams, may reveal "retrospective intuitions" (CW8, par. 98) with respect to the lives of the child's ancestors.

"The longer a dream remains spontaneously in the memory, the greater is the importance to be attributed to it" (CW4, par. 475), according to Jung. A clergyman reported a dream he had had when he was about 5 years old; he dreamed that

> he was in a water-closet which was outside the house, and suddenly somebody forced him to take the whole little house upon his back. . . . He had to carry that water-closet with all the contents. (Z10, p. 56)

Jung saw the dream as very appropriate for a future clergyman: It pointed out the necessity for him to carry "this corruptible body of dirt" (Z10, p. 56). (The relation between dreams remembered from childhood and adult personality variables, including adult dream-content, might be studied empirically.)

In practical work with children, Jung advised educators to tell the child something about the image, such as that the figure is a good fairy, so that the child can deal with it. At the same time, he recommended refraining from going into "psychological details" (CW17, par. 211), by which he seemed to mean interpretation, to avoid penetrating "deep into the [child's] unconscious" (CW17, par. 179).

Jung's caution against telling children the interpretations of their dreams was due to his observation that adaptation of the child to the environment is possible only after the withdrawal of attention from archetypal dreams and fantasies. "If these . . . contents remain conscious too long, the individual is threatened by an incapacity for adaptation; he is haunted by a constant yearning to remain with or to return to the original vision [of the psychological condition of early childhood]" (CW18, par. 204). It is important that this "connection with the primordial unconsciousness [be] severed" (CW17, par. 211), in order for the child to adapt to the surroundings. Failure to do so is often the precursor of an early death.

An example of a child with such a problem was a girl who, at age 8^1, was still having many archetypal dreams. Her father brought to Jung a series of her dreams (D18); they were mainly of death or life-threatening situations, such as falling into the water. Jung did not tell the father that he thought they "contained an uncanny prognosis" (CW18, par. 205). Evidently he expected the child's death, which occurred a year later.

Although Jung had relatively little to say about the interpretation of children's dreams as such, all his statements on the topic seem to be consistent with his statements about dream interpretation in general. Where explicit guidelines are lacking, therefore, one can extend to children's dreams the rather complete interpretive method that Jung developed for adult dreams.

Note

[1] In CW9-I, par. 623, Jung stated that the child was 10. From later information he was able to clarify (CW18, par. 525) that she was 8 when she had the dreams, 10 when her father brought them to Jung, and 11 when she died.

Chapter 15

THE DREAM
INTERPRETATION

Hypothesizing the Interpretation

When the dream context has been established, the dream images character-ized, and the situational factors (the therapeutic situation and the age of the dreamer) noted, the optimal time has come for attempting an interpretation. Actually, at any time during the dream analysis procedures the interpreter may have an intuition of the dream's meaning. One who has had little experience with dream interpretation may be excited by an intuitive idea and want to blurt out what he or she thinks the dream means. Jung warned, however, against premature interpretation. His warning is based, first, on the need for gathering as much evidence as possible before the formulation of an interpretation in order to avoid the imposition of preconceived ideas, and, second, on the importance of coopera-tion between dreamer and interpreter in developing the interpretation. The careful interpreter who proposes a dream interpretation is not stating a conclusion but formulating an hypothesis which will be assessed against the dream facts and the verification tests before it is accepted or rejected.

Discovering the meaning of a dream was likened by Jung to translating a language.[1] Each element in the dream is a "word." The equivalence of the "word" in the dreamer's psychological language can be discovered only from the amplifications, not in a predetermined word-for-word sense. If the dream element elicits only one amplification, the translation is simple: For example, if "ferocity" is the dreamer's only association to the image of a tiger, the translation is established accordingly. In order to take into account multiple amplifications, Jung adapted his analogy of philology. Translating a dream element with multiple amplifications can be compared to finding the meaning of a rare word that appears in several passages in a text. One studies the passages and hypothesizes the meaning of the word in each passage; from the various meanings one hypothesizes a definition and, finally, one tests the last hypothesis by inserting the definition into all the original passages. If the hypothesis is correct, the textual passages become meaningful. In interpreting a dream, each image is treated like a word. For example, if a dreamer has had dreams in which a certain friend stole from him or her, the appearance of the friend in subsequent dreams would be translated as an unconscious force that robs the dreamer of something valuable.

Sometimes, despite the careful work prescribed in previous chapters, the interpreter and the dreamer fail in their effort to hypothesize an interpretation of the dream. In that case, Jung warned against forcing an explanation and he recommended treating the dream like an unknown object: Carry it around; look at it from all sides; talk with others about it; let your imagination play with it; ask yourself, Why am I telling myself this story? Then adopt a waiting attitude. Subsequent dreams will give further clues, or a hint of the dream's meaning will arise in the interpreter's mind. Further patience and perseverance will allow the hint to develop.

> Certain portions of the dream gradually grow clearer, and we begin to see, in the apparently meaningless jumble of images, some glimmerings of a script—only disconnected sentences at first, then more and more . . . . (CW17, par. 264)[2]

The entire process is expedited by telling the dream story in different words. For example, the dreamer may describe a dream image as one figure hitting another and being hit in return. By rephrasing the scene as one in which the first figure is "starting a fight," a relevant analogy to a verbal fight may be drawn. The procedure is not always so simple, of course; nevertheless, when the interpreter and dreamer try to translate each dream element into a concept or image that is recognizably related to the dreamer's waking life, the meaning often becomes clear.

Occasionally, an external event explains the dream, especially if the dream is precognitive. If so, the connection is likely to become evident only long after the dream occurred.

Although Jung rejected Freud's hypothesis that the dream is a "mere symptom" (CW8, par. 703) of repression, he admitted that repression can deform and distort the dream. Nevertheless, we have no criterion to help us recognize the existence of such distortion. The hypothesis of distortion, therefore, is of little practical help in dream analysis.

Some dream theorists surmise, contrary to Jung's view, that not all dreams are meaningful: "some dreams may be just plain woolgathering, with the mind idly wandering and making jokes with itself (Kiester, 1975, p. 19). Kiester also suggested that the remembered dream may be too fragmentary; since the dreamer may "recall only portions of the final dream, we do not understand its meaning just as we would be baffled by the closing act of a play if we missed the earlier acts" (p. 18). Nevertheless, in therapy, an attempt should be made to hypothesize an interpretation of each dream that the dreamer wishes to pursue. Often, an interpretation that eludes one when the dream is fresh, emerges at a later time.

There are interpretations that fail to explain some of the dream details despite the application of all the guidelines discussed in this book. These interpretations can serve still as useful hypotheses, if they take into account the dream's general tendency and emotional atmosphere.

Jung warned against being "satisfied with a vague feeling of having understood [a dream]" (CW18, par. 577). Like all hypotheses, a tentative dream interpretation must be tested against the relevant facts: the dream elements, their interrelations, the amplifications that have been gathered, and the interconnections among the amplifications. If any element of the dream has not been taken into account, or if the interpretation does not fit the elements as they are presented in the dream, the hypothesis must be revised and the modified hypothesis tested against the dream text. Testing against the dream images and modification of the hypothesis are repeated until the inadequacies are overcome.

An example of testing and modification is found in the dream of the *man shooting at a wolf* (MAM Files). The first interpretation was that the man was taking action to kill the wolf side of himself, and that his missing the animal probably was deliberate. That interpretation would have fit a dream image of the man carrying the gun. However, it was the dreamer's wife who carried the gun into the woods. This image, plus his taking the gun from her, required that the interpretation be modified to recognize that his threat to the wolf was an attitude he was taking over from his wife. Thus the interpretation is deepened if not radically changed: It exposed to the dreamer both his own threat to the wolf side of himself, and the origin of that attitude in his wife's influence on him.

Finally, if the interpretation can be stated simply—in a nutshell, so to speak—it is likely to have a greater impact on the dreamer than would a more complex statement, and it can be tested more readily for verification.

The Dreamer and the Interpretation

The most creative and accurate dream interpretation result, probably, from a cooperative process in which both interpreter and dreamer participate fully and emerge with an interpretation that is satisfactory to both. There are many occasions, however, when the interpreter hypothesizes mentally an interpretation and then wonders what to say to the dreamer about it. An estimation of the dreamer's emotional strength at the moment may warn that harm could be done if the dreamer hears more than he or she can understand and accept.

Dream interpretations that reveal illusions are of no use to the dreamer who is not yet able to accept the truth, according to Jung. When the dreamer's self-esteem is precarious, being confronted by a dream interpretation too rapidly can be dangerous. In the case of an initial dream, Jung said that if the dreamer could understand it when it occurred, he or she would know too much too soon. Some dreamers may use the interpretation, moreover, to ward off the impact of the dream or to reveal less in the next dream.

A patient of Jung's recounted several "indecent dreams" (CW8, par. 533) and then asked why some of his dreams should be so disgusting. It is better, according to Jung, to give no answer to the question if the analyst feels that the dreamer is not ready to understand the interpretation and a possible clumsy answer may do more harm than good. Also calling for silence is a dream that produces an inflation (personal exaltation) in the dreamer; the dream is likely to be compensating severe inferiority feelings and a sense of worthlessness, and an interpretation could be destructive to the dreamer.

Whatever is done with material from the personal unconscious, Jung warned that "at the beginning of a treatment . . . [the dreamer] would be completely bewildered if the collective aspect of his dreams were pointed out to him" (CW13, par. 478). The general rule advocated by Jung was "never to go beyond the meaning which is effective for the [dreamer] ; . . ." (CW16, par. 99).

Still another dream interpretation that probably should not be shared with the dreamer, because of the possibility that the interpretation is wrong, is one that indicates unavoidable impending catastrophe, such as the girl's dreams of the *deaths of her mother and of a horse* (D11). The diagnosis and prognosis of fatal organic illness, which Jung derived from these dreams, were shared only with the girl's physician.

Communication of the interpretation to the dreamer is likely, then, to be introduced only gradually into the therapy, except perhaps (in my view) with persons who have been interested enough in dreams to record their dreams on their own; they may be able to undertake dream interpretation more quickly. Moreover, such persons often have been making their own, perhaps erroneous, interpretations. Their therapy could be slowed by postponing dream interpretation in the sessions.

Even when the interpreter does arrive at an interpretation which he or she decides to share with the dreamer, it is important to refrain from insisting that the dreamer accept the interpretation if it fails to win assent. When such a failure occurs, an interpretation that is otherwise correct becomes incorrect "because it anticipates and thus cripples the patient's development" (CW16, par. 314; see Ch. 16 for full discussion of verification of dream interpretations). Jung seemed to mean that the dreamer may surmise that a certain direction is desirable for his or her psychological development. Seeking within for the appropriate feelings or attitudes may result in repression of some genuine feelings. The dream interpretation thus becomes incorrect because it prevents the genuine development from occurring.

Although Jung advised caution in telling the dreamer the interpreter's view of the dream's message, he found that an incorrect interpretation was unlikely to convince the dreamer. "The [dreamer] is not an empty sack into which we can stuff whatever we like; he brings his own particular contents with him which stubbornly resist suggestion and push themselves again and again to the fore. Analytic 'suggestions' merely distort the expression, but not the content" (CW4, par. 648); people are susceptible only to suggestions with which they tend to agree.

In my experience, it is often helpful for the interpreter to introduce his or her interpretation in the form of a question or tentative statement, for example, "Perhaps the dream is saying. . . ." In this way the dreamer is given something to consider that leaves the way open for discussion or disagreement and shows consideration for the dreamer's point of view. The dreamer, in turn, may feel safe enough to be open to disturbing revelations from the dreams which he or she might reject if they were stated more dogmatically.

At other times, although it may be desirable to give an interpretation, it is important for the therapist to admit not understanding the dream. The client may mature more quickly by knowing that the therapist does not always understand the dreams and that the patient must develop the capacity to understand his or her own dreams.

When archetypal figures appear in a person's dreams, Jung advised explaining to the dreamer "that his case is not particular and personal, but that his psychology is approaching a level which is universally human. That outlook is very important, because a neurotic feels tremendously isolated and ashamed of his neurosis. But if he knows his problem to be general and not merely personal, it makes all the difference" (CW18, par. 233). Jung restricted his advice to dreams occurring in the later stages of analysis, but it seems to me to apply also to the earlier stages, even if Jung was right in stating that archetypal images are less frequent then.

In nearly every circumstance, according to Jung, it is important for the interpreter to say something about the dream to indicate being with the dreamer and listening to the message of the unconscious, not just to the conscious purposes of the dreamer. Jung, as a therapist, tried to express himself in a way that was brief, practical, and personal.

Particular care must be taken in interpreting dreams to a person with an unbalanced mental condition. In such persons, consciousness usually is very one-sided and the unconscious is correspondingly irrational. Such a person may appear "super-normal," as if to compensate artificially for a latent psychosis. Indeed, a dream may warn the analyst of the threat, thus enabling guidance of the patient in choosing a course of action which is least likely to precipitate a psychotic break. Such was the physician's dream of the *idiot child smeared with feces* (D15). The dream restrained Jung from accepting the man for analytic training. In most such instances, including this one, the interpretation should not be shared with the dreamer.

When the dreamer has a less precarious mental state, on the other hand, the interpreter should bring to awareness the transpersonal (archetypal) meaning of a dream because, if the meaning is not discovered, the dreamer may take the problem too personally, thus diminishing awareness of its similarity to those of other human beings and thereby remaining isolated. An example is the dream in which *the young officer was bitten in the heel by a snake and instantly paralyzed* (CW8, par. 305). He was unable to admit his distress at being rejected by the young woman with whom he was in love. Because he could not acknowledge that his feelings were like those of other human beings, a dream was required to show him the universality of his experience through its mythological dimensions.

Should the analyst dream of the patient, it is best to recount the dream to him or her, Jung held, on the ground that the patient may understand something about it or come to some new understanding because of it. Jung used as an example his own dream in which *he saw a woman, whom he recognized as his patient, sitting high above him, on the balustrade of a castle* (CW7, par. 189). He concluded that he must have been looking down on her in waking life. When he told her the dream and the interpretation, "a complete change came over the situation . . . and the treatment shot ahead . . ." (CW7, par. 190).

Despite Jung's view of the matter, I would hesitate to generalize on the advisability of telling the patient the analyst's dream because there are situations in which it can be destructive to the patient. The difference in perspective on this subject may be because Jung remembered dreaming of his patients only when they were fairly well advanced in the analytic process. My experience is that such dreams can occur at any time in the patient's analytic work.

Jung placed considerable stress on dream analysis in psychotherapy, to the point of stating that the analytical method consists primarily of dream analysis. It seems to me that this view can give the analysand the impression that by discussing dreams with the analyst, psychological development is assured. In my experience, both as an analyst and as an analysand, more than dream analysis is necessary for psychological development. However valuable the dream interpretations, the analysand still must deal with waking life, including emotions and relationships with other persons, often beginning with feelings toward the analyst.

Notes

[1] Berry (1974) challenged the practice of translating images into words, on the ground that "any form into which the image is cast is a transposition of it, perhaps a step away from it" (p. 68). She advocated "sticking to the image." Her approach seems quite harmonious with Jung's, perhaps even the best possible application of Jung's understanding of the dream language. In my experience, however, images do not speak directly to many dreamers, and verbal translations are often necessary in order for the dreamer to acquire the value of his dreams.

[2] Jung actually wrote, "more and more of the context," but the emerging "script" refers more accurately to the succession of images than to the context.

Chapter 16

VERIFYING
THE DREAM
INTERPRETATION

As dream interpretation becomes of interest to more people and in increased use in and out of psychotherapy, the question becomes more pressing, "How can one know that a dream interpretation is correct?" For some dream interpreters, an interpretation is assumed to be correct if it is true to the theories of personality and dreams accepted by the interpreter. Jung rejected the view that dream interpretation could be verified by a theory and sought a basis of verification elsewhere. His efforts were tentative because he recognized that dream interpretation is an "attempt to explain nature [and that every such attempt] is a hazard. A reliable method does not come into being until long after the pioneer work has been accomplished" (CW10, par. 319).

Jung found some hindrance of objective verification in the greater importance he placed on the contribution of dream interpretation to the therapeutic process. That is, his long experience demonstrated to him that, optimally, dream interpretations result from a "dialectical process" (CW18, par. 492) between dreamer and interpreter which does not necessarily issue in "scientifically verifiable" (CW16, par. 86) results. The purpose of dream interpretation for Jung was the dreamer's psychological development.

He seemed to find, however, that the fewer the errors in a dream interpretation, the more it contributes to the therapeutic process. Consequently, he proposed four tests of the truth of an interpretation, to be applied after the hypothesis has been tested against the dream facts. In order of application, the tests are:

1. Does the interpretation "click" with the dreamer?
2. Does the interpretation "act" for the dreamer?
3. Is the interpretation confirmed (or not disconfirmed) by subsequent dreams?
4. Do the events anticipated by the interpretation occur in the dreamer's waking life?

An affirmative answer to any one or more of these questions serves to verify an interpretation.

Tests for Verifying a Dream Interpretation

Test 1: Does the interpretation "click" with the dreamer?

Jung applied routinely the test of whether the interpretation "clicked" (CW18, par. 505) with the dreamer, that is, whether the dreamer endorsed it. (Some dreamers experience an "aha!" reaction; others give quieter assent.) For example, when Jung interpreted for a young man the dream in which *his father was driving while drunk* (CW16, par. 335) as compensatory to the dreamer's too-positive feelings toward his father, the interpretation "struck home [and] won the spontaneous assent of the dreamer" (CW16, par. 337).

When an interpretation does not "click" immediately with the dreamer, it is not necessarily incorrect. He or she may reject it because of discomfort with its implications or it may be simply unconvincing. Often the nonacceptance is due to a temporary inability to understand and accept that particular message from the unconscious. If so, the dreamer may confirm it later, or one of the other three tests may verify it. Consequently, each interpretation should be kept in mind by the interpreter.

Test 2: Does the interpretation "act" for the dreamer?

A dream interpretation can be verified by its "set[ting the dreamer's] life in motion again" (CW16, par. 86), whether or not it is accepted cognitively by the dreamer. The new vitality may become apparent in the stimulation given to the therapeutic process and the flow of positive feelings between therapist and patient. The obverse occurs also, Jung found: Errors in dream interpretation are reflected in the "bleakness, sterility, and pointlessness" (CW7, par. 189) of the sessions.

An example of verifying a dream interpretation on the basis of its acting for the dreamer is found in the dream in which *the dreamer's giant-size father held her in his arms like a little child* (D16). Her strong attachment to Jung was unaffected by the seemingly likeliest interpretation: that it was a transference of her strong tie to her father.[1] Jung pursued the problem with the interpretation that the dreamer's attachment to him was due to a deep yearning for a god. This "hypothesis was not entirely plausible" (CW7, par. 217) to her, that is, it did not "click" with her. But it acted for her, as evidenced by the fact that the attachment to Jung diminished. The interpretation, together with an accompanying deepening of her relationship with a friend, made it possible for her to terminate the analysis with Jung without great distress.

The capacity of a dream interpretation to act for a dreamer can be confirmed "negatively" as well as "positively." Jung described a dreamer who displayed a set of symptoms that returned when he ignored the message of a particular dream and disappeared when he attended to it. The text of the dream is, in part, as follows:

> *I come to a strange, solemn house—the "House of the Gathering."* ... *A voice says: "What you are doing is dangerous. Religion is not a tax to be paid so that you can rid yourself of the woman's image, for this image cannot be got rid of.* ... *Out of the fulness of life shall you bring forth your religion; only then shall you be blessed!"* (D19)

The dreamer was a highly educated scientist with a severe neurosis (not specified by Jung). Although he had been brought up in the Roman Catholic faith, he had paid no attention to religion for most of his life. In discussions of religion, the dreamer was inclined to take what Jung called (but did not define) "a traditional attitude," apparently to defend against his emotions. Jung interpreted the "woman's image," that is, the anima, to refer to the dreamer's emotional needs. The dream itself was a numinous experience revealing to the dreamer the fact that in attempting to deal with life entirely intellectually, he had rejected his emotions along with his sterile, traditional religion. By re-admitting his emotions into his life he could experience a true, vital religion and a fuller life. Jung noted that whenever the dreamer "tried to be disloyal to his experiences or to deny the voice, the neurotic condition instantly came back" (CW11, par. 74).

Test 3: Is the interpretation confirmed (or disconfirmed)
by subsequent dreams?

A third test is that of subsequent dreams. When a dream has been interpreted incompletely or incorrectly, the dreamer sometimes brings in a subsequent dream in which the major motif of the first dream is repeated more clearly or given a negative twist through "ironic paraphrase" (CW7, par. 189), or the interpretation of the first dream is clearly opposed. Jung likened a wrong interpretation to giving the patient psychic poison; the system rejects it just as it rejects a toxic substance.

An example of an interpretation that was shown by a subsequent dream to be incorrect occurred in the therapy of a woman who was estranged from the man with whom she was deeply involved. In one dream, *she and her man friend went to one part of a show, then found that the second part was in another place* (MAM Files). The analyst inferred that the dreamer's relationship with the man would have to be continued "in another place," and interpreted this statement to mean that the breach in the patient's relationship with the flesh-and-blood man must be accepted. Then the struggle could become an inward one with the dreamer's "masculine" qualities—aggressiveness and competitiveness—which her friend personified. After hearing the interpretation, the patient dreamed that *she was to have an abortion; the doctor made an incision in her abdomen, and nature did the rest* (MAM Files). When the second dream was understood to mean that the analyst (doctor) was the agent of the destruction (abortion) of a psychological new life, it seemed evident that the interpretation of the first dream was incorrect. The first dream was reinterpreted to mean simply that there was to be a transition (literally "change of site," that is, place) in the relationship between the dreamer and her friend. Such a transition could occur only if the relationship was continued. The new interpretation was verified by the fact that a transition occurred: The relationship deepened as the dreamer and her friend struggled effectively with the conflicts between them.

Dreams verifying interpretations of previous dreams can be expected to be less frequent than those challenging earlier interpretations, according to Jung's theory of the compensatory function of dreams: A correct interpretation does not require the modification supplied through compensation by a new dream. Confirming dreams do occur, however, perhaps in response to a conscious attitude that is not yet firm. For example, a person who is depressed might have a dream which is interpreted to mean that the depression is due to dissatisfaction with a job. A second dream, confirming the interpretation of the first, might be one in which the dreamer is working effectively and contentedly at a different kind of job.

A special case of verification by subsequent dreams is that of the traumatic (reactive) dream. A traumatic dream cannot be interpreted in the sense of translating the dream images into words. It simply recurs until the emotional impact of the waking experience depicted in the dream has been assimilated. Thus, if a traumatic-appearing dream continues to occur, the conclusion that it was traumatic is probably correct. If it has been interpreted by the method described in this book for compensatory (non-traumatic) dreams and ceases to occur, it was not traumatic, and the interpretation probably was correct.

*Test 4: Do the events anticipated by the interpretation occur
in the dreamer's waking life?*

Jung's fourth test for the verification of dream interpretations consists of facts from the dreamer's waking life: events that are anticipated by dreams, including the occurrence or avoidance of difficulties; the persistence or disappearance of symptoms; and other physical events, such as accidents, organic illness, or death.

Subsequent difficulties verified Jung's interpretation of the professor's dream that *a train moved too fast out of a curve and was derailed* (D14). The dream seemed to mean that the dreamer was determined to advance his career at a headlong pace despite the danger of "going off the rails," and wrecking his future. He insisted on pursuing a prestigious professorship, and the catastrophe predicted by the dream occurred: He achieved the position, then lost it.

Another of the professor's dreams, that of *visiting his home village and hearing his classmates say that he did not come there very often* (CW18, par. 163) was interpreted as meaning that he had climbed too high. This interpretation was validated by the disappearance of his symptoms of mountain sickness when his status was lowered.

Sometimes a dream interpretation diagnosing organic illness is verified by medical tests or by death. For example, the dream of T. M. Davie's patient included the image of *draining a pond* (CW18, par. 135n). Jung interpreted the image as describing some of the physiological facts of periventricular epilepsy, from which the patient later was found to be suffering.

A dream interpretation providing a differential diagnosis between organic and hysterical symptoms may be verified by the subsequent course of the illness. An example is the young woman's dreams of the *self-inflicted deaths of her mother and of a horse* (D11). Jung's diagnosis, based on his dream interpretation, that the dreamer's symptoms were organic, proved to be correct.

Other Possible Verification Tests

The tests for the verification of dream interpretations which have been described so far are those that Jung actually used to confirm interpretations of dreams brought to him. Some other possible methods, which he considered worthy of investigation, follow.

The Word Association Test, which Jung used a great deal early in his career, revealed the complexes of the person taking the test. Jung published a detailed study of his testing of one young woman. He presented also nine of her dreams and his interpretation of them, which he found to confirm the results of the Word Association Test (CW2, pars. 793–862). Similar experiments could be performed, but in reverse order: administering the Word Association Test for confirmation of the dream interpretations that identify complexes. Other personality tests might be used in comparable fashion, insofar as they reflect day-by-day emotional states.[2]

Farber and Fisher (1943) used an additional method: asking the dreamer under hypnosis to interpret his or her dreams; 20% of their hypnotized subjects were adept at interpretation. Agreement of the interpretations under hypnosis and those in the waking state, with or without the help of a therapist, might constitute verification. The validity of this method could be studied by comparing its verification of interpretations that win the assent of the dreamer with those that do not.

Whether or not a dream interpretation can be verified by one of the tests suggested, the therapeutic value of dream analysis remains. By providing various points of view, alternative dream interpretations enhance the therapeutic process by stimulating interaction between therapist and patient. Thus, even the usual uncertainty regarding the correctness of an interpretation has value, wrote Jung. Valuable or not, uncertainty is inescapable because

> Target practice on a shooting range is far from being a battlefield, but the doctor has to deal with casualties in a real war. Therefore he has to concern himself with psychic realities even if he cannot define them in scientific terms. (CW18, par. 571)

Notes

[1] Jung did not specify whether he verbalized this dream interpretation to her but he indicated that the idea had been proposed to her repeatedly, on the basis of non-dream material.

[2] Additional methods of verification were suggested but not recommended by Jung. Two are in published works.

> One method—which, however, is not scientific—would be to predict future happenings from the dreams by means of a dream-book and to verify the interpretation by subsequent events, assuming of course that the meaning of dreams lies in their anticipation of the future. [Since Jung referred elsewhere to "vulgar little dream books" (CW8, par. 543), his evaluation of this method as "not scientific" is understated.]

> Another way to get at the meaning of the dream directly might be to turn to the past and reconstruct former experiences from the occurrences of certain motifs in the dreams. While this is possible to a limited extent, it would have a decisive value only if we could

discover in this way something which, though it had actually taken place, had remained unconscious to the dreamer, or at any rate something he would not like to divulge under any circumstances. If neither is the case, then we are dealing simply with memory-images whose appearance in the dream is (a) not denied by anyone, and (b) completely irrelevant so far as a meaningful dream function is concerned, since the dreamer could just as well have supplied the information consciously. (CW8, pars. 537–538)

(Although Jung indicated that the second procedure is a method of verification, its reads to me more like a method of interpretation.)

A third method of verification that Jung suggested but did not recommend appeared in an unpublished work. The method is that of applying an interpretation to "parallel cases" (CD38, p. 2)–evidently the dreams of other dreamers–and then deciding whether it explains them as well. It appears that Jung was referring to specific dream images, presumably relatively fixed symbols, rather than to entire dreams.

Chapter 17

A DREAM AND
ITS INTERPRETATION

Background of the Dreamer

J.K., the daughter of Jewish parents, is a 30-year-old woman who converted to Christianity at age 18. Four years later she married a Protestant who was planning to enter the ministry; the marriage ended in divorce after two years.

After her conversion, which was distressing to her parents, J.K. moved to a distant state. For two years she attended a nonaccredited Lutheran college that trains religious workers and missionaries. A few years later she became disenchanted with the evangelistic approach to religion and shifted her affiliation to the Episcopal Church. She entered a state university and graduated at age 29 with a degree in history. At the time she reported the dream, she had been in analysis for about three years and was half-way through a Master of Arts (M.A.) program in history. At the time of the dream, J.K.'s analytic work centered around a painful complex that took the form of wanting to dominate others and, at the same time, wanting to be dominated. She and I referred to it simply as "The Complex."

The Dream

I am holding my Passover plate from Israel, which is encased in a cube of glass or plastic. It is understood that this had been given to me by Queen Elizabeth I (image of her coming toward me). I say to Margaret and Elaine: "This is the Great Plate of England and I can't afford to have anything happen to it—not touched, or broken, lost, chipped, or even looked at!" I clutch it, and then I think I put it in the trunk of my car for safekeeping. (MAM Files)

Identifying the Dream

J.K. had written the dream, and the text seemed complete. But in giving her associations to the Passover Plate, she mentioned that *it was turquoise ("the color of deep water") and with two bronze or brass handles, indentations for the ritual foods, and gold Hebrew letters in each indentation naming the food to be placed there.* This description was incorporated into the dream text.

Structure of Dream

The *structure* of the dream is recognizable although it is somewhat irregular.

The *exposition* is incomplete in that no statement of place or time is present.

The *protagonists* include the following: (1) the dreamer; (2) Margaret and Elaine; (3) Queen Elizabeth I.

The *plot development* has occurred already: the Plate has been given to the dreamer by Queen Elizabeth I.

The *culmination* of the dream is the dreamer's statement to Margaret and Elaine that the Plate must not be damaged, lost, or looked at.

The *lysis* is the dreamer's putting the Plate in the trunk of her car for safekeeping.

Amplifications

Most of the amplifications are the dreamer's personal associations, some are from generally available information, and a few are mythological parallels. (The mythological parallels brought to the images of this dream all happen to be from the Jewish-Christian tradition.)

PASSOVER

J.K.'s associations to Passover began with its being the one Jewish holiday she could remember celebrating as a child; the celebration was held at her grandfather's house. Until her conversion, all she knew of Passover was that it celebrated the Jews' getting out of Egypt. It figured in her introduction to Christianity, however: She heard a Hebrew-Christian evangelist draw parallels between Passover and Communion: the lamb's blood on the doorposts and the blood of Christ. Now, she connects Passover with Maundy Thursday and Good Friday, major Christian observances. Their importance to her is reflected in her statement. "That's my time of year." She added that Passover is the oldest continuously celebrated religious festival in Western history, and that she feels "very Jewish" during the period of the festival.

PLATE

J.K. received the Passover Plate as a gift from a friend at the Lutheran college who thus expressed her respect for J.K.'s Jewish origin, "neither playing it down nor building it up." She elaborated the association with the fact that some of her schoolmates at the college had been uncomfortable about her being Jewish and seemed not to know what to say to her about it. During discussions of Christianity and the New Testament, they talked down to her; when Judaism and the Old Testament came up, they assumed that she was the expert. They seemed in awe of J.K.'s conversion to the faith that was traditional to them.

The Plate, to the dreamer, was associated further with antiquity; it was a holy relic. Having the Plate was, she said, like having a piece of Israel.

ISRAEL

Her associations to Israel began with the fact that it is the Holy Land. Since her conversion, J.K. has been determined to make a pilgrimage to Jerusalem. She sees Israel as belonging to her in a way that it does not to non-Jews. During the "Six-Day War" in 1967, she became very excited and had a moving dream of being in Israel. She considers herself a "political" but not a "religious" Zionist; that is, she believes that Israel has a political right to exist, but not all Jews need live there, and non-Jews who want to live in Israel should be permitted to do so. J.K. elaborated her associations with the statement that, in converting to Christianity, she was aware of manifesting a certain rejection of her Jewish heritage, and she is aware of some negative feelings toward Jews, especially when they take the attitude that just being a Jew is somehow a virtue.

CUBE OF GLASS OR PLASTIC

In associating to the cube of glass or plastic enclosing the Plate, she noted its characteristics of being solid but transparent, and three dimensional. It provided an indestructible protective covering for the Plate.

QUEEN ELIZABETH I

As a student of history, J.K. has a particular interest in Queen Elizabeth I. The fact that Elizabeth's name was given to an era reflects the Queen's special place in history. J.K. sees the Queen as well educated and possessing an excellent sense of humor. By remaining a virgin, she "overcame the crushing male dominance" that might have manifested itself in a marriage, retained her hereditary power, and was able to rule and handle very difficult problems. For example, she defeated Spain through the destruction of the Armada, avoided entanglement with France, made an effort to control inflation, and imposed a settlement of England's religious conflicts in what was a tolerant manner for the times: Both Catholics and Protestants were required to conform outwardly by attending the Anglican Church but their private opinions on religious questions could not be subjected to public or state scrutiny.

Further, to J.K. the Queen is a "heroic figure, almost a goddess, not quite human." On the historical level, the Queen is "very human"; in J.K.'s fantasy, Elizabeth is "super-human, capable of almost anything, [possessing] wisdom and authority." The dreamer added the nonpersonal amplification that there are myths and legends of gods giving gifts to humans, such as Yahweh giving the Ten Commandments to Moses.

MARGARET

J.K. described Margaret, her housemate, as her closest friend and an intense person, and associated to her a "deep feeling for things Jewish, as if this [feeling] were for me." Margaret seems to expect J.K. to respond with equal intensity, and sometimes presumes to "know" J.K.'s values. Furthermore, Margaret seems not to take seriously J.K.'s Complex.

ELAINE

Elaine is Margaret's friend and a frequent visitor to the home of J.K. and Margaret. J.K. sees Elaine as a person who analyzes everything, including values and numinous experiences. J.K. described herself as once having done the same.

THE GREAT PLATE OF ENGLAND

The Great Plate suggested to the dreamer the name of a horse race called "The Queen's Plate," in which the prize for the winner is a plate. J.K. learned about this race after the dream. She gets very excited over horse races, finding them "awesome." Her fascination with horse racing centers on the animals' genealogies; she likes to predict winners on the basis of lineage. This interest, she feels, stems in part from her lack of knowledge of her own forebears and her desire for continuity. Her interest in horse races reflects also her seeking for the "perfect horse." As a child, J.K. rode horseback a great deal during visits to her grandfather. She considers a horse race to be a test of endurance; riding a horse is "controlling nature."

To England, the dreamer associated monarchy and royalty. She elaborated this idea with the fact that many Hebrew blessings begin with addressing God as the King of the Universe. Christianity is a monarchy, she added; she was impressed with Jesus' claim to the throne on the basis of His being in the lineage of David. This claim contributed to her conversion.

I pointed out that the English people are said to be the Ten Lost Tribes of Israel. J.K. acknowledged this legend and added her impression that "British Israelism" is anti-Semitic in nature.

NOT TOUCHED, BROKEN, LOST, OR CHIPPED

The dreamer's associations to these images took the form of feelings. The dream statement that she did not want anything to happen to the Plate meant "hands off," and the Plate was so important to her that "the transpersonal becomes terribly personal."

OR EVEN LOOKED AT

I offered as an amplification the Old Testament injunction that one cannot look on the face of God and live. ("But [the Lord] said, 'You cannot see my face, for man shall not see me and live'," Exodus 33:20.)

CAR TRUNK

The dreamer stated that the trunk of her car is the only movable thing she owns that has a lock. Her car is a source of power and mobility.

THE DREAM AS A WHOLE

In addition to associating to specific dream elements, the dreamer volunteered her feelings about the dream as a whole. She said she had experienced awe. She "felt honored, and chosen for a special responsibility which had been given to [her]." The dream, to her, was encouraging; it was saying good things about the future. She felt that she was "on the right track," and had a new surge of self-confidence. "Somebody or something greater than I had entrusted me with a valuable object. I was keeper of the Queen's Plate."

Interconnecting Themes

Four themes, indicated by the interconnections among amplifications, can be identified in the dream:

1. The tension between religious loyalties is the major interconnecting theme. These loyalties are Jewish and Christian, Lutheran and Episcopalian. The theme connects the amplifications of Passover, the Passover Plate, Israel, England, and, in the Catholic-Protestant conflict of her era, Queen Elizabeth I.

2. The theme of continuity interconnects the amplifications of Judaism and Christianity, the antiquity of the Plate, hereditary rulers, genealogy and endurance of horses, celebration of Passover, and the role of J.K.'s grandfather (her link to her ancestors) in her early experiences with the celebration of Passover and her appreciation of horses.

3. The theme of special responsibility appears in the dreamer's response to the receipt of the Plate, in the responses of herself and others to her identity as a Jew and a Christian, and in her view of Queen Elizabeth.

4. The theme of the meeting of the divine and the human appears in the amplifications to Queen Elizabeth, the Plate (made by human hands but too numinous to be looked at), and in the amplifications that mention Christianity, the central figure of which is the God-man Jesus Christ).

The Conscious Situation

At the time of the dream, J.K. was depressed and finding it difficult to work on her M.A. thesis, the subject of which was penance. She attributed her depression in part to the discomfort of a severely painful knee, the restriction of movement resulting from it, and the fact that no medical diagnosis had been made. The possible psychogenic origin of this disability, as an expression of her Complex, had been discussed in several analytic sessions: The use of the knee in kneeling connects it with submissiveness—with being dominated. Also contributing to her depression were conflicts between her and Margaret, and J.K.'s feeling of being neglected emotionally by Margaret.

Hypothesizing the Interpretation

The lack of place or time specifications for the setting of J.K.'s dream suggests that it is a long-range response to her problems rather than a compensation of the moment. Corroboration of this suggestion may be found in an association to Queen Elizabeth I—that she gave her name to an entire era.

The dream text begins with the statement that the dreamer is holding something; that is, she possesses something and is attending to it. The object J.K. is holding in the dream is her Passover Plate from Israel. It reflects the tension in the duality of her religious background and orientation, which has been suggested by her associations: learning from a Hebrew-Christian about the significance of Passover, and the direct connection of Passover, a Jewish religious festival, with the Christian observances of Maundy Thursday and

Good Friday; the gift of the Plate from a friend as an expression of the giver's valuing J.K.'s dual background; the development out of J.K.'s Christian experience of her interest in the Jewish state of Israel; and the Plate's connection with Judaism through Passover and Israel in conjunction with its being presented in the dream by the head of the (Christian) Church of England.

The Passover Plate also suggests the continuity of Judaism and Christianity, historically and theologically. The interpretation of the Plate as indicating continuity is supported by the association of Passover with J.K.'s grandfather, the bearer for her of the continuity in her family. Moreover, Passover is the oldest continuously celebrated religious festival in Western history. Continuity points to the phenomenon of time: past, present, and future.

The Plate's roundness and its status in the dream as a gift from a numinous royal figure suggest wholeness. In addition, J.K. identified its color as that of water, a relatively fixed symbol of the collective unconscious, which is the source of psychological wholeness.

The three-dimensionality of the cube of glass or plastic in which the Plate is enclosed gives it depth; the encasement indicates inaccessibility to touch. The Plate's inaccessibility hints at the dreamer's desire to protect the numinous object, which is expressed later in the dream, but it points also to a reluctance to touch—give attention to—the problems with which the dream confronts her.

The interpretation of Queen Elizabeth I, the presenter of the Plate, as a divine-human figure, is based on the amplification of myths of gods making gifts to human beings. Add to this the fact of Elizabeth's remarkable achievements and royal status and it becomes apparent that for J.K., Elizabeth is an image of the Self. The Queen resolved the interreligious conflict of her day, dealt successfully with male (animus) dominance, and is both human and divine. All of these amplifications suggest strongly that for J.K. the tension between Judaism and Christianity and her Complex define the arena of her individuation process. The image of Queen Elizabeth coming toward the dreamer indicates the initiative of the Self in the process. The interconnecting theme of special responsibility corroborates the individuation process as a part of the dream message.

The Great Plate of England seems to be a condensation of the images of the Passover Plate and a horse race. The amplifications to these two images support the hypothesis that the dream anticipates the furthering of J.K.'s individuation process. This hypothesis is based on the suggestion of continuity, the roundness of the Passover Plate, and the characteristic striving of the horse race. When the hypothesis was tested against all of the dream images, however, some modifications had to be made. The seeking for perfection (mentioned in relation to a horse, implying a striving in the dreamer) is antithetical to wholeness (in Jung's view) because perfection excludes the dark side. Moreover, the competitive spirit inherent in a horse race would seem not to be concordant with individuation. Thus, J.K.'s drive toward individuation is diminished by conflicting wishes.

England, to which the Great Plate "belongs," is amplified by the anti-Semitic British Israelism, which bring to mind J.K.'s own "anti-Semitism" in the partial rejection of her Jewish heritage and her negative feelings toward ethnocentric Jews. This "anti-Semitism" of the dreamer is a further reminder of the dreamer's problem of reconciling her dual membership in the Jewish and Christian communities.

When the dreamer says she cannot afford to have anything happen to the Plate, she seems to be expressing a determination not to lose the values it embodies. In fact, she specifies the mishaps that conceivably could befall the Plate, as if to say that it must not be so diminished. Since looking at the Plate does not in itself diminish it, the prohibition against looking at it must be understood in a different way. Not looking at the Plate—a representation of the dreamer's problems—suggests that she is facing squarely neither her conflicts and complexes, nor the potential responsibility inherent in a glimpse of the Self. Based on the amplification of the prohibition against looking on the face of God, and the dreamer's feeling response to the Plate, the latter can be seen as numinous and hence, taboo. Thus, the religious conflict is great but important for her development.

To Margaret, who sometimes "knows" J.K.'s values, the dreamer says, in her statement that this is the Great Plate of England, "I am putting my own value on the Plate." To Elaine, who tends to analyze everything, the dreamer says in the words, "I can't afford to have anything happen to it," that its value is not to be analyzed—broken and reduced.

By clutching the valuable object, the dreamer demonstrates that she is exceedingly anxious and protective of it. At the same time, she keeps it close and thus takes it to herself.

The dreamer then puts (stated as, "I think I put it") the Plate into the trunk of her car for safekeeping. By so doing, she guards it; the car trunk can be locked, hence it provides safety. She can carry the Plate with her wherever she goes but it is hidden from view; thus, perhaps, it is not subject to the dangers she lists but it is not kept in consciousness either. That is, she may not be ready yet to deal fully with either the problems or the possibilities expressed in her dream.

Highlighting the Application of Jung's Theory

Any one dream illustrates only a portion of Jung's theory of dream interpretation. The points exemplified by J.K.'s dream are specified here.

AMPLIFICATIONS

The interpretive process made use of all the major types of amplifications. The dreamer provided personal amplifications to nearly every image, such as descriptions of Margaret and Elaine. Information from the environment took the form of a fact the dreamer had not known at the time of the dream, that there is a horse race called "The Queen's Plate." Archetypal amplifications included several from the Bible. The amplifications that were used in the interpretation were those that served to identify the interconnecting themes.

RELEVANT CONSCIOUS SITUATION

The relevant aspects of the conscious situation were ascertained by the fact that they had an emotional impact on the dreamer, making her depressed: the sore knee and its implications for the Complex, and her feeling emotionally neglected by Margaret. That the conscious situation was that of an era in the dreamer's life was confirmed by the interconnecting theme of continuity.

DREAM SERIES

No previous or subsequent dreams could be found which amplified this dream or verified its interpretation.

APPROACHING THE DREAM INTERPRETATION

Avoiding Assumptions

Since Queen Elizabeth can be seen as a Self figure, it would be tempting to assume that her gift of the Passover Plate from Israel, a Jewish-sounding image, was a support of the Jewish heritage over the Christian, as an instrument of the individuation process. Such an assumption would violate the dreamer's feeling for her Christian commitment and would let her avoid the tension of religious loyalties which emerged in the careful process of interpretation that was followed.

Dream Images as Symbols

The dream images were treated as symbols in that they were interpreted on the basis of amplifications, including the dreamer's individual experience; some were found to have multiple meanings. For example, the Plate was interpreted as indicating wholeness but, also, the striving for perfection (which is antithetical to wholeness in excluding the dark side of the personality).

The Dream Is Not a Disguise, but a Set of
Psychic Facts

The interpretation took the images as they were, with no assumption that they were concealing something. Queen Elizabeth I, for example, has a specific meaning for the dreamer and is not a disguise for a "problem woman" (e.g., a mother figure) in the dreamer's life.

The Dream Does Not Tell the Dreamer What To Do

The dream states what is, not what should be done. In the dreamer's statement that she "can't afford" to have the Plate looked at, for example, she expresses her reluctance to look at the problems brought into awareness by the Plate. It may be that her development would be enhanced by her looking at them, but the dream does not direct her to do so.

The Personalities of Interpreter and Dreamer

My inclination, as a person with a less romantic approach to life than the dreamer's, might be to underemphasize the numinosity of the figure of Queen Elizabeth I. The value of the dream might have been damaged, therefore, if I had followed my inclination rather than the dreamer's associations and feeling response to the dream.

OBJECTIVE AND SUBJECTIVE CHARACTERIZATION

The analysis of the dream images shows them to be almost all subjective. The dream ego, the Passover Plate, Queen Elizabeth I, Elaine, and the dreamer's car all must be taken almost certainly as aspects of the dreamer's psyche. The sole objective element is the need, implied in the statement to Margaret and Elaine, for dealing with Margaret's not taking seriously enough the dreamer's Complex. Characterizing the figure of Margaret objectively is consonant with characterizing objectively the dream images of persons close to the dreamer.

REDUCTIVE AND CONSTRUCTIVE ANALYSIS

Reductive interpretation confronts the dreamer with her problems, such as her reluctance to face her religious conflict. The constructive interpretation points the direction to individuation for the dreamer. Both interpretations are included in the interpretive hypothesis.

COMPENSATION

The compensatory aspects of the dream include its focus on the tension in the dreamer between her Jewish background and Christian convictions. A conscious attitude of the dreamer is that she has come to terms with this problem by seeing Christianity as the culmination of Judaism and, consequently, not separate from it. The dream's compensation confirms the tension but indicates that it can be transcended, by showing the Passover Plate from Israel as identical with the Great Plate of England. Since the Plate is encased in glass or plastic, however, the reconciliation is not now accessible. Further, the dream says that the dreamer is not yet ready to "look at" the problem. The prognosis is positive, in that the Plate is a gift from the Self figure, Queen Elizabeth.

Further compensation is found in the impetus for the dreamer to guard against the attitudes associated with Margaret and Elaine, which correspond to attitudes in herself, that is, the premature evaluating and the overanalyzing of the tension symbolized by the Plate.

The interpretation can be stated "in a nutshell" as a translation of the dream language: The dreamer possesses, in her Jewish and Christian affiliations, a source of great tension and great value. It was given to her by the Self as a means of individuation. She is determined to protect it by placing her own value on it, and not allowing it to be reduced by intellectual questioning. She is not ready to face the problem, however, and puts it in a safe place to carry around with her.

VERIFYING THE INTERPRETATION

The interpretation as stated was verified by winning the assent of the dreamer, who had participated actively in developing the interpretation. This assent was especially significant in that the dream already had "acted for" the dreamer and she had a firm basis for giving her assent. The dreamer's action affected J.K.'s depression, which centered around her difficulty in working on her M.A. thesis. The thesis was on the medieval system of penance, which aroused her Complex whenever she tried to work on it; hence the thesis had lain untouched for some weeks. After the dream, her depression lifted and she was able to resume working. Apparently, a release of psychic energy resulted from (a) bringing to consciousness the tension of religious loyalties and (b) a glimpse of the Self.

Chapter 18

APPRAISAL
OF JUNG'S THEORY
OF DREAM
INTERPRETATION

In appraising Jung's theory of dream interpretation, I am aware that I live, work, and write in a time, place, and culture and out of a personal background that differ from Jung's. His formative years were spent in the last quarter of the nineteenth century, in the stability of pre-World War I Europe; mine were spent in the second quarter of the twentieth century, in the political and economic turmoil of the interwar period in America. I share with Jung a semi-rural background, but his was in a small mountainous nation rooted in the Middle Ages and characterized by a stable class structure; mine was in a prairie state that was still close to its pioneer history (symbolized, perhaps, by the covered wagon) and characterized by social mobility. Jung's family background and mine had some similarities in form if not in content: a sense of history, a high valuation of education, a conventional religiosity, and firm ideas on matters important to them. But his education was classical; mine, pragmatic.

Despite these differences, Jung's approach to dream interpretation works for me and my analysands, as attested to by the many examples I have used to illustrate aspects of Jung's theory. The beauty of Jung's theory, in my experience, is that it is so comprehensive that it can be adapted readily and well to dreams of a later time and another culture. Thus, it has much to offer the dream interpreter in today's world.

Jung did not set out to formulate a theory of dream interpretation; rather, he developed a series of hypotheses and procedures by which the meaning of dreams could be ascertained. His basic assumption was that each dream (and series of dreams) is unique to the dreamer and, hence, can be understood only in terms of the dreamer's psychological make-up, conscious experiences, and personal relationships. He deviated from this assumption only in the analysis of a few archetypal dreams, which required an interpretation germane to a large group of people.

Jung's conception of the collective unconscious, in which archetypal dream images originate, was the logical development of his search for an explanation for dream images that cross the boundaries of time and culture. With his long-standing interest in archaeology and religion, it is understandable that he was fascinated by dream images that related to humankind's history and even prehistory, and that he devoted considerable time to the exploration and discussion of archetypes. But it would be a mistake to infer that in dream analysis he subordinated his basic assumption (that dreams are unique to the dreamers) to his fascination with the archetypal. Other than expecting archetypal dreams to reflect the individuation process more than nonarchetypal dreams (perhaps because so many of his patients brought in archetypal dreams late in the therapeutic process), he appears, essentially, to have treated such dreams no differently from others. Jung's basic assumption for dream analysis, coupled with the hypotheses and procedures he formulated for use in the interpretive process, thus makes his "theory" (for want of a better inclusive term) applicable to all dreams.

The comprehensiveness of Jung's theory of dream interpretation grew out of the many challenges that were presented to him by the almost unimaginable number of dreams—67,000 is the number often cited—that he analyzed during his professional career. Jung's empirical approach, taking into account the psychic facts presented by so many dreams, forced him to modify, clarify, and expand his theory (or method) repeatedly, over many years. Thus the theory grew and changed organically.

Despite Jung's flexible approach, his theory remained remarkably stable over the years. Many of his ideas germinated as expansions, modifications, or counterhypotheses to ideas of Freud, most of which Jung had advocated, with reservations, before he broke with Freud. The reservations increased in importance until they helped to precipitate the break. Subsequently, Jung developed his own approach to dreams, beginning with a burst of ideas during the five years that followed the break from Freud. The stability of Jung's theory reflects the fact that nearly all the rudiments were present in his initial post-Freudian works on dreams and their interpretation, although another 20 to 30 years were required for clarification and restatement. (For a full discussion of the Freudian precursors of Jungian dream theories, see Frey-Rohn, 1974.)

The frequent modification carries with it some difficulties, however, for Jung's interpreters. In confronting various situations and audiences, Jung used different sets of words in which to express the same idea. Furthermore, because he was a poetic speaker and writer, he frequently expressed himself in terms that are notable more for literary expression than clarity. Hence, one often cannot be sure whether Jung was repeating an idea he had presented earlier, or modifying it.

Differences of opinion arise among Jungian dream interpreters regarding the intent of some of Jung's statements because of his various expressions of the same ideas. As a result, the temptation is great to use those parts of the theory that are congenial and to ignore the rest. For example, some interpreters construe virtually all dreams subjectively and constructively and fail to consider the other alternatives that are integral to Jung's theory: objective and reductive interpretations.

In this book, I present Jung's theory as comprehensively as possible. Although I differ with the theory on specific points, the differences do not interfere with my concurrence with the preponderance of the concepts. Because the theory is not monolithic, it is possible to challenge parts of it without rejecting the whole. My agreements, disagreements, and evaluations of Jung's ideas are given in this appraisal. It would be niggling to criticize the consistency and effectiveness with which he applied his ideas, as reflected in his examples. In the same way, I do not state my questions about Jung's facts, such as the frequency of certain kinds of dreams. They can be tested empirically but they do not add to or detract from the theory.

A major asset of Jung's method is its breadth, which makes possible individualized application: The dream is interpreted in its own context, which includes the dreamer's associations and conscious situation; the dream images are treated as a language to be translated, rather than a disguise; the correctness of the interpretation is verified by the responses of the dreamer. This involvement of the dreamer in the analysis of the dream prevents, to a large extent, the imposition of the interpreter's biases or preconceptions.

The breadth of Jung's theory of dream interpretation is matched by its depth, which is an attribute of his understanding of dream images as symbols rather than signs. The depth of the interpretation is enhanced, also, by the inclusion of archetypal amplifications in the repertoire of possibilities.

The major defect of Jung's theory, for me, is the lack of precision that accompanies its breadth, probably necessarily. In attempting to account for the widest possible range of dreams, Jung developed concepts that, in use, lend themselves to limitless possible definitions. The hypothesis of the compensatory function of dreams is the prime example. Because it has been expanded to apply to nearly every dream, it is defined less rigorously than I would like. For example, a dream image that is similar to waking reality can be understood as confirming or opposing it, depending on the judgment of the interpreter. (Since most dream interpretation is integral to psychotherapy, little is known about the degree to which interpreters agree.)

The lack of precision is evident also in the overgeneralized guidelines for dream interpretation in Jung's body of work. This overgeneralization could be corrected, perhaps, if the criteria for the application of the various guidelines were defined more firmly. Also, some of Jung's statements sound more sweeping than I believe they were meant. An example is his assertion that a dream does not tell the dreamer what to do. There are times when the dream seems to imply or even state what the dreamer should do: e.g., take steps to avoid catastrophe; or a dream figure may specify an instruction, such as to resign from a job. The dreamer is free to act or not act on the directions, of course, but when, as in a very small proportion of dreams, the instructions are given by a dream figure that is highly authoritative, the dreamer may feel that the choice has been made by the dream.

At the same time, Jung's overgeneralization is accompanied by what I consider to be too-restrictive pairings of interpretive categories and descriptions. For example, Jung implied that a reductive interpretation is always negative because it criticizes the dreamer's behavior or values. In my view, a reductive interpretation may be critical but it may be positive, also, in that it presses the dreamer to become aware of some previously repressed instinctual or other shadow motivations which, if accepted, can be positive assets as well as a push in the direction of wholeness.

Another of Jung's pairings, which seems to be unnecessarily limiting for the range of possible interpretations of a dream, is that of objective with reductive interpretation and subjective with constructive. The same criticism can be made of his inclination to interpret archetypal dreams always constructively, and prospective dreams always positively.

An exception to the lack of precision in Jung's theory is found in the distinction between objective and subjective characterizations of dream images. Jung defined the alternatives clearly and gave quite specific guidelines for their application.

Even the very helpful distinction between objective and subjective characterizations, however, requires further clarification when the rubrics directing one or the other interpretation conflict. For example, when can the dream image of a person be said to be a representation of someone else (for the purpose of displacing the accompanying emotionality)? Such clarification would increase the usefulness of the subjective-objective distinction.

The worth of a theory of dream interpretation is measured, in part, by its therapeutic value. In this realm, the empirical evidence for Jung's theory is overwhelming. In addition to his own clinical data, a sampling of which is presented in this book, nearly every work on Jungian psychology contributes to the amassing of case material in which Jungian dream interpretation has been used therapeutically.

The value of a theory of dream interpretation, like any theory, also is measured by its heuristic value—its capacity to stimulate investigation. Although Jung's theory of dream interpretation has inspired little experimental work, it has been the focus of a great deal of scholarly research, especially on archetypal motifs (e.g., the Great Mother). In addition, it is highly significant as the first theory of dream interpretation to hypothesize many of the ideas now accepted by most dream theorists, including theorists who are not aware that Jung is their precursor.

Many possibilities for empirical research are mentioned in this book in connection with specific aspects of Jung's theory. Some additional empirical research could be done with existing methods. For example, the content analysis method (Hall & Van de Castle, 1966) is useful in comprehending the data from large numbers of dreams. A further method applicable to studying dreams and their interpretation is the "idiopathic" method pioneered by Allport, exemplified in his *Letters from Jenny* (1965). With it, one can examine unique experiences, or at least individual cases, as psychological variables.

The main thrusts of this book have been that the dream is an important aspect of human experience, which must be taken into account in the search for wholeness, and that dream interpretation is an art that can be learned. The frontier, however, probably lies in using dreams and their interpretation to study the workings of the human mind. A great deal of research has been devoted to discovering when and how people dream, but virtually all dream research scientists would agree, I believe, that the most important question is *why* we dream.

The "why" of dreaming probably will not be answered until considerable attention is given to the interpretation of dreams. Since remembered "home dreams" seem to be different in content from remembered laboratory dreams, and the dreams we remember play a different role in our lives from those we do not remember, the experimentalists may have to move out of the laboratory into the clinical setting to study the meaning—interpretation—of dreams for leads to resolving the question of why we remember some dreams and not others, and the related question of why we dream.

The argument that the generally accepted scientific method cannot be applied to material as subjective and internal as dreams seems to me to be a delaying action. Comparable arguments have been used frequently in the history of science, and especially of psychology, only to prove spurious when unprejudiced minds went to work on the problem. For example, Piaget's theory of child development was dismissed for many years as unscientific; it was based on observations of his own children only. Nevertheless, when American psychologists became interested in Piaget's work, they devised methods of testing empirically his considerable body of theory. Something similar can happen with Jung's theories, especially his theory of dream interpretation. Although much of Jung's work on dream interpretation is more method than theory, the method is based on such theoretical premises as the self-regulation of the psyche and the collective unconscious. These premises can become testable hypotheses.

In considering Jung's work as unscientific, psychologists overlook the fact that the scientific enterprise has, according to philospher of science Reichenbach (1938), two basic components: the "context of discovery" and the "context of justification" (p. 239). Most American psychologists concentrate on the context of justification: testing hypotheses experimentally against data they are skilled at gathering. Jung's primary interest was in the context of discovery: framing hypotheses by induction from clinical data he happened to encounter. Both experimentation and hypothesizing are empirical in that they make use of data, but they use data in different ways and for different purposes.

Thus, it is possible for research on dream interpretation to join other scientific endeavors, such as those of mapping the brain and observing overt behavior, in adding to our understanding of the workings of the human mind. It may be that dreams will lead us first to an understanding of the mysterious realm of creativity because dreaming is the creative activity experienced by the most people.

APPENDIX

D1. (Chs. 1, 3, 11)

"... A colleague of mine ... always teased me about my dream-interpretations. Well, I met him one day in the street and he called out to me, 'How are things going? Still interpreting dreams? By the way, I've had another idiotic dream. Does that mean something too?' This is what he had dreamed: *'I am climbing a high mountain, over steep snow-covered slopes. I climb higher and higher, and it is marvelous weather. The higher I climb the better I feel. I think, "If only I could go on climbing like this for ever!" When I reach the summit my happiness and elation are so great that I feel I could mount right up into space. And I discover that I can actually do so: I mount upwards on empty air, and awake in sheer ecstasy.'*

"After some discussion, I said, 'My dear fellow, I know you can't give up mountaineering, but let me implore you not to go alone from now on. When you go, take two guides, and promise on your word of honor to follow them absolutely.' 'Incorrigible!' he replied, laughing, and waved good-bye .... Two months later ... when out alone, he was buried by an avalanche, but was dug out in the nick of time by a military patrol that happened to be passing. Three months afterwards ... he went on a climb with a younger friend, but without guides. A guide standing below saw him literally step out into the air while descending a rock face. He fell on the head of his friend, who was

203

waiting lower down, and both were dashed to pieces far below. That was *ecstasis* with a vengeance!" (CW16, pars. 323-24)

Jung recounted the same dream elsewhere with some additional information: "The dreamer was a man with an academic education, about fifty years of age .... I knew that he was ... an experienced [and] ardent mountain climber .... He told me how he loved to go alone without a guide, because the very danger of it had a tremendous fascination for him. He also told me about several dangerous tours, and the daring he displayed ... he added, becoming at the same time more serious, that he had no fear of danger, since he thought that death in the mountains would be something very beautiful .... he [said] very emphatically that he would never 'give up his mountains,' that he had to go to them in order to get away from the city and his family. 'This sticking at home does not suit me,' he said .... Also he seemed disgusted with his professional work. It occurred to me that his uncanny passion for the mountains must be an avenue of escape from an existence that had become intolerable to him.

"I therefore privately interpreted the dream as follows: Since he still clung on to life in spite of himself, the ascent of the mountain was at first laborious. But the more he surrendered himself to his passion, the more it lured him on and lent wings to his feet. Finally it lured him completely out of himself: he lost all sense of bodily weight and climbed even higher than the mountain, out into empty space. Obviously this meant death in the mountains.

"... I told him quite frankly what I thought, namely that he was seeking his death in the mountains, and that with such an attitude he stood a remarkably good chance of finding it.

"But that is absurd,' he replied, laughing. 'On the contrary, I am seeking my health in the mountains.' " (CW17, pars. 117-122)

In still another account, Jung stated that the man "was inextricably involved in a number of shady affairs. He developed an almost morbid passion for dangerous mountain-climbing as a sort of compensation: he was trying to 'get above himself' .... A mountain guide watched him and [his] friend letting themselves down on a rope in a difficult place. The friend had found a temporary foothold on a ledge, and the dreamer was following him down. Suddenly he let go of the rope 'as if he were jumping into the air,' as the guide reported afterwards." (CW18, par. 471)

Jung mentioned the dream a fourth time in briefer form, with no additional information (CW8, par. 164).

D2. (Ch. 2)

"I was in [the] meadow [of the vicarage which stood quite alone near Laufen castle]. Suddenly I discovered a dark, rectangular, stone-lined hole in the ground. I had never seen it before. I ran forward curiously and peered down into it. Then I saw a stone stairway leading down. Hesitantly and fearfully, I descended. At the bottom was a doorway with a round arch, closed off by a green curtain. It was a big, heavy curtain of worked stuff like brocade, and it looked very sumptuous. Curious to see what might be hidden behind, I pushed it aside. I saw before me in the dim light a rectangular chamber about thirty feet long. The ceiling was arched and of hewn stone.

The floor was laid with flagstones, and in the center a red carpet ran from the
entrance to a low platform. On this platform stood a wonderfully rich golden
throne. I am not certain, but perhaps a red cushion lay on the seat. It was a
magnificent throne, a real king's throne in a fairy tale. Something was
standing on it which I thought at first was a tree trunk twelve to fifteen feet
high and about one and a half to two feet thick. It was a huge thing, reaching
almost to the ceiling. But it was of a curious composition: it was made of
skin and naked flesh, and on top there was something like a rounded head
with no face and no hair. On the very top of the head was a single eye, gazing
motionlessly upward.

"It was fairly light in the room, although there were no windows and no
apparent source of light. Above the head, however, was an aura of brightness.
The thing did not move, yet I had the feeling that it might at any moment
crawl off the throne like a worm and creep toward me. I was paralyzed with
terror. At that moment I heard from outside and above me my mother's
voice. She called out, 'Yes, just look at him. That is the man-eater!' That
intensified my terror still more, and I awoke sweating and scared to death.
For many nights afterward I was afraid to go to sleep, because I feared I
might have another dream like that.

"This dream haunted me for years. Only much later did I realize that what
I had seen was a phallus, and it was decades before I understood that it was a
ritual phallus. I could never make out whether my mother meant, '*That* is the
man-eater,' or, 'That is the *man-eater*.' In the first case she would have meant
that not Lord Jesus or the Jesuit [whose black robe had frightened me, and at
whose presence my father had seemed irritated and fearful] was the devourer
of little children, but the phallus; in the second case that the 'man-eater' in
general was symbolized by the phallus, so that the dark Lord Jesus, the Jesuit,
and the phallus were identical.

"The abstract significance of the phallus is shown by the fact that it was
enthroned by itself, 'ithyphallically' (. . . 'upright'). The hole in the meadow
probably represented a grave. The grave itself was an underground temple
whose green curtain symbolized the *meadow*, in other words the mystery of
Earth with her covering of green vegetation. The carpet was *blood-red*. What
about the vault? Perhaps I had already been to the Munôt, the citadel of
Schaffhausen? This is not likely, since no one would take a three-year-old
child up there. So it cannot be a memory-trace. Equally, I do not know where
the anatomically correct phallus can have come from. The interpretation of
the *orificium urethrae* as an eye, with the source of light apparently above it,
points to the etymology of the word phallus (. . . shining, bright).

"At all events, the phallus of this dream seems to be a subterranean God
'not to be named,' and such it remained throughout my youth, reappearing
whenever anyone spoke too emphatically about Lord Jesus. Lord Jesus never
became quite real for me, never quite acceptable, never quite lovable, for
again and again I would think of his underground counterpart, a frightful
revelation which had been accorded me without my seeking it. The Jesuit's
'disguise' cast its shadow over the Christian doctrine I had been taught. Often
it seemed to me a solemn masquerade, a kind of funeral at which the
mourners put on serious or mournful faces but the next moment were secretly
laughing and not really sad at all. Lord Jesus seemed to me in some ways a
god of death, helpful, it is true, in that he scared away the terrors of the

night, but himself uncanny, a crucified and bloody corpse. Secretly, his love and kindness, which I always heard praised, appeared doubtful to me, chiefly because the people who talked most about 'dear Lord Jesus' wore black frock coats and shiny black boots which reminded me of burials. They were my father's colleagues as well as eight of my uncles—all parsons. For many years they inspired fear in me—not to speak of occasional Catholic priests who reminded me of the terrifying Jesuit who had irritated and even alarmed my father. In later years and until my confirmation, I made every effort to force myself to take the required positive attitude to Christ. But I could never succeed in overcoming my secret distrust.

"The fear of the 'black man,' which is felt by every child, was not the essential thing in that experience; it was, rather, the recognition that stabbed through my childish brain: 'That is a Jesuit.' So the important thing in the dream was its remarkable symbolic setting and the astounding interpretation: 'That is the man-eater.' Not the child's ogre of a man-eater, but the fact that *this* was the man-eater, and that *it* was sitting on a golden throne beneath the earth. For my childish imagination it was first of all the king who sat on a golden throne; then, on a much more beautiful and much higher and much more golden throne far, far away in the blue sky, sat God and Lord Jesus, with golden crowns and white robes. Yet from this same Lord Jesus came the 'Jesuit,' in black women's garb, with a broad black hat, down from the wooded hill. I had to glance up there every so often to see whether another danger might not be approaching. In the dream I went down into the hole in the earth and found something very different on a golden throne, something non-human and underworldly, which gazed fixedly upward and fed on human flesh. It was only fifty years later that a passage in a study of religious ritual burned into my eyes, concerning the motif of cannibalism that underlies the symbolism of the Mass. Only then did it become clear to me how exceedingly unchildlike, how sophisticated and oversophisticated was the thought that had begun to break through into consciousness in those two experiences. Who was it speaking in me? Whose mind had devised them? What kind of superior intelligence was at work?

"Who spoke to me then? Who talked of problems far beyond my knowledge? Who brought the Above and Below together, and laid the foundation for everything that was to fill the second half of my life with stormiest passion? Who but that alien guest who came both from above and from below?

"Through this childhood dream I was initiated into the secrets of the earth. What happened then was a kind of burial in the earth, and many years were to pass before I came out again. Today I know that it happened in order to bring the greatest possible amount of light into the darkness. It was an initiation into the realm of darkness." (MDR, pp. 12–15)

D3. (Ch. 3)

"Dream: *'I was in a boat with some man. He said, 'We must go to the very end of the lake, where the four valleys converge, where they bring down the flocks of sheep to the water.' When he got there, he found a lame sheep in the flock, and I found a little lamb that was pregnant. It surprised me because it seemed too young to be pregnant. We tenderly took those two sheep in our*

arms and carried them to the boat. I kept wrapping them up. The man said,
'They must die, they are shivering so.' So I wrapped them up once more.'

"... [The dreamer] is on the move .... She is in the boat with a man. The situation in the dream refers to a lake which obviously is the Lake of Zurich, as the boy [in the previous dream] is Swiss. The situation then, is located here—the actual situation, no memory situation and that unknown man with her is the music teacher [of a previous dream] .... This time ... he is the man who sails the boat, ... the man at the tiller takes the lead, and he says, 'We must go to the very end of the lake.' It is a higher necessity, a *must*, we must go to the end of the thing, the whole length of the lake. It is a sort of enterprise, an undertaking, and it must be done thoroughly, to the very end. And now there comes something most amazing: the dream says, 'where the four valleys converge.' Here things are getting quite mythological .... Traveling with an unknown man in a boat has a mythological connotation. It could be a metaphor. One is in the same boat with somebody—it is the same enterprise .... The man ... is the new spirit she has learned or created in Switzerland, and that spirit now takes her along. He is taking her by the hand, saying, 'You go where I go, you follow me,' and she accepts it, and the next enterprise is an adventure, traveling on the lake and going to the very end of it. ... In mythology [that would be] the Argonauts, the seeking of the Golden Fleece . . . at the other end there is no fleece, but there are sheep .... The Argonauts ... [had] to pass through the rocks where the pigeon loses its tail, and all that. They take an exceedingly psychological trip: ... the night sea-journey. The lake is the unconscious ... because when you try to look into the unconscious you see nothing—you only see your ego, ... because it is dark underneath and light above and you see only yourself. Yet you know thousands of things are sunken there, monsters are there, eternal night down there .... The world of our ancestors, even the world of our childhood, is still going on down in those depths. It is like the shining surface of a sheet of water which at the same time is deep and dark. We may assume that the whole world is sunk in the depths of the sea—like Atlantis—and we see nothing but our own image reflected in that shining surface. That is the reason the unconscious is expressed by the sea or by any body of water, even stagnant water.

"Now that trip to the end of the lake is a serious experience .... It ... takes you to the very end and there you would expect to find something definite, something new. And this thing that is so new and definite is symbolized by four valleys that ... come together, ... and flocks of sheep are coming down to drink the water of life. This is almost a Biblical image ... I cannot remember a place where four valleys converge, and when I asked the patient, she was completely stumped .... Well, one thinks of the four directions; in the Indian Pueblos one hears of the four cardinal points of the horizon, one thinks of the orientation of temples according to the four cardinal points. Also there is a ... dynamic element in [this image]: ... Flocks of sheep are traveling down from all the four corners in order to come to the center, to drink from the water .... Something similar ... [is in the] legend that when Jesus was born and the three wise men are supposed to have come together from the four corners of the world, there were not three men, but four, but the fourth did not come in time. Jesus is the source of life and his followers are the sheep. This is the place of the waters of life where people will seek their salvation . . . . [Another analogy is the Garden of Eden,] the reverse picture: the center, and the waters of life coming out in four rivers . . . . Then another picture, flocks of humanity streaming in [in the City of the Four Gates] . . . in Revelation, the Last Judgment, where all the peoples of the earth stream together, like sheep. They separate the sheep from the goats. And the center of the whole performance is the Heavenly Jerusalem where the Judgment is rendered . . . . You find [the four-fold symbol also] in the Pueblos, in India, in China . . . . You find it even in the *tetraktys* of Pythagoras . . . .

"... When the man picks up the lame sheep, he is picking up something that ... expresses himself in a way, . . . as the prophets in the Old Testament acted prophetically or symbolically . . . . When the dream figures take up those animals, it is as if they were speaking through their action, . . . as if they said, for instance, 'This I do to show you that one should feel compassion' . . . .

"... These sheep might be of Christian origin, because sheep, particularly the lamb, play a very great role in Christian symbolism, and it is quite certain that Christian symbols would come up somewhere with our patient . . . . She simply could not solve her problems with the typical Protestant point of view . . . . This lamb symbolism is a piece of Catholicism in our patient which is quite unexpected . . . .

"... [The symbolism is an analogy to] the figure of the shepherd who picks up a little lamb and carries it . . . . The man assumed the role of the good shepherd. Already, he is a guide—he guides the dreamer to the place of the four valleys and when he comes to his flock picks up a lame sheep. He is a figure that can be likened to a very interesting early figure of the primitive church, called the *Poimen*, which has now vanished from ecclesiastical terminology. The good shepherd has remained, but the other figure has vanished with a certain book that was almost canonical at the time called *The Shepherd of Hermas*. When the New Testament writings were gathered together, that was omitted. I must use the Greek word Poimen here because this Poimen is a pre-Christian figure. It is not a Christian invention, it is a pagan invention, and has a direct historical relation to Orpheus. And Orpheus is another figure related to Christ; he was understood to be an anticipation of Christ because he tamed wild passions in the form of wild animals by his delicate music. He is also like a shepherd, and moreover he is called 'the Fisher,' and as such he played a great role in the Dionysian mysteries which were of course pre-Christian. So we see the Christ figure in heathen cults. We even find in certain inscriptions Christ almost identical with Bacchus, absolutely on the same level . . . . In the early days the figure of Christ was quite hazy, our idea of him is an absolutely new invention . . . . That very impersonal figure was never called Christ. That name was taboo. He was called the Shepherd of Men . . . .

"... Our good lady ... returns here to the archetypal pattern ... of the spirit-like leader of men. It goes right back to the spirit-leaders of primitive tribes—where certain men called medicine men are at times possessed by spirits, chiefly ancestral spirits, who lead them and tell what is good for the people . . . .

"... You can't see it from this dream exactly. You only get a hint, ...He comes in later on and ... slowly develops into the primitive spirit-leader, a seer, who sees ahead all the things which she is meant to go through later on .... The spirit-leader ... will take the lead, will foresee and experience by anticipation, and she will go the same way and will experience it in her own life.

"Now picking up one of the lame sheep denotes his quality as a good shepherd. There is something wrong with both of these sheep; one is lame and the one she picks up is pregnant which is an abnormality, a thing that should not be actually, and so both may die as the shepherd intimates. He says that they may die because they shiver so much; they are already quite cold. Now if we take that sheep symbolism as indicating a specific Christian way of solving the great problem of how to live, then we could say that it is demonstrated here in a twofold way.

"... Here in the dream, this woman is with the sheep inasmuch as she is still an instinctual member of the Christian church. Her mind is lame and she is pregnant. She is still too young to carry and yet she is pregnant with the future. That means that she is too young as a person, not ripe, not mature, she is pregnant with the future but she cannot carry it ....

"After this dream, the patient was attacked by an extraordinary feeling of lassitude and weariness. This was perfectly inexplicable to her but the reason is quite obvious from the dream. The lameness and illness of the sheep is a living fact in her. One has such a feeling of weariness, a sort of resignation, of despair, when one has lost a hope—a form in which one could live, for instance. When that possibility is gone, one is overcome by this kind of psychogenic fatigue. It is a direct consequence of the dream, or of the realization that has taken place in the dream. And, mind you, this reaction came before we had analyzed it. She did not know what the dream conveyed but she felt the effect of it, which is often the case." (VSI, pp. 19–21, 23–28)

D4. (Chs. 5, 11)

"... A young man dreams: *'I was standing in a strange garden and picked an apple from a tree. I looked about cautiously, to make sure that no one saw me.'*

"The associated dream-material is a memory of having once, when a boy, plucked a couple of pears surreptitiously from a neighbour's garden. The feeling of bad conscience, which is a prominent feature of the dream, reminds him of a situation experienced on the previous day. He met a young lady in the street—a casual acquaintance—and exchanged a few words with her. At that moment a gentleman passed whom he knew, whereupon he was suddenly seized with a curious feeling of embarrassment, as if he were doing something wrong. He associated the apple with the scene in the Garden of Eden, and also with the fact that he had never really understood why the eating of the forbidden fruit should have had dire consequences for our first parents. This had always made him feel angry; it seemed to him an unjust act of God, for God had made men as they were, with all their curiosity and greed.

"Another association was that sometimes his father had punished him for certain things in a way that seemed to him incomprehensible. The worst punishment had been bestowed on him after he was caught secretly watching girls bathing. This led up to the confession that he had recently begun a love-affair with a housemaid but had not yet carried it through to its natural conclusion. On the evening before the dream he had had a rendezvous with her.

"Reviewing this material, we can see that the dream contains a very transparent reference to the last-named incident. The associative material shows that the apple episode is obviously intended as an erotic scene. For various other reasons, too, it may be considered extremely probably that this experience of the previous day has gone on working in the dream. In the dream the young man plucks the apple of Paradise, which in reality he has not yet plucked. The remainder of the material associated with the dream is concerned with another experience of the previous day, namely the peculiar feeling of bad conscience which seized the dreamer when he was talking to his casual lady acquaintance. This, again, was associated with the fall of man in Paradise, and finally with an erotic misdemeanour of his childhood, for which his father had punished him severely. All these associations are linked together by the idea of *guilt*.

"We shall first consider this material from the causal standpoint of Freud; in other words, we shall 'interpret' the dream, to use Freud's expression. A wish has been left unfulfilled from the day before. In the dream this wish is fulfilled under the *symbol* of the apple episode. By why is this fulfilment disguised and hidden under a symbolical image instead of being expressed in a clearly sexual thought? Freud would point to the unmistakable element of guilt in this material and say that the morality inculcated into the young man from childhood is bent on repressing such wishes, and to that end brands the natural craving as something painful and incompatible. The repressed painful thought can therefore express itself only 'symbolically.' As these thoughts are incompatible with the moral content of consciousness, a psychic authority postulated by Freud, called the censor, prevents this wish from passing undisguised into consciousness.

"Considering a dream from the standpoint of finality, which I contrast with the causal standpoint of Freud, does not—as I would expressly like to emphasize—involve a denial of the dream's causes, but rather a different interpretation of the associative material gathered round the dream. The material facts remain the same, but the criterion by which they are judged is different. The question may be formulated simply as follows: What is the purpose of this dream? What effect is it meant to have? These questions are not arbitrary inasmuch as they can be applied to every psychic activity. Everywhere the question of the 'why' and the 'wherefore' may be raised, because every organic structure consists of a complicated network of purposive functions, and each of these functions can be resolved into a series of individual facts with a purposive orientation.

"It is clear that the material added by the dream to the previous day's erotic experience chiefly emphasizes the element of guilt in the erotic act. The same association had already shown itself to be operative in another experience of the previous day, in that meeting with the casual lady acquaintance, when the feeling of a bad conscience was automatically and inexplicably aroused, as if in that instance too the young man was doing something wrong. This feeling also plays a part in the dream and is further intensified by the association of the additional material, the erotic experience of the day before being depicted by the story of the Fall, which was followed by such severe punishment.

"I maintain that there exists in the dreamer an unconscious propensity or tendency to represent his erotic experiences as guilt. It is characteristic that the dream is followed by the association with the Fall and that the young man had never really grasped why the punishment should have been so drastic. This association throws light on the reasons why he did not think simply: 'What I am doing is not right.' Obviously he does not know that he might condemn his conduct as morally wrong . . . . His conscious belief is that his conduct does not matter in the least morally, as all his friends were acting in the same way, besides which he was quite unable on other grounds to understand why such a fuss should be made about it.

"In this dream we can discern a compensating function of the unconscious whereby those thoughts, inclinations, and tendencies which in conscious life are too little valued, come spontaneously into action during the sleeping state, when the conscious process is to a large extent eliminated . . . .

"The theft of the apple is a typical dream-motif that occurs in many different variations in numerous dreams. It is also a well-known mythological motif, which is found not only in the story of the Garden of Eden but in countless myths and fairytales from all ages and climes." (CW8, pars. 457–464, 466, 476)

D5. (Ch. 5)

"*I was with an unknown, brown-skinned man, a savage, in a lonely, rocky mountain landscape. It was before dawn; the eastern sky was already bright, and the stars fading. Then I heard Siegfried's horn sounding over the mountains and I knew that we had to kill him. We were armed with rifles and lay in wait for him on a narrow path over the rocks.*

"*Then Siegfried appeared high up on the crest of the mountain, in the first ray of the rising sun. On a chariot made of the bones of the dead he drove at furious speed down the precipitous slope. When he turned a corner, we shot at him, and he plunged down, struck dead.*

"*Filled with disgust and remorse for having destroyed something so great and beautiful, I turned to flee, impelled by the fear that the murder might be discovered. But a tremendous downfall of rain began, and I knew that it would wipe out all traces of the dead. I had escaped the danger of discovery; life could go on, but an unbearable feeling of guilt remained.*

"*. . .* A voice within me said, 'You *must* understand the dream, and must do so at once! The inner urgency mounted until the terrible moment came when the voice said, If you do not understand the dream, you must shoot yourself! In the drawer of my night table lay a loaded revolver, and I became frightened . . . . Suddenly the meaning of the dream dawned on me. 'Why, that is the problem that is being played out in the world.' Siegfried, I thought, represents what the Germans want to achieve, heroically to impose their will, have their own way. 'Where there is a will there is a way!' I had wanted to do the same. But now that was no longer possible. The dream showed that the attitude embodied by Siegfried, the hero, no longer suited me. Therefore it had to be killed.

"After the deed I felt an overpowering compassion, as though I myself had been shot: a sign of my secret identity with Siegfried, as well as of the grief a man feels when he is forced to sacrifice his ideal and his conscious attitudes. This identity and my heroic idealism had to be abandoned, for there are higher things than the ego's will, and to these one must bow.

"These thoughts sufficed for the present, and I fell asleep again.

"The small, brown-skinned savage who accompanied me and had actually taken the initiative in the killing was an embodiment of the primitive shadow. The rain showed that the tension between consciousness and the unconscious was being resolved." (MDR, pp. 180–181)

D6. (Ch. 8)

"The dreamer is at a social gathering. On leaving he puts on a stranger's hat instead of his own.

"The hat, as a covering for the head, has the general sense of something that epitomizes the head. Just as in summing up we bring ideas 'under one head' (*unter einen Hut*), so the hat, as a sort of leading idea, covers the whole personality and imparts its own significance to it. Coronation endows the ruler with the divine nature of the sun, the doctor's hood bestows the dignity of a scholar, and a stranger's hat imparts a strange nature. Meyrink uses this theme in his novel *The Golem* . . . , where the hero puts on the hat of Athanasius Pernath and, as a result, becomes involved in a strange experience. It is clear enough in *The Golem* that the thing that entangles the hero in fantastic adventures is the unconscious. Let us stress at once the significance of *The Golem* parallel and assume that the hat in the dream is the hat of an Athanasius, an immortal, a being beyond time, the universal and everlasting man as distinct from the ephemeral and 'accidental' mortal man. Circumscribing the head, the hat is round like the sun-disc of a crown and therefore contains [an] allusion to the mandala. The unconscious with its figures is . . . standing like a shadow behind the dreamer and pushing its way into consciousness." (CW12, par. 53)

D7. (Ch. 8)

"An actor smashes his hat against the wall, where it looks like this: [diagram of a circle with 8 spokes and a solid black center].

"As certain material not included here shows, the 'actor' refers to a definite fact in the dreamer's personal life. Up to now he had maintained a certain fiction about himself which prevented him from taking himself seriously. This fiction has become incompatible with the serious attitude he has now attained. He must give up the actor in him who rejected the self." (CW12, par. 255)

D8. (Ch. 8)

". . . The first dream contains his whole problem and a hint as to its solution.

" '*I hear that a child of my youngest sister is ill and my brother-in-law comes and asks me to go with him to the theatre and dine afterwards. I have eaten already, yet I think I can go with him.*

" '*We arrive in a large room, with a long dining-table in the centre already spread; and on the four sides of the big room are rows of benches or seats like an amphitheatre, but with their backs to the table,—the reverse way. We sit down and I ask my brother-in-law why his wife has not come; than I think it is probably because the child is ill and ask how she is. He says she is much better, only a little fever now.*

" '*Then I am at the home of my brother-in-law, and I see the child, a little girl one or two years old*' (he adds: there is no such girl in reality, but there was a boy of two). '*The child looks rather ill, and some one informs me that she would not pronounce the name of my wife, Maria. I pronounce that name and ask the child to repeat it, to say 'Aunt Mari-ah ah', like yawning, despite the protests of the people around me against the way of pronouncing my wife's name.*'

"This ordinary dream introduces us into the home atmosphere of the patient . . . . He is obviously caught in the terminology of his family, so perhaps his unconscious tends to emphasize the fact that his problem is there.

"*Child of his youngest sister:* Two years ago her first child died, a beautiful boy of two. He said: 'We very much participated in the sorrow of the parents during the illness and at his death from dysentery—he was my godchild.' The sister is connected with the dreamer chiefly through that loss, and there is a similar situation in the dream: the illness of the little girl recalls the time when the boy was ill and died . . . . He is connected with the sister through an emotional memory of loss; . . . . He is threatened now with a similar loss but this one is psychological, a symbolical facon de parler, represented by a girl child. Therefore the situation is somewhat similar, but in reality there is nothing of the kind, no illness in the family . . . .

"*His youngest sister* was always his particular pet, she is 11 years younger . . . . she is the link with the ill child, and the child belongs to his own psychology . . . . So the sister is symbolic, she lives abroad in a far-off country and he has no actual correspondence with her . . . . She represents an unknown woman, or a feminine factor of unknown nature in himself, that has an imaginary child who is ill . . . .

"*Illness of child:* His sister's first child had suffered from intestinal trouble and died of it . . . . After the death of this child, his sister became quite anxious lest the second boy might fall ill, but he did not. She became rather serious and went in for Christian Science, and it was as if the boy were really made better; the man does not know whether that was coincidence or a consequence of the fact that the sister was quieter and treated the child with more self-assurance . . . . The connotation of Christian Science has also to do with that female character in his own psychology, ... The female factor underwent a certain conversion, and [the dreamer] within the last two or three years has begun to be interested in philosophy, occultism, theosophy, and . . . . spiritualism . . . . There was a change in him. He was a business man, and all his 'pep' was associated with business matters, but these other interests filtered into him, he was slowly imbued by philosophical ideas . . . .

"His *brother-in-law* is the second figure in the dream. They had been friendly [even] before his marriage with his sister; they had been in the same business and went to the opera together, his brother-in-law being very musical. He said, 'I got all my music—not much—from my brother-in-law, as he came through me into my business firm; he has now a position as director; I was rather disappointed that he took so long to get au fait with the new business, yet he has more facility in dealing with people than I have' . . . . His brother-in-law . . . had withdrawn from the business altogether and left the country. So actually the brother-in-law also lives far away, there are very few letters, and he plays no part worth mentioning in his life . . . . He was on better terms with his wife in [the dreamer's] own case. The patient is not artistic at all; . . . . The brother-in-law, through his musical and less businesslike qualities, symbolizes another side of the dreamer; he is not as efficient as the patient but has plus on the artistic side. Music is symbolical of a more rounded outlook for the dreamer, it is the art of feeling par excellence . . . .

"*Brother-in-law . . . asks him to go the theatre and to dine afterwards:* The patient says: 'I cannot remember having been to the theatre with my brother-in-law since his wedding; if so, then together with our wives; or that I have ever dined with him except in his own house.' Again this . . . never happened in reality, and is therefore a symbolic invention. The theatre is the place of unreal life, it is life in the form of images, one can see there how these things work . . . . So in inviting him to the theatre, his brother-in-law invites him to the staging of his complexes,—where all the images are the symbolic or unconscious representations of his own complexes. *And to dine afterwards:* . . . . Communion means eating a complex, originally a sacrificial animal, the totem animal, the representation of the basic instincts of that particular clan. You eat your unconscious or ancestors and so add strength to yourself . . . . integrate them . . . .

"Theatre and dining is an anticipation of the process of analysis . . . . The feeling side of his personality, that side of himself which was not in business, was shut away from life, it was not even in his marriage. The brother-in-law is like a second unconscious personality, who invites him in the dream to dine alone with him, without the . . . wives: they are the emotions, for that is the way man usually becomes acquainted with woman. He must leave at home the emotional factor or there will be no objectivity; he cannot look at the pictures or think about himself when emotional . . . .

"*He thinks he has already dined*, and it is therefore superfluous to dine again. He has no associations so we are free to guess. Perhaps he thinks that he has already assimilated himself, feels that he is complete, a perfectly normal, up-to-date individual, with no need to come to me nor to assimilate anything more,—some resistance against analysis. Nevertheless he agrees and goes with his brother-in-law. 'It is not a habit of mine to go out in the evening, I prefer to remain at home. It must be a particular condition that would induce me to go out, for instance, a play in which my wife would be interested, when, if I don't go, she would go to bed early.' He accepts the fact that he could see more of himself and go through analysis; yet he emphasizes the fact that he does not like to go out, and would only go to something especially interesting or something that would interest his wife. This is his correctness; a man out of his home is suspect, a husband should only be interested in public affairs or in things his wife likes, and never go to out-of-the-way plays or places. His last remark—that she goes to bed early—opens up a vista. His wife would rather sleep than bore herself to death with him. Most exciting evening! Therefore yawning with internal resistance—Mari—and yawn! Obviously this is the situation at home—that association with 'a' at the end of 'Mari' . . . .

"The big room in which our patient and his brother-in-law were to eat was like a village hall in an inn, like those where the Vereins [clubs] meet in Switzerland . . . . On two official occasions the patient remembers he has participated in such meetings in a room like this.

"*The long dining-table in the middle of the room was spread* as though for a great number of people. Then he discovers *the peculiar arrangement of the seats, rising on the four sides like an amphitheatre, but with their backs turned to the table.* [It was his private theatre, where he would see his own inner drama stages.] . . . Most probably eating, in connection with the theatre, means the assimilation of the images seen in the private theatre, that is, the phantasy material or other material revealed through introspection . . . .

"The big room . . . and the theatre: . . . both are public places, the table is spread; . . . he went to the theatre and to a certain place to dine, so we may be perfectly sure that this part of the dream belongs to the same theme.

"Now we come to those *seats which are turned away from the table.* He said: 'We had to climb a stair beginning at the door as if going up to a sort of tribunal, and from the stair we had access to rows of benches turned to the walls of the room. I saw how people were sitting down on those seats and noticed no one near the table in the middle of the room, dinner was not to begin yet, apparently.' He remembered having seen a room like that in an Algerian town, where they were playing *jeu de paume,* a king of *pelote de Basque,* like the old English tennis. That room also suggested an amphitheatre, but the seats were arranged along only two sides of the room, coming almost to the middle, but leaving an open space for the game. In this game a ball is beaten against a wall with tremendous force so that the arm gets swollen up to the shoulder. It is somewhat like the English 'fives', the forerunner of the English tennis. He also had an association with a clinic, where there were amphitheatre seats in the lecture-hall. He had seen a picture of such a room and also been in one in reality where a professor demonstrated on a blackboard an operation which was to be done on his wife.

"Remember that a dining-room is a place where things ought to be assimilated; but eating has not begun, and it seems to be meant that it should not yet begin . . . . That dining-room is a public place . . . . The dream says: 'Assume that you are in a public place where there are other people, as at a concert, theatre, or ballgame, and you have to do 'like so many other people', a collective job, by no means an individual one; here are the phantoms of your dreams, and it is very difficult to have to swallow that you are a coward, a lazy dog, etc.! . . . . This seems to the patient to be an almost impossible job. He takes it with so much hesitation, so little appetite, because he assumes that he is the only individual from the beginning of the world who has had to do it . . . .

"So the dreams says to the man: 'This thing you are doing is a collective job; you think you are doing it privately in the doctor's room but many other people are doing the same thing' . . . . The patient suffers particularly from the fact that he cannot tell the truth, and the dream says this is a collective task.

"Now why this ball game? A table would be the place where eating takes place, and the seats would serve the people who are attending that collective eating,—really a psychological communion table. The psychological root of communion, and the necessary preliminary, is always confession; we must confess before we are worthy to receive communion . . . . Why are these seats turned with their backs to the table? This obviously means something very abnormal, . . . that you are refusing to enter into the communion . . . . The dream says: 'What you are doing in your secrecy, is what everyone else is doing, everybody is turning his back on his fellow-beings.'

" *'We sit down and I ask my brother-in-law why his wife has not come.* While I ask I remember at the same time the reason of her being absent; I did not wait for an answer because I wanted to show my brother-in-law that I had not forgotten that the child was ill.' As to *the illness* he says: 'My wife is never social, never goes out for pleasure if one of the children is not perfectly well, or if she thinks the children would be insufficiently controlled while she is away.' As they had lived so much in tropical countries where much care is required with young children, bringing them up had been more difficult than if they had lived in Switzerland . . . . The *sick child* is now much better, only a little fever. In his association with this fact he referred to the boy of his brother-in-law: 'Before the boy died I had repeatedly asked my brother-in-law how the child was.' All this discussion about his brother-in-law's wife of course refers to his own personal problem, to the fact that his wife does not come with him, that they have no communion. He said: 'When a child is ill, my wife is always terribly troubled, out of proportion.' The illness of the child is the most obvious reason why he and his wife turn their backs on each other; but the illness of a real child would not create an obstacle between a man and his wife . . . . Just as in fact a wife is called elsewhere by the sickness of a child, just so psychologically she does not join him because of the illness of the child in the dream. Now since the illness of the child goes all through the dream, we must assume that it means more than the mere opportunity for the wife not to be in the game. And it is important that the ill child is a girl.

"The real child who died was a boy and has no actual importance here . . . . The allusion to the dead boy is an allusion to the patient's own dead youth. He has arrived in the second part of life, where one's psychology changes: youth is dead, the second part of life is beginning. But this is only an allusion; our interest now is in the sickness of the girl-child . . . .

"I should like now to come back to the *jeu de paume*, that *pelote de Basque* . . . . From mediaeval manuscripts we learn that the old ritual *jeu de paume* was played up to the 12th century, and in certain remote places, at Auxerre in France for instance, up to the 16th century . . . . These games were played 'for the consolation and recreation of the soul' . . . . Possibly there is a connection with the ceremony of the '*bride-ball*' which was thrown between bride and groom. And in other games in the churches the ball was kicked or torn to pieces as the god of the past years . . . . It is quite probable that his ball symbolizes the sun . . . . The dining, the seats, the pelote, all that material comes together in the dream and his associations . . . .

". . . The dreamer is now at the house of his brother-in-law, where he sees the child, a little girl, one or two years old . . . . The scene has shifted to a private place inside the individual . . . . He said about the house of his brother-in-law: 'My father lived several years in that house, and my sister inherited it; it is only about 100 paces away from my own house, so we often [saw] each other. The house and shutters are all monotonously painted grey, and it gives a dreary, monotonous aspect. I wish they would paint the shutters at least a different colour to animate it a bit' . . . .

". . . We get the important information from his association that his house is not far away, which means that it is not very far from conciousness . . . . The house of his brother-in-law would be of course the unconscious aspect of his own house, the place where the drama is going on. The house . . . means the habitual or inherited attitude, the habitual way of living, or something acquired like a house, or perhaps the way one lives with the whole family. His habitual attitude is uninteresting and grey as the house of his brother-in-law, and he longs for more colour in it . . . .

"*The child:* In reality it was a boy of two who was ill and died, and the dreamer's two other sisters have each a little girl in her 7th year whom he likes. He says, 'I like little girls much better than little boys, they are much nicer and more expressive, I like my own little daughter better than the boys.' There are no other associations so I call his attention to the age of the child . . . . 'What about two years ago?' 'Two years ago I came back from abroad and settled in Switzerland. I began then the study of occult literature, spiritism, theosophy, all sorts of things; only lately I gave it up more or less, because I was not quite satisfied, not just lack of interest, but some odium around such study. When my little nephew died two years ago, I was just reading a book by Dennis Bradley, 'Towards the Stars', (evidently a religious book). I liked it particularly and gave it to my sister after the death of the boy.'

"He had also read German occult literature: 'I read a famous German book: 'The Visionary of Prevorst,' written by Dr. Justinus Kerner, 1829, . . . the first history of a case of somnambulism psychologically observed, and most interesting.' He . . . wanted a certain doctor to write a study of her but . . . [feared] that the man would be injured by it.

"*The little girl is the child of his anima*, and has to do with creative energy, and coming from the occult side is spiritual . . . . He gave up the study himself becaue it had a bad influence on him. He thought occult studies made people very unreal; there was so much doubtful matter, so speculative and yet so impressive, that it filled people's heads with all sorts of vapourous ideas; there was a poisonous unreality in those things very often . . . . So one side of himself is concerned with a decided spiritually creative factor that is two years old, and the doctor represents his rational side which he is using in studying this poetical element expressed by the child. In the last two years a new thing has been growing in this man, not only this interest in occult matters which kept his mind busy, but also a creative interest and intention, which would be the expression not of thoughts but of feeling, and which would give colour to his house.

". . . .The colour of this child's face is bad, and her features are distorted exactly like the boy who died. And he adds without apparent connection: 'I am reading very little about occultism now.' The occult stuff transcended his digestive powers, he suffered from mental indigestion. Then because the girl is linked up with the boy who died, we must assume she suffers from intestinal trouble too; she has been fed with occult literature, and that is not the proper kind of food for the little poetic soul developing in him.

" '*Someone informs me that the child would not pronounce the name of my wife,*' and on account of that he pronounces the name of his wife to the child and tries to make her repeat it. He says: 'My wife is most beloved by all her nephews and nieces; usually the first name that the children succeed in pronouncing is hers.' And he mentions that not long ago he received a letter from one of his other sisters in which she told him that her little boy had composed a melody to which he sang: 'Aunt Mary is a dear boy.' In contradistinction with reality this dream child will not or cannot pronounce the name of his wife, she is evidently in opposition to her. We know that the relation between the dreamer and his wife is rather monotonous, and within two years a development has begun in him which produces a living being that deviates from his wife. This child of his anima is linked up with occult interests and a possible sort of scientific or artistic activity. He is puzzled by this, and tries to teach the child to pronounce the name properly, rather shocked that something should develop in him that is not in accordance with his wife, that does not fit into marriage. 'I often made the effort to teach my own children or my sisters' to pronounce words in the right way which they pronounced wrongly.' He stands for proper form; there should be nothing in his mind or in his heart that is not correct. So that something in him does not want to pronounce the name of his wife is a fact which should not be. . . .

"His wife's name is Maria and he mentions: 'An old aunt of my wife is also called Aunt Maria, but she is quite remote, we have nothing to do with her.' Then he goes on: 'While I was teaching the child to pronounce the word 'Maria' properly, I was amused that I only said "Mari–" and instead of pronouncing the "a" was yawning, adding a yawn to the name instead of the last vowel; in the dream I found myself extremely witty in doing so, but cannot see the joke in waking life.' All *the family protests* against his so-called joke, and he says: 'Yes, they are quite right, one should not show the children such bad manners, because they cannot, like adults, make a distinction between reality and a joke.' Again the correct attitude. This part of the dream was anticipated in the house with shutters painted grey. The house is grey and he is bored, and his unconscious expresses this by that funny allusion,–that he yawns in pronouncing the name of his wife . . . .

"... *The brother-in-law:* The dreamer has been in an important position, a director of a business company, and his brother-in-law, being a younger man, has succeeded him; so he followed him, he is the representative of the one that follows us, the shadow . . . . If the brother-in-law represents a shadow, it follows that the wife of the shadow is a very definite figure and must have the characteristics of that figure, the wife is the anima . . . .

"... The anima is a definite entity, and so is this child a definite entity, and all the more dangerous because it is an imaginary child. She is dangerous because she might reflect back on the patient himself . . . . She is about two years old, . . . she is pale and ill, and . . . she is the product of the union of the shadow and the anima,–they come together somehow . . . . [Two years ago] he began his occult studies which led him into analysis . . . .

"The occult science he was trying to study would represent symbolically the dark and unknown side of things; since that interest was born out of the union of the shadow and anima it would naturally be expressed by something occult . . . . Now the unconscious says it is an unsound kind of occupation and therefore the child is ill . . . . The fact that he goes to dinner with the shadow means that he accepts the existence of the shadow . . . . The child is ill because he has begun his studies in the wrong way, he ought to begin [with] the shadow . . . .

"... There was the association of the *jeu de paume* and *pelote de Basque.* They were not quite the same. The *jeu de paume* was played in the middle ages, not with a racquet, but with the palm of the hand; and the same idea was in the *pelote de Basque* but the ball was played against the wall; then a third version was the *jeu de paume* as it was played in the church, the clerics throwing the ball to one another. I don't know what kind of figures they made but all were playing the same game. And we play it too, the ball game has become almost a figure of speech with us; we often use the similes 'throw the ball', 'play the game', 'I catch it', etc. It simply means playing together; we all play together and since we react, we are all in it, responsible and alive . . . .

"Then there is a particular version here, a mere association so we must not press it too hard; in the case of the pelote played against the wall where the ball is caught not by other people but by oneself, there may be an element of self-isolation or auto-eroticism . . . .

"If the dreamer follows the intimation of the shadow he will see his problem as a collective one which ought to be brought into general connection with the spirit of his own time, and not hidden away, assuming it to be the mistake of a single individual . . . .

"Now after this general statement, which prepares him for an entirely different attitude to his particular problem, the dream returns again to the personal aspect of things, the pathological condition of the child. Its condition is morbid because occult studies lead nowhere; they are just an attempt at sublimation, a sublimation which never answers the real, urgent problem of the times. What must be done now with the child? It is all very well to say that this is a collective problem, . . . come back to your own problem, your own child, come and admit you are bored with your dear wife at home. Psychologically that means he must *acknowledge his shadow*, the inferior man who does not live up to rational conditions, a sort of primitive more aware of the needs of nature, who forces him to admit his boredom . . . . Then the shadow will be detached from his anima, because as he becomes conscious of his shadow, it is released from his unconscious. Then between the shadow and anima a real relation can take place with the outcome that the child will be normal.

". . . When the shadow and anima have a proper relationship, there is a chance that his relation to his wife will become better, that he can have an individual relationship with her. For he can only establish a real relationship when he is aware of his shadow . . . . Our man must give up his illusions, admit he is not respectable and that he is bored; and he must tell his wife he is bored to death and at the same time 'sometimes my sublimation fails to work'. If he only knew his wife this would be easier."

". . . [The illness of the child was acute.] the association with that child's disease was that the sister of the dreamer had lost a child by intestinal dysentery. According to this association we can assume that the dream child is ill as the sister's actual child is ill . . . . Nothing is said directly in the dream about the duration of the illness, but we can conclude from the parallel that it must have been pretty quick, that the occult studies did not trouble the child for long. It is probably an acute disease which came from indigestion. He told me he felt 'peculiarly empty' after a time and threw away the books: 'I became sick of it.' " (DA1, pp. 9-15, 18-21, 23-24, 27-29, 31-34, 38-39, 42-43, 50-52, 55)

D9. (Ch. 8)

"The second dream was four days later and dreamed on the basis of his knowledge of the first dream. Here is the dream: *My wife asks me to come with her to pay a call on a poor young woman, a tailoress. She lives and*

*works in an unhealthy hole, she is suffering from T.B. I go there and say to
the girl that she should work in the open. I tell her that she could work in
my garden–but she says she has no machine. I tell her that she can have my
wife's machine.*

"... In his associations he says 'in spite of the fact that there is nothing
erotic in the dream I felt that it had that atmosphere. When my wife asked
me to pay the visit I felt that something might happen.... My wife played a
completely passive role but I apparently acted as though I were quite alone.
She (the tailoress) was dressed in dark colours and I remembered that
someone had told me that people who had T.B. were often erotic. When
people have unused libido the erotic comes up. The sewing-machine belongs to
my wife and I had the feeling that she should say the first word.'

"He associates his own imprisoned life with the girl's life. He cannot allow
his feelings to work in the open,–the only thing to do is to have the girl work
in his own garden with his wife's sewing machine. The feelings of a
respectable man cannot work in the open, hence 'in his own garden' means
pressing his feelings back into his marriage. One of his motives for respect-
ability is the fear that his health might be affected by venereal disease.... It
is very difficult for a rational man to admit what his Eros really is....

"... He is lonely with his problem.... When the dream says 'my wife
asked me to go to see the girl' it mitigates the man's trouble. If the man can
feel that his wife is not against him, it begins to make him feel less
lonely....

"... The girl represents his feelings which go abroad, the wife the feeling at
home, the respectable feeling. The interpretation is 'my feelings, which are with
my wife, have an interest in trying to deal with those other feelings.' Actually
his wife has no interest in those feelings towards other women, but the dream
says it will make his feeling towards his wife more individual, more real if he
deals with these. He has perhaps been thinking of his wife in a rigid and
inflexible way because he has done a similar injustice to his feelings. If he can
learn to deal with his feelings that go abroad, which are creative feelings, his
relation towards his wife becomes living, because doubtful....

"When he pays attention to his feelings, he finds them associated with a
girl who is infected with a serious illness. Feelings and thoughts can grow sick
and die....

"The girl in the dream is a tailoress, meaning a maker of clothes; the maker
of new attitudes....

"There are two machines, two methods. One the girl's, the other the
wife's.... The girl says 'I have my own way.' He offers the method of his
wife.... Sewing is fastening things together.... That which should be joined
together in the man, psychologically, is the conscious and the unconscious.

"... The sewing-machine method would mean a mechanical way, purely of
cause and effect, a soulless way....

"... In his associations the dreamer says–'could it be that the girl, who is
infected with T.B., represents my sick feelings, that they must live in a dark
hole? I had the feeling that the sewing-machine really belonged to my wife
and that she should say the first word'....

"He understands the method as purely mechanical and that is the way he
looks at sex....

"... The patient's feelings do not permit him to come out into the open.

As the sewing-machine belongs to his wife, the sex mechanism belongs to his wife. He got a tremendous kick out of this dream, although he is confronted with the fact that it would be awkward for him to be in love with this girl." (DA1, pp. 66-72)

D10. (Ch. 8)

"The next dream of the next night. The patient says: *'I possess a sort of cage on a wagon, a cage which might be for lions or tigers. The cage consists of different compartments. In one of them I have four small chickens. I must watch them carefully because they are always trying to escape, but in spite of my frantic efforts they do escape near the hind wheel. I catch them in my hand and put them in another compartment of the cage, the one I believe to be the safest. It has a window but it is secured by a fly screen. The lower end of the screen is not properly fastened so I make up my mind to get some stones and put them on the lower edge of the screen to keep the animals from escaping. Then I put the chickens in a basin with smooth, high sides, assuming that they will find it difficult to get out. They are down at the bottom of the basin and I see that one does not move and I think that it is because I have pressed it too hard. I think that if the chicken is dead it cannot be eaten. While I watch it it begins to move and I smell an aroma of roast chicken.'*

"His associations are very few. *Cage:* 'wild animals of a circus are kept in such cages. We human beings are the keepers of our thoughts and we ought to be careful that our thoughts do not run away, because if they do it would be very difficult to catch them again.' He asks himself, are the birds thoughts or feelings, psychological factors which try to liberate themselves and which he tries to hold back even at the risk of pressing them too hard so that they die and are no longer eatable? But the fact that they are animals seems to point to something instinctive.

"*Hind wheel:* In an automobile this is a very important part because it is the motive part and indispensable to the car . . . .

". . . These little animals . . . represent the dissociation of . . . individuality . . . . There is something in him that fights against concentration. He is obviously sick of constraint, he has so much in his present life. This is the reason for his dissociation, he thinks he has had enough of concentration, and he would hate to hold himself together still more. His unconscious is showing him in the actual process of holding these animals together, so the unconscious obviously wishes him to hold his individuality together. His resistance is in the way of a false analogy. We might conclude that this holding together is like his life, but there is nothing in the dream to show it. He needs to concentrate on the center of individuality, . . . the Self, and these four chickens obviously belong to that center; and the patient's interference and his greatest care are needed or else the center is always disintegrating and separating . . . . It has to do with four chickens to be assembled in a basin, and also the idea of roast chickens. It is a funny way of representing this center.

"In the Yi-King there is a sign, No. 50 which is called 'The Pot'. According to Prof. Wilhelm a cooking pot with three legs is the sign of yogi technique for the producing of the new man. There is something very good in the pot, it is the meal for the king, the fat of pheasants is in it. There you have the chicken. This part of the dream suggests that the non-ego center does not really exist by itself, it has to be produced by the patient himself and with great care.

"... The Yi-King ... suggests that you must collect rare things from all over the world, cook them together in the pot, and something may appear, perhaps the gold. That is the idea in the dream. There are four animals which try to escape, and they must be hunted and put into the pot. It seems to the patient that one of them is all ready to eat. The meal is ready for the perfect man. Instincts are the food to be held and transformed over the fire . . . . After such a process one is no longer torn by the pairs of opposites, but is at one with himself . . . .

"The patient had almost no associations with 'chicken' except for eating. Chickens are animals for which we can have no great respect. They are usually panicky, blind, dumb creatures which run into the road just as an automobile comes along. They are an excellent simile for fragmentary tendencies repressed or never come across by us, living autonomous lives quite apart from our knowledge. These bits of fragmentary soul, like the chickens, are working up terrible nonsense, all the foolish things wise people do . . . .

"... Why is he pressing the chicken so violently that it seems dead? This chicken is obviously one of his functions which tried to escape, so we may assume that it is his inferior function, the one most out of control. He is an intellectual type and his inferior function is feeling. He has squeezed his feeling too much; he has been squeezing it to please his wife, but the apparent gain is not worth it . . . . He caught his feeling, squeezed it, nearly killed it and then he looked at it . . . . When the gods want to bring something about they brood over it, make Tapas, contemplate it. So in this case when the patient begins to look at the chicken which he thinks is dead, it comes to life again . . . ." (DA1, pp. 79–82)

D11. (Chs. 9, 15, 16)

"The patient [said]: '. . . I have terrible dreams. Only recently I dreamt *I was coming home at night. Everything is as quiet as death. The door into the living-room is half open, and I see my mother hanging from the chandelier, swinging to and fro in the cold wind that blows in through the open windows.* Another time I dreamt that *a terrible noise broke out in the house at night. I get up and discover that a frightened horse is tearing through the rooms. At last it finds the door into the hall, and jumps through the hall window from the fourth floor into the street below. I was terrified when I saw it lying there, all mangled.'*

"The gruesome character of the dreams is alone sufficient to make one pause. All the same, other people have anxiety dreams now and then. We must therefore look more closely into the meaning of the two main symbols, 'mother' and 'horse.' They must be equivalents, for they both do the same thing: they commit suicide. 'Mother' is an archetype and refers to the place of origin, to nature, to that which passively creates, hence to substance and matter, to materiality, the womb, the vegetative functions. It also means the unconscious, our natural and instinctive life, the physiological realm, the body in which we dwell or are contained; for the 'mother' is also the matrix, the hollow form, the vessel that carries and nourishes, and it thus stands psychologically for the foundations of consciousness. Being inside or contained in something also suggests darkness, something nocturnal and fearful, hemming one in. These allusions give the idea of the mother in many of its mythological and etymological variants; they also represent an important part of the Yin idea in Chinese philosophy . . . .

"The word 'mother,' which sounds so familiar, apparently refers to the best-known, the individual mother—to 'my mother.' But the mother-symbol points to a darker background which eludes conceptual formulation and can only be vaguely apprehended as the hidden, nature-bound life of the body. Yet even this is too narrow and excludes too many vital subsidiary meanings . . . .

"If we apply our findings to the dream, its interpretation will be: The unconscious life is destroying itself . . . .

" 'Horse' is an archetype that is widely current in mythology and folklore. As an animal it represents the non-human psyche, the subhuman, animal side, the unconscious. That is why horses in folklore sometimes see visions, hear voices, and speak. As a beast of burden it is closely related to the mother-archetype (witness the Valkyries that bear the dead hero to Valhalla, the Trojan horse, etc.). As an animal lower than man it represents the lower part of the body and the animal impulses that rise from there. The horse is dynamic and vehicular power: it carries one away like a surge of instinct. It is subject to panics like all instinctive creatures who lack higher consciousness. Also it has to do with sorcery and magical spells—especially the black night-horses which herald death.

"It is evident, then, that 'horse' is an equivalent of 'mother' with a slight shift of meaning. The mother stands for life at its origin, the horse for the merely animal life of the body. If we apply this meaning to the text of our dream, its interpretation will be: The animal life is destroying itself." (CW16, pars. 344–348)

D12. (Ch. 9)

"[The scene was] a mountainous region on the Swiss-Austrian border. It was toward evening, and I saw an elderly man in the uniform of an Imperial Austrian customs official. He walked past, somewhat stooped, without paying any attention to me. His expression was peevish, rather melancholic and vexed. There were other persons present, and someone informed me that the old man was not really there, but was the ghost of a customs official who had died years ago. 'He is one of those who still couldn't die properly.'

". . . In connection with 'customs' I at once thought of the word 'censorship.' In connection with 'border' I thought of the border between consciousness and the unconscious on the one hand, and between Freud's views and mine on the other. The extremely rigorous customs examination at the border seemed to me an allusion to analysis. At a border suitcases are opened and examined for contraband. In the course of this examination, unconscious assumptions are discovered. As for the old customs official, his work had obviously brought him so little that was pleasurable and satisfactory that he took a sour view of the world. I could not refuse to see the analogy with Freud.

"At that time Freud had lost much of his authority for me. But he still meant to me a superior personality, upon whom I projected the father, and at the time of the dream this projection was still far from eliminated . . . . I still thought highly of Freud, but at the same time I was critical of him. This divided attitude is a sign that I was still unconscious of the situation and had not come to any resolution of it . . . . The dream urged upon me the necessity of clarifying this situation.

"Under the impress of Freud's personality I had, as far as possible, cast aside my own judgments and repressed my criticisms. That was the prerequisite for collaborating with him. I had told myself, 'Freud is far wiser and more experienced than you. For the present you must simply listen to what he says and learn from him.' And then, to my own surprise, I found myself dreaming of him as a peevish official of the Imperial Austrian monarchy, as a defunct and still walking ghost of a customs inspector. Could that be the death-wish which Freud had insinuated I felt toward him? I could find no part of myself that normally might have had such a wish, for I wanted at all costs to be able to work with Freud, and, in a frankly egotistic manner, to partake of his wealth of experience. His friendship meant a great deal to me. I had no reason for wishing him dead. But it was possible that the dream could be regarded as a corrective, as a compensation or antidote for my conscious high opinion and admiration. Therefore the dream recommended a rather more critical attitude toward Freud. I was distinctly shocked by it, although the final sentence of the dream seemed to me an allusion to Freud's potential immortality.

"The dream had not reached its end with the episode of the customs official; after a hiatus came a second and far more remarkable part. *I was in an Italian city, and it was around noon, between twelve and one o'clock. A fierce sun was beating down upon the narrow streets. The city was built on hills and reminded me of a particular part of Basel, the Kohlenberg. The little streets which lead down into the valley, the Birsigtal, that runs through the city, are partly flights of steps.* In the dream, *one such stairway decended to Barfüsserplatz. The city was Basel, and yet it was also an Italian city, something like Bergamo. It was summertime; the blazing sun stood at the zenith, and everything was bathed in an intense light. A crowd came streaming toward me, and I knew that the shops were closing and people were on their way home to dinner. In the midst of this stream of people walked a knight in full armor. He mounted the steps toward me. He wore a helmet of the kind that is called a basinet, with eye slits, and chain armor. Over this was a white tunic into which was woven, front and back, a large red cross.*

"One can easily imagine how I felt; suddenly to see in a modern city, during the noonday rush hour, a crusader coming toward me. What struck me as particularly odd was that none of the many persons walking about seemed to notice him. It was as though he were completely invisible to everyone but me. I asked myself what this apparition meant, and then it was as if someone answered me—but there was no one there to speak: 'Yes, this is a regular apparition. The knight always passes by here between twelve and one o'clock, and has been doing so for a very long time [for centuries, I gathered] and everyone knows about it.'

"The knight and the customs official were contrasting figures. The customs official was shadowy, someone who 'still couldn't die properly'—a fading apparition. The knight, on the other hand, was full of life and completely real. The second part of the dream was numinous in the extreme, whereas the scene on the border had been prosaic and in itself not impressive; I had been struck by my reflections upon it.

"In the period following these dreams I did a great deal of thinking about the mysterious figure of the knight. But it was only much later, after I had been meditating on the dream for a long time, that I was able to get some idea of its meaning. Even in the dream, I knew that the knight belonged to the twelfth century. That was the period when alchemy was beginning and also the quest for the Holy Grail. The stories of the Grail had been of the greatest importance to me ever since I read them, at the age of fifteen, for the first time. I had an inkling that a great secret still lay hidden behind those stories. Therefore it seemed quite natural to me that the dream should conjure up the world of the Knights of the Grail and their quest—for that was, in the deepest sense, my own world, which had scarcely anything to do with Freud's. My whole being was seeking for something still unknown which might confer meaning upon the banality of life." (MDR, pp. 163–165)

D13. (Ch. 9)

"Spiders, like all animals that are not warm-blooded or have no cerebro-spinal nervous system, function in dreams as symbols of a profoundly alien psychic world. So far as I can see, they express contents which, though active, are unable to reach consciousness; they have not yet entered the sphere of the cerebrospinal nervous system but are as though lodged in the deeper-lying sympathetic and parasympathetic systems . . . .

"In this connection I rememeber the dream of a patient who had the greatest difficulty in conceiving the idea of the supraordinate totality of the psyche and felt the utmost resistance to it. He . . . was unable to distinguish between the ego and the self, and, because of his hereditary taint, was threatened with a psychological inflation. In this situation he dreamt that *he was rummaging about in the attic of his house, looking for something. In one of the attic windows he discovered a beautiful cobweb, with a large garden-spider sitting in the centre. It was of a blue colour, and its body sparkled like a diamond.*

". . . The dream, . . . like the Delphic oracle, turns out to be ambivalent. It says in effect: 'What is troubling you in the head (attic) is, though you may not know it, a rare jewel. It is like an animal that is strange to you, forming symbolically the centre of many concentric circles, reminiscent of the centre of a large or small world, like the eye of God in medieval pictures of the universe.' . . . . Anyone who gets into the spider's net is wrapped around like a cocoon and robbed of his own life. He is isolated from his fellows, so that they can no longer reach him, nor he them. He lives in the loneliness of the world creator, who is everything and has nothing outside himself. If, on top of all this, you have had an insane father, there is the danger that you will begin to 'spin' yourself, and for this reason the spider has a sinister aspect that should not be overlooked.

"The round metallic spider of our dreamer probably has a similar meaning. It has obviously devoured a number of human beings already, or their souls, and might well be a danger to earth dwellers. That is why the prayer, which recognizes the spider as a 'divine' being, requests it to lead the souls 'downwards' and 'keep them safe below,' because they are not yet departed spirits but living earthly creatures. As such they are meant to fulfil their earthly existence with conviction and not allow themselves any spiritual inflation, otherwise they will end up in the belly of the spider. In other words, they should not set the ego in the highest place and make it the ultimate authority, but should ever be mindful of the fact that it is not sole master in its own house and is surrounded on all sides by the factor we call the unconscious . . . ." (CW10, pars. 671–673)

D14. (Chs. 9, 11, 13, 16)

"Here is the second dream: *'I am in a great hurry because I want to go on a journey. I keep on looking for things to pack, but can find nothing. Time flies, and the train will soon be leaving. Having finally succeeded in getting all my things together, I hurry along the street, only to discover that I have forgotten a brief-case containing important papers. I dash back all out of breath, find it at last, then race to the station, but I make hardly any headway. With a final effort I rush on to the platform only to see the train just steaming out of the station yard. It is very long, and it runs in a curious S-shaped curve, and it occurs to me that if the engine-driver does not look out, and puts on steam when he comes into the straight, the rear coaches will still be on the curve and will be thrown off the rails by the gathering speed. And this is just what happens: the engine-driver puts on steam, I try to cry out, the rear coaches give a frightful lurch and are thrown off the rails. There is a terrible catastrophe.* I wake up in terror.'

". . . No effort is needed to understand the message of the dream. It describes the patient's frantic haste to advance himself still further. But since the engine-driver in front steams relentlessly ahead, the neurosis happens at the back: the coaches rock and the train is derailed.

"It is obvious that, at the present phase of his life, the patient has reached the highest point of his career; the strain of the long ascent from his lowly origin has exhausted his strength. He should have rested content with his achievements, but instead of that his ambition drives him on and on, and up and up into an atmosphere that is too thin for him and to which he is not accustomed. Therefor his neurosis comes upon him as a warning.

". . . The fate depicted in the dream ran its course. He tried to exploit the professional openings that tempted his ambition, and ran so violently off the rails that the catastrophe was realized in actual life.

"Thus, what could only be inferred from the conscious anamnesis—namely that the mountain sickness was a symbolical representation of the patient's inability to climb any further—was confirmed by the dreams as a fact." (CW16, pars. 299–303)

Jung recounted the same dream in different words in CW18, pars. 165–6.

D15. (Chs. 13, 15)

"He dreamt that *he was traveling by railroad. The train had a two-hour stop in a certain city. Since he did not know the city and wanted to see something of it, he set out toward the city center. There he found a medieval building, probably the town hall, and went into it. He wandered down along corridors and came upon handsome rooms, their walls lined with old paintings and fine tapestries. Precious old objects stood about. Suddenly he saw that it had grown darker, and the sun had set. He thought, I must get back to the railroad station. At this moment he discovered that he was lost, and no longer knew where he exit was. He started in alarm, and simultaneously realized that he had not met a single person in this building. He began to feel uneasy, and quickened his pace, hoping to run into someone. But he met no one. Then he came to a large door, and thought with relief: That is the exit. He opened the door and discovered that he had stumbled upon a gigantic room. It was so huge and dark that he could not even see the opposite wall. Profoundly alarmed, the dreamer ran across the great, empty room, hoping to find the exit on the other side. Then he saw—precisely in the middle of the room—something white on the floor. As he approached he discovered that it was an idiot child of about two years old. It was sitting on a chamber pot and had smeared itself with feces.* At that moment he awoke with a cry, in a state of panic . . . .

"What the dream says is approximately this: the trip on which he sets out is the trip to Zürich. He remains there, however, for only a short time. The child in the center of the room is himself as a two-year-old child. In small children, such uncouth behavior is somewhat unusual, but still possible. They may be intrigued by their feces, which are colored and have an odd smell. Raised in a city environment, and possibly along strict lines, a child might easily be guilty of such a failing.

"But the dreamer, the doctor, was no child; he was a grown man. And therefore the dream image in the center of the room is a sinister symbol. When he told me the dream, I realized that his normality was a compensation . . . . The latent psychosis was within a hair's breadth of breaking out and becoming manifest." (MDR, pp. 135–136)

D16. (Chs. 13, 16)

". . . *Her father* (who in reality was of small stature) *was standing with her on a hill that was covered with wheat-fields. She was quite tiny beside him, and he seemed to her like a giant. He lifted her up from the ground and held her in his arms like a little child. The wind swept over the wheat-fields, and as the wheat swayed in the wind, he rocked her in his arms.*

"From this dream and others like it . . . I got the impression that her unconscious was holding unshakably to the idea of my being the father-lover, so that the fatal tie we were trying to undo appeared to be doubly strengthened. Moreover one could hardly avoid seeing that the unconscious placed a special emphasis on the supernatural, almost 'divine' nature of the father-lover, thus accentuating still further the over-valuation occasioned by the transference. I therefore asked myself whether the patient had still not understood the wholly fantastic character of her transference, or whether perhaps the unconscious could never be reached by understanding at all, but must blindly and idiotically pursue some nonsensical chimera . . . .

". . . As I turned the dreams over and over in my mind, there dawned on me another possibility. I said to myself: it cannot be denied that the dreams continue to speak in the same old metaphors with which our conversations have made both doctor and patient sickeningly familiar. But the patient has an undoubted understanding of her transference fantasy. She knows that I appear to her as a semi-divine father-lover, and she can, at least intellectually, distinguish this from my factual reality. Therefore the dreams are obviously reiterating the conscious standpoint minus the conscious criticism, which they completely ignore. They reiterate the conscious contents, not *in toto,* but insist on the fantastic standpoint as opposed to 'sound common sense.'

"I naturally asked myself what was the source of this obstinacy and what was its purpose? ... A careful examination and analysis of the dreams, especially of the one just quoted, revealed a very marked tendency—in contrast to conscious criticism,- ... to endow the person of the doctor with superhuman attributes. He had to be gigantic, primordial, huger than the father, like the wind that sweeps over the earth—was he then to be made into a god? Or, I said to myself, was it rather the case that the unconscious was trying to *create* a god out of the person of the doctor, as it were to free a vision of God from the veils of the personal, so that the transference to the person of the doctor was no more than a misunderstanding on the part of the conscious mind, a stupid trick played by 'sound common sense.'? ... Could the longing for a god be a *passion* welling up from our darkest, instinctual nature, a passion unswayed by any outside influences, deeper and stronger perhaps than the love for a human person? Or was it perhaps the highest and truest meaning of that inappropriate love we call transference, a little bit of real *Gottesminne*, that has been lost to consciousness ever since the fifteenth century? ...

"This new hypothesis was not entirely plausible to my very critical patient. The earlier view that I was the father-lover, and as such presented an ideal solution of the conflict, was incomparably more attractive to her way of feeling. Nevertheless her intellect was sufficiently clear to appreciate the theoretical possibility of the new hypothesis. Meanwhile the dreams continued to disintegrate the person of the doctor and swell him to ever vaster proportions. Concurrently with this there now occurred something which at first I alone perceived, and with the utmost astonishment, namely a kind of subterranean undermining of the transference. Her relations with a certain friend deepened perceptibly, notwithstanding the fact that consciously she still clung to the transference. So that when the time came for leaving me, it was no catastrophe, but a prefectly reasonable parting.... I saw how the transpersonal control-point developed—I cannot call it anything else—a *guiding function* and step by step gathered to itself all the former personal overvaluations; how, with this afflux of energy, it gained influence over the resisting conscious mind without the patient's consciously noticing what was happening. From this I realized that the dreams were not just fantasies, but self-representations of unconscious developments which allowed the psyche of the patient gradually to grow out of the pointless personal tie." (CW7, pars. 212–214, 217)

D17. (Ch. 14)

"... A little girl about nine years old ... had run a subnormal temperature for three months and was unable to attend school. [She suffered] loss of appetite and increasing listlessness. The doctor could find no reason for this condition. The father and mother were both sure they had the child's full confidence, and that she was not worried or unhappy in any way. The mother finally admitted to the psychologist that she and her husband did not get on together, but said that they never discussed their difficulties in front of the child, who was completely unconscious of them. The mother wanted a divorce, but could not make up her mind to face the unheaval it would involve ... the parents made no effort to solve any of the difficulties causing their unhappiness. Both [parents] had an unduly possessive attachment to the child, . . . She slept in her father's room in a little bed next to his and got into his bed in the mornings. She gave the following dream:

" 'I went with Daddy to see Granny. Granny was in a big boat. She wanted me to kiss her and wanted to put her arms round me, but I was afraid of her. Daddy said, 'Well then, I'll kiss Granny!' I didn't want him to do it, as I was afraid something might happen to him. Then the boat moved off and I couldn't find anybody and I felt frightened.'

"Several times she had dreams about Granny. Once Granny was all mouth, wide open. Another time she dreamt of a 'big snake, which came out from under my bed and played with me.' She often spoke of the snake dream, and had one or two others like it. The dream about her Granny she told with reluctance, but then confessed that every time her father went away she was frightened he would never come back. She had sized up her parents' situation, and told the psychologist that she knew her mother did not like her father, but she did not want to talk about it, 'because it would make them feel bad.' When her father was away on business trips she was always afraid he would leave them. She had also noticed that her mother was always happier then . . . . Eventually [the parents decided to separate] and explained the situation to the child . . . . her health improved as soon as the real situation came out into the open . . . ." (CW17, pars. 216–217)

D18. (Ch. 14)

". . . Here are the salient motifs from the dreams:

"1. The 'bad animal': a snakelike monster with many horns, that kills and devours all other animals. But God comes from the four corners, being really four gods, and gives rebirth to all the animals.

"2. Ascent into heaven where pagan dances are being celebrated, and descent to hell where angels are doing good deeds.

"3. A horde of small animals frightens the dreamer. The animals grow to enormous size, and one of them devours her.

"4. A small mouse is penetrated by worms, snakes, fishes, and human beings. Thus the mouse becomes human. This is the origin of mankind in four stages.

"5. A drop of water is looked at through a microscope: it is full of branches. This is the origin of the world.

"6. A bad boy with a clod of earth. He throws bits of it at the passers-by, and they all become bad too.

"7. A drunken woman falls into the water and comes out sober and renewed.

"8. In America many people are rolling in an ant heap, attacked by the ants. The dreamer, in a panic, falls into a river.

"9. The dreamer is in a desert on the moon. She sinks so deep into the ground that she reaches hell.

"10. She touches a luminous ball seen in a vision. Vapours come out of it. Then a man comes and kills her.

"11. She is dangerously ill. Suddenly birds come out of her skin and cover her completely.

"12. Swarms of gnats hide the sun, moon, and stars, all except one star which then falls on the dreamer.

"In the unabridged German original, each dream begins with the words of the fairytale: 'Once upon a time . . . .' With these words the little dreamer suggests that she feels as if each dream were a sort of fairytale, which she wants to tell her father as a Christmas present. Her father was unable to elucidate the dreams through their context, for there seemed to be no personal associations . . . .

". . . [The dreams'] leading thoughts are in a way like philosophical problems. The first dream, for instance, speaks of an evil monster killing all other animals, but God gives rebirth to them through a kind of *apocatastasis*, or restitution. In the Western world this idea is known through Christian tradition. It can be found in the Acts of the Apostles 3:21: '(Christ,) whom the heaven must receive until the times of restitution of all things . . . .' The early Greek Fathers of the Church (Origen, for instance) particularly insisted on the idea that, at the end of time, everything will be restored by the Redeemer to its original and perfect state. According to Matthew 17:11, there was already an old Jewish tradition that Elias 'truly shall first come, and restore all things.' I Corinthians 15:22 refers to the same idea in the following words: 'For as in Adam all die, even so in Christ shall all be made alive' . . . .

"Nine of the twelve dreams are concerned with the theme of destruction and restoration. We find the same connection in I Corinthians 15:22, where Adam and Christ, i.e., death and resurrection, are linked together. None of these dreams, however, shows anything more than superficial traces of a specifically Christian education or influence. On the contrary, they show more analogy with primitive tales. This is corroborated by the other motif—the cosmogonic myth of the creation of the world and of man, which appears in dreams 4 and 5 . . . .

"The idea of Christ the Redeemer belongs to the world-wide and pre-Christian motif of the hero and rescuer who, although devoured by the monster, appears again in a miraculous way, having overcome the dragon or whale or whatever it was that swallowed him. How, when, and where such a motif originated nobody knows . . . . Our only certainty is that every generation, so far as we can see, has found it as an old tradition . . . . The milieu in which our little dreamer lived was acquainted only with the Christian tradition, and very superficially at that. Christian traces may be represented in her dreams by such ideas as God, angels, heaven, hell, and evil, but the way in which they are treated points to a tradition that is entirely non-Christian.

"Let us take the first dream, of the God who really consists of four gods, coming from the 'four corners'. . . . The quaternity itself is a strange idea, but one that plays a great role in Eastern religions and philosophies . . . .

". . . The horned serpent appears in Latin alchemy as the *quadricornutus serpens* (four-horned serpent), a symbol of Mercurius and an antagonist of the Christian Trinity . . . .

"In dream 2 a motif appears that is definitely non-Christian and a reversal of values: pagan dances by men in heaven and good deeds by angels in hell. This suggests, if anything, a relativization of moral values. . . .

". . . Such dreams . . . are in a way analogous to the doctrines taught to young people in primitive tribes when they are initiated into manhood. At such times they learn about what God or the gods or the 'founding' animals have done, how the world and man were created, what the end of the world will be, and the meaning of death. And when do we, in our Christian civilization, hand out similar instructions? At the beginning of adolescence.

But many people begin to think of these things again in old age, at the approach of death.

"Our dreamer, as it happened, was in both these situations, for she was approaching puberty and at the same time the end of her life. Little or nothing in the symbolism of the dreams points to the beginning of a normal adult life, but there are many allusions to destruction and restoration.... Their atmosphere recalls the old Roman saying, *vita somnium breve* (life is a short dream), rather than the joy and exuberance of life's springtime ....

"... The dreams ... were a preparation for death, expressed through short stories, like the instruction at primitive initiations, or the *koans* of Zen Buddhism. It is an instruction that does not resemble the orthodox Christian doctrine but is more like primitive thought ....

"... It was as if future events were casting their shadow ahead by arousing thought-forms that, though normally dormant, are destined to describe or accompany the approach of a fatal issue." (CW18, pars. 525-527, 529-534, 536-539)

Jung recounted two of the dreams in detail and commented on them. In one, the child " *'saw an animal that had lots of horns. It spiked up other little animals with them. It wriggled like a snake and that was how it lived. Then a blue fog came out of all the four corners, and it stopped eating. Then God came, but there were really four Gods in the four corners. Then the animal died, and all the animals it had eaten came out alive again.'*

"This dream describes an unconscious individuation process: all the animals are eaten by the one animal. Then comes the enantiodromia: the dragon changes into pneuma, which stands for a divine quaternity. Thereupon follows the apocatastasis, a resurrection of the dead." (CW9-1, pars. 623-624)

In the second detailed dream, the dreamer *"is in empty cosmic space, walking on something like a path, and far in the distance ahead of her, she sees a round light, which as she approaches becomes bigger and finally is an enormous globe that comes nearer and nearer, and of course she grows afraid. Then when the globe is close to her, the path bifurcates and she doesn't know whether she should go to the right or to the left*, and in that moment she wakes up; it is a nightmare. This is a very typical dream of that kind, I call them cosmic dreams of childhood; they are the archetypal experiences of children with strong memories of what the Tibetans would call the Bardo life, a pre-natal condition of the mind, the conditions before the birth into this spatial world. That shows itself first under its absolute aspect, an empty dead world to which life is absolutely strange, particularly human life, and it explains also why man has a mind or a consciousness at all. He must have something different, not of the same kind, or he would not be conscious; he must have something which is at variance with the conditions of our space and it is a fact that the psyche is at variance with the conditions of our space." (Z8, p. 153)

D19. (Ch. 16)

"I come to a strange, solemn house—the 'House of the Gathering.' Many candles are burning in the background, arranged in a peculiar pattern with four points running upward. Outside, at the door of the house, an old man is posted. People are going in. They say nothing and stand motionless in order

to collect themselves inwardly. The man at the door says of the visitors to the house, 'When they come out again they are cleansed.' I go into the house myself and find I can concentrate perfectly. Then a voice says: 'What you are doing is dangerous. Religion is not a tax to be paid so that you can rid yourself of the woman's image, for this image cannot be got rid of. Woe unto them who use religion as a substitute for another side of the soul's life; they are in error and will be accursed. Religion is no substitute; it is to be added to the other activities of the soul as the ultimate completion. Out of the fulness of life shall you bring forth your religion; only then shall you be blessed!' While the last sentence is being spoken in ringing tones I hear distant music, simple chords on an organ. Something about it reminds me of Wagner's Fire Music. As I leave the house I see a burning mountain and I feel: 'The fire that is not put out is a holy fire' (Shaw, St. Joan).

"The dreamer notes that this dream was a 'powerful experience.' Indeed it has a numinous quality and we shall therefore not be far wrong if we assume that it represents a new climax of insight and understanding. The 'voice' has as a rule an absolutely authoritative character . . . .

"The house probably corresponds to the square, which is a 'gathering place' . . . . The four shining points in the background again indicate the quaternity. The remark about cleansing refers to the transformative function of the taboo area. The production of wholeness, which is prevented by the 'tax evasion,' naturally requires the 'image of the woman,' since as anima she represents the fourth, 'inferior' function, feminine because contaminated with the unconscious. In what sense the 'tax' is to be paid depends on the nature of the inferior function and its auxiliary, and also on the attitude type. The payment can be either concrete or symbolic, but the conscious mind is not qualified to decide which form is valid.

"[In] the dream's view that religion may not be a substitute for 'another side of the soul's life' . . . . religion is equated with wholeness; it even appears as the expression of a self integrated in the 'fulness of life.'

"The faint echo of the Fire Music—the Loki motif—is not out of key, for . . . there is every reason here for some anxiety, since man as a whole being casts a shadow. The fourth was not separated from the three and banished to the kingdom of everlasting fire for nothing. But does not an uncanonical saying of our Lord's declare: 'Who so is near unto me is near unto the fire'? . . .

"The theme of the Fire Mountain . . . is to be met with in the Book of Enoch. Enoch sees the seven stars chained 'like great mountains and burning with fire' at the angel's place of punishment. In contrast to this menacing theme there is a connection with the miracles of Jehovah revealed on Mount Sinai, while according to other sources the number seven is by no means sinister, since it is on the seventh mountain of the western land that the tree with the life-giving fruit is to be found, i.e., the *arbor sapientiae*." (CW12, pars. 293–298)

REFERENCES
AND BIBLIOGRAPHY

REFERENCES

AP refers to *Analytical Psychology*, notes on the seminar conducted by Dr. C. G. Jung, Zurich, March 23–July 6, 1925. Compiled by F. de Angulo. (Typescript)

CD refers to Jung's lectures on children's dreams, given at the Eidgenössische Technische Hochschule, Zürich.*

    36. Seminar on children's dreams and older works on dream interpretation, Winter semester 1936-7. Edited by Hans H. Baumann. (Mimeo)

    38. Psychological Interpretation of Children's Dreams. Notes on Lectures, Autumn-Winter 1938-9. Edited by L. Frey and R. Schärf. Translated by M. Foote with C. Brunner. (Mimeo)

    40. Psychologische interpretation von Kinderträumen. Winter semester 1939-40. Edited by L. Frey and A. Jaffé. (Mimeo)

CW refers to Jung's *Collected Works*, Vols. 1–18. Editors: Sir Herbert Read, Michael Fordham, Gerhard Adler, and William McGuire. Bollingen Series XX. Published initially by Pantheon and, then, Princeton University Press. Except where indicated, the translator was R. F. C. Hull.

Vol. 1. *Psychiatric studies* (2nd ed.), 1957.

Vol. 2. *Experimental researches* (trans. by L. Stein with D. Riviere), 1973.

Vol. 3. *The Psychogenesis of mental disease*, 1960.

*Copyright C. G. Jung Heirs.

Vol. 4. *Freud and psychoanalysis*, 1961.
Vol. 5. *Symbols of transformation* (2nd ed.), 1956.
Vol. 6. *Psychological types* (trans. by H. G. Baynes, revised by R. F. C. Hull), 1971.
Vol. 7. *Two essays on analytical psychology* (2nd ed. rev. & augmented), 1966.
Vol. 8. *The structure and dynamics of the psyche* (2nd ed.), 1960.
Vol. 9 (Part 1). *The archetypes and the collective unconscious* (2nd ed.), 1959.
Vol. 9 (Part 2). *AION: Researches into the phenomenology of the self* (2nd ed.), 1959.
Vol. 10. *Civilization in transition* (2nd ed.), 1964.
Vol. 11. *Psychology and religion: West and east* (2nd ed.), 1958.
Vol. 12. *Psychology and alchemy* (2nd ed.), 1953.
Vol. 13. *Alchemical studies*, 1967.
Vol. 14. *Mysterium coniunctionis* (2nd ed.), 1963.
Vol. 15. *The spirit in man, art, and literature*, 1966.
Vol. 16. *The practice of psychotherapy* (2nd ed.), 1954.
Vol. 17. *The development of personality*, 1954.
Vol. 18. *The symbolic life: Miscellaneous writings*, 1976.
DA refers to Jung's *Dream Analysis* seminars, Vols. 1 & 2 (3rd ed.), 1958. Notes of the seminars in Analytical Psychology, Zurich, 1928-1930. Compiled and edited by M. Foote, C. H. Deady, and C. F. Baumann. Published privately by The Committee of the Psychological Club of Zurich.*
(Dreams) refers to *Dreams from the Collected Works of C. J. Jung*, translated by R. F. C. Hull. Bollingen Series XX. Princeton, N.J.: Princeton University Press, 1974.
FJ refers to *The Freud/Jung letters*. (See McGuire, W., in following list.)
KY refers to *Psychological commentary on Kundalini Yoga, Spring* 1975, pp. 1-32, and *Spring* 1976, pp. 1-31.*
Let 1 & 2 refers to *C. G. Jung letters*, Vols. 1 & 2. (See Adler, G., in following list.)
MAM Files refers to the clinical files of Mary Ann Mattoon.
MDR refers to *Memories, Dreams, Reflections*. (See Jaffé; A. in following list.)
MHS refers to *Man and His Symbols*. (See Jung, C. G., et al., in following list.)
MP refers to Jung's lectures, *Modern Psychology*, Vols. I-II (2nd ed.), 1959. Notes on lectures given at Zurich, 1933-1935. Compiled and edited by E. Welsh & B. Hannah (Jan. 1938). Privately printed.*
par. = paragraph.
SE refers to The Standard Edition of the Complete Psychological Works of Sigmund Freud. (See Freud, S. in following list.)
SW refers to *Dreams and Symbolism*, lectures at Swanage by C. G. Jung. Unauthorized notes taken in longhand by M. W. Harding, Swanage, England, July-August 1925. (Typescript)*
VS refers to *The Visions Seminars*, Vols. 1 & 2, by C. G. Jung. Zurich: Spring Publications, 1976.*
Z refers to Jung's seminar given in Zurich, *Psychological Analysis of Nietzche's Zarathustra*. Parts 1-10, 1934-39. M. Foote, Editor. Private publication. (Mimeo)*

*Copyright C. G. Jung Heirs.

BIBLIOGRAPHY

Adler, A. *What life should mean to you.* New York: Capricorn, 1931, 1958.

Adler, G. *The living symbol.* New York: Pantheon, 1961.

Adler, G. Letter to the editor. *Psychological Perspectives*, 1977, 8(1), 117.

Adler, G. (Ed.) with Jaffé, A. *C. G. Jung letters*, Vol. 1 (1906-1950); Vol. 2 (1951-1961). Princeton: Princeton University Press, Bollingen Series XCV, 1973, 1975.

Allport, G. W. (Ed.). *Letters from Jenny.* New York: Harcourt, Brace & World, 1965.

Anderson, H., & Anderson, G. *An introduction to projective techniques.* Englewood Cliffs, N.J.: Prentice-Hall, 1951.

Antrobus, J. S., Dement, W., & Fisher, C. Patterns of dreaming and dream recall: An EEG study. *Journal of Abnormal and Social Psychology*, 1964, 69, 341-344.

Barker, C. *Healing in depth.* London: Hodder & Stoughton, 1972.

Bash, K. W. Zur experimentellen Grundlegung der Jungschen Traumanalyse. *Schweizerische Zeitschrift für Psychologie und ihre Anwendungen*, 1952, 11(4), 282-295.

Baynes, H. G. *Analytical Psychology and the English mind.* London: Methuen, 1950.

Bell, A. P., & Hall, C. S. The personality of a child molester. Chicago: Aldine-Atherton, 1971.

Bell, J. E. *Projective techniques.* New York-London-Toronto: Longmans, Green, 1948.

Bennet, E. A. *C. G. Jung.* New York: E. P. Dutton, 1962.

Bennet, E. A. *What Jung really said.* New York: Schocken, 1967.

Berry, P. An approach to the dream. *Spring*, 1974, 58-79.

Bolgar, H. Consistency of affect and symbolic expression: A comparison between dreams and Rorschach responses. *American Journal of Orthopsychiatry*, 1954, 24, 538-545.

Boss, M. *The analysis of dreams.* (Trans. by A. J. Pomeranz.) London: Rider, 1957.

Bradway, K. Jung's Psychological Types. *The Journal of Analytical Psychology*, 1964, 9(2), 129-35.

Bradway, K. & Detloff, W. Incidence of psychological types among Jungian analysts. *Journal of Analytical Psychology*, 1976, 21(2).

Breger, L., Hunter, I., & Lane, R. W. *The effect of stress on dreams.* New York: International Universities Press, 1971.

Caligor, L., & May, R. *Dreams and symbols.* New York: Basic Books, 1968.

Campbell, J. *The portable Jung.* New York: Viking, 1971.

Cartwright, R. D. Dreams, reality, and fantasy. In J. Fisher & L. Breger. *The meaning of dreams: Recent insights from the laboratory.* State of California Department of Mental Hygiene Research Symposium No. 3, 1969, 101-119.

Cattell, R. B. *Personality and motivation structure and measurement.* Yonkers: World Book, 1957.

Dallett, J. The effect of sensory and social variables on the recalled dream: complementarity, continuity, and compensation. Abstract of the Dissertation, 1973. (Mimeo)

Davie, T. M. Comments upon a Case of 'Periventricular Epilepsy'. *British Medical Journal* (London), 1935, 2, 293–297.

Dement, W., & Wolpert, E. A. The relation of eye movement, body motility, and external stimuli to dream content. *Journal of Experimental Psychology*, 1958, **55**(6), 543–553. (a)

Dement, W., & Wolpert, E. A. Relationships in the manifest content of dreams occurring on the same night. *Journal of Nervous and Mental Disease*, 1958, **126**, 568–578. (b)

Diamond, E. *The science of dreams.* London: Eyre & Spottiswoode, 1962.

Dieterich, A. *Eine Mithrasliturgie* (2nd. ed.) Leipzig: Tübner, 1910. (First published 1903.) Translated by G. R. S. Mead: A mithraic ritual. London, 1907.

Domhoff, B. A quantitative study of dream content using an objective indicator of dreaming. Unpublished doctoral dissertation, University of Miami, 1962.

Domhoff, B. Home dreams versus laboratory dreams. In M. Kramer (Ed.), *Dream psychology and the new biology of dreaming.* Springfield, Ill.: C. C. Thomas, 1969, 199–217.

Domhoff, B. & Kamiya, J. Problems in dream content study with objective indicators. I, II, and III. *Archives of General Psychiatry*, 1964, **11**(5), 519–532.

Dunne, J. W. *An experiment with time* (2nd ed.). New York: Macmillan, 1938.

Edinger, E. F. *Ego and Archetype.* New York: Putnam's, 1972.

Ellenberger, H. F. *The discovery of the unconscious.* New York: Basic Books, 1970.

Eysenck, H. J., & Eysenck, S. B. *Personality structure and measurement.* San Diego: Knapp, 1969.

Faraday, A. *Dream power.* New York: Coward, McCann & Geoghegan, 1972.

Faraday, A. *The dream game.* New York: Harper & Row, 1974.

Farber, L. & Fisher, C. An experimental approach to dream psychology through the use of hypnosis. *Psychoanalytic Quarterly*, 1943, 12:202–216.

Fiss, H., Klein, G. S., & Bokert, E. Waking fantasies following interruption of two types of sleep. *Archives of General Psychiatry*, 1966, **14**, 543–551.

Fodor, J. A., Garrett, F., & Brill, S. L., Pi Ca Pu; The perception of speech sounds by prelinquistic infants. *Perception & Psychophysics*, 1975, **18**(2), 74–78.

Fodor, N. *Freud, Jung, and occultism.* New Hyde Park, N.Y.: University Books, 1971.

Fordham, F. *An Introduction to Jung's psychology.* Baltimore, Md.: Penguin Books, 1953.

Fortier, R. A Study of the relationship of the response to color and some personality functions. Unpublished doctoral dissertation, Western Reserve University, 1952. (Cited In Suinn, 1967.)

Foulkes, D. *The psychology of sleep.* New York: Charles Scribner's Sons, 1966.

Foulkes, D., & Rechstschaffen, A. Presleep determinants of dream content: Effects of two films. *Perceptual and motor skills*, 1964, **19**, 983–1005.

French, T. & Fromm, Erika. *Dream interpretation: A new approach.* New York: Basic Books, 1964.

Freud, S. *The complete psychological works of Sigmund Freud*, Vols. 4 & 5, (Standard Edition). London: Hogarth, 1953.

Freud, S., & Jung, C. G. *The Freud/Jung letters*. Princeton: Princeton University Press, Bollingen Series XCIV, 1974.

Frey-Rohn, L. *From Freud to Jung*. New York: Putnam's, 1974. (Originally published as *Von Freud zu Jung*. Rascher: Zurich and Stuttgart, 1969.)

Fromm, Erich. *The forgotten language of dreams*. New York: Grove, 1951.

Garfield, P. *Creative dreaming*. New York: Simon & Schuster, 1974.

Goldbrunner, J. *Individuation: A study of the depth psychology of Carl Gustav Jung*. South Bend, Ind.: Notre Dame Press, 1964.

Goodenough, D. R., Shapiro, A., Holden, M., & Steinschriber, L. A comparison of "dreamers" and "nondreamers": Eye movements, electroencephalograms, and the recall of dreams. *Journal of Abnormal and Social Psychology*, 1959, **59**, 295–302.

Hall, C. S. *What people dream about*. Scientific American, 1951, **184**, 60–63.

Hall, C. S. *The meaning of dreams*. New York: Harper & Bros., 1953.

Hall, C. S., & Nordby, V. J. *A primer of Jungian psychology*. New York: New American Library (A Mentor Book), 1973.

Hall, C. S., & Van de Castle, R. L. *The content analysis of dreams*. New York: Appleton-Century-Crofts, 1966. (a)

Hall, C., & Van de Castle, R. Studies of dreams reported in the laboratory and at home. *Monograph Series*, No. 1, 1966, Institute of Dream Research, Santa Cruz. (b)

Hannah, B. *Jung: His life and work*. New York: Putnam's, 1976.

Harding, M. E. *Woman's mysteries: Ancient and modern*. London: Longmans, Green, 1935.

Harding, M. E. *The parental image: Its injury and reconstruction*. New York: Putnam's, 1965.

Hartmann, E. *The biology of dreaming*. Springfield, Ill.: C. C. Thomas, 1967.

Hawkes, J. *History of mankind: Cultural and scientific development*, Vol. 1, Part 1: *Prehistory*. New York: New American Library (Mentor Book), 1963. Published in cooperation with UNESCO.

Hillman, J. *Insearch: Psychology and religion*. New York: Charles Scribner's Sons, 1967.

Hillman, J. *Re-Visioning psychology*. New York: Harper, 1975.

Hochheimer, W. *The psychotherapy of C. G. Jung*. New York: Putnam's, 1969.

Jacobi, J. *The psychology of C. G. Jung*. (Trans. from the German by Ralph Mannheim.) New Haven: Yale University Press, 1942.

Jaffé, A. From the life and work of C. G. Jung. New York: Harper & Row, 1971. (Originally published as *Aus Leben und Werkstatt von C. G. Jung: Parapsychologie, Alchemie, Nationalsozialismus, Errinerungen aus den letzten Jahren*. Zurich: Rascher, 1971.)

Jaffé, A. (Rec. & Ed.). *Memories, dreams, reflections by C. G. Jung*. New York: Pantheon, 1963.

Janet, P. Les obsessions et al psychasthénie (2 vols.). Paris: F. Lacan, 1903.

Johnson, H., & Ericksen, C. W. Preconscious perception: A reexamination of the Poetzl phenomenon. *Journal of Abnormal and Social Psychology*, 1961, **62**, 497–503.

Jones, R. M. *The new psychology of dreaming*. New York: Grune & Stratton, 1970.

Jouvet, M. Recherches sur les structures nerveuses et les mecanismes respons-
ables des différentes phases du sommeil physiologique. *Archives Italiennes
de Biologie*, 1962, **100**, 125–206.

Jouvet, D., Valatx, J. L., & Jouvet, M. Etude polygraphique du sommeil du
chat. *C.R. Soc. Biol.*, 1961, **155**, 1660–1664.

Jung, C. G., von Franz, M.-L., Henderson, J. L., Jacobi, J., & Jaffé, A. *Man
and his symbols*. Garden City, N.Y.: Doubleday, 1964.

Jurgevich, R. M. The hour of Freudianism: A study of brainwashing the
American professionals and laymen. Philadelphia: Dovance, 1974.

Kahn, E., Dement, W., & Fisher, C. Incidence of color in immediately recalled
dreams. *Science*, 1962, **137**, 1054–1055.

Kant, O. Dreams of schizophrenic patients. *Journal of Nervous and Mental
Disease*, 1942, **95**, 335–347.

Kelsey, M. T. *Dreams: The dark speech of the spirit*. Garden City, N.Y.:
Doubleday, 1968.

Kiester, E., Jr. Dream world. *Human Behavior*, Dec. 1975, 16–23.

Kirsch, J. *The reluctant prophet*. Los Angeles: Sherbourne, 1973.

Kluger, H. Y. Archetypal dreams and everyday dreams: A statistical investigation into Jung's theory of the collective unconscious. *The Israel Annals of
Psychiatry and Related Disciplines*, 1975, **13**(1), 6–47.

McGuire, W. (Ed.), *The Freud/Jung letters*. Princeton: Princeton University
Press, Bollingen Series XCIV, 1974.

Maeder, A. The dream problem. *Nervous and Mental Disease Monograph
Series*, No. 22, 1916. (New York: Nervous and Mental Disease Publishing
Co.)

Mahoney, M. F. *The meaning in dreams and dreaming*. New York: Citadel
Press, 1966.

Marjasch, S. The "I" in dreams. *Spring*, 1966, 60–75. (a)

Marjasch, S. On the dream psychology of C. G. Jung. In G. E. Von
Grunebaum & R. Caillois (Eds.), *The dream and human societies*. Berkeley:
University of California Press, 1966. (b)

Masserman, J. H. *Principles of dynamic psychiatry*. Philadelphia: W. B.
Saunders, 1946.

Mattoon, M. A. *The Christian concept of sin as an approach to the shadow*.
Unpublished diploma thesis, C. G. Jung Institute, Zurich, Switzerland, 1965.

Mattoon, M. A. *The theory of dream interpretation according to C. G. Jung:
an exposition and analysis*. Unpublished doctoral dissertation, University of
Minnesota, 1970.

Meier, C. A. *Die Bedeutung des Traumes*. Olten: Walter, 1972.

Meier, C. A. The challenge posed to dream theories by the new biology of
dreaming: A Jungian view. In M. Kramer (Ed.), *Dream psychology and the
new biology of dreaming*. Springfield, Ill.: Charles C Thomas, 1969.

Nell, R. Interpretation of dreams on the subjective level. In E. F. Hammer
(Ed.), *Use of interpretation in treatment*. New York: Grune & Stratton,
1968.

Neumann, E. *Art and the creative unconscious*. Princeton: Princeton University Press, Bollingen Series LXI, 1959.

Neumann, E. *The origins and history of consciousness*. New York: Pantheon,
1954, 1964.

New Larousse Encyclopedia of Mythology. London: Hamlyn, 1959.

Noone, R., & Holman, D. *In search of the dream people.* New York: Morrow, 1972.

Offenkrantz, W. & Rechtschaffen, A. Clinical studies of sequential dreams. I. A Patient in Psychotherapy. *Archives of General Psychiatry,* 1963, **8**, 497-508.

Otto, R. *The idea of the holy.* New York: Oxford University Press, 1958. (Originally published, 1923.)

Penfield, W. Memory mechanisms. *A.M.A. Archives of Neurology and Psychiatry,* 1952, **67**, 178-198.

Perls, F. *Gestalt therapy verbatim.* New York: Bantam, 1969.

Pirsig, R. M. *Zen and the art of motorcycle maintenance.* New York: Morrow, 1974.

Plaut, A. Analytical psychologists and psychological types. *The Journal of Analytical Psychology,* 1972, **17**(2), 137-149.

Pulver, S. E., & Eppes, B. The Poetzl phenomenon: Some further evidence. *Journal of Nervous and Mental Disease,* 1963, **136**, 527-534.

Rapaport, A. Mathematics and cybernetics. In S. Arieti (Ed.), *American Handbook of Psychiatry,* Vol. II. New York: Basic Books, 1959.

Rechtschaffen, A., & Verdone, P. Amount of dreaming: Effect of incentive, adaptation to laboratory, and individual differences. *Perceptual and Motor Skills,* 1964, **19**, 947-958.

Reed, H. The art of remembering dreams. *Quadrant,* Summer 1976, **9**(1).

Reichenbach, H. *Experience and prediction.* Chicago: University of Chicago Press, 1938.

Ross, J. The resources of binocular perception. *Scientific American,* March 1976, **234**, 80-86.

Rossi, E. L. *Dreams and the growth of personality.* New York: Pergamon (General Psychology Series), 1972.

Sanford, J. A. *Dreams, God's forgotten language.* Philadelphia: J. B. Lippincott, 1968.

Schonbar, R. Temporal and emotional factors in the selective recall of dreams. *Journal of Consulting Psychology,* 1961, **25**, 67-73.

Sheppard, E. Systematic dream studies: Clinical judgment and objective measurement of ego strength. *Comprehensive Psychiatry,* 1963, **4**, 263-270.

Sheppard, E. & Saul, J. An approach to a systematic study of ego function. *Psychoanalytic Quarterly,* 1958, **27**, 237-245.

Shurley, J. T. Paper presented at the meeting of the American Psychiatric Association, Atlantic City, N.J., May 1960.

Singer, J. *Boundaries of the Soul.* New York: Doubleday, 1972.

Stern, P. J. *C. G. Jung: The haunted prophet.* New York: Braziller, 1976.

Stewart, K. Mental Hygiene and world peace. *Mental Hygiene,* July 1954, **38-3**, 387-403.

Stoyva, J. M. Posthypnotically suggested dreams and the sleep cycle. *Archives of General Psychiatry,* 1965, **12**, 287-294.

Suinn, R. M. Jungian personality typology and color dreaming. *Psychiatric Quarterly,* 1966, **40**(4), 659-666.

Suinn, R. M. Anxiety and Color Dreaming. *Mental Hygiene,* 1967, **51**, 27-29.

Tatibana, T. Psychologie Folia, 1938, **6**, 127. (Cited in Suinn, 1967.)

Thass-Thienemann, T. *The interpretation of language,* Vols. I & II. New York: Jason Aronson, 1968, 1973.

Trotter, R. J. From language to linguistics and beyond. *Science News*, 1975, **108**(21), 321–336.

Ullman, M. & Krippner, S. with Vaughan, A. *Dream Telepathy*. New York: Macmillan, 1973.

Van de Castle, R. L. His, hers and the children's. *Psychology Today*, 1970, **4**(1), 37–39.

Van der Post, L. *Jung & the story of our time*. New York: Pantheon, 1975.

Von Franz, M.-L. *C. G. Jung: His myth in our time*. New York: Putnam's, 1975.

Waxenberg, S. E., Dickes, R., & Gottesfeld, H. The Poetzl phenomenon re-examined experimentally. *Journal of Nervous and Mental Disease*, 1962, **135**, 387–398.

Whitman, R. M., Pierce, C. M., Maas, J. W., & Baldridge, B. J. The dreams of the experimental subject. *Journal of Nervous and Mental Disease*, 1962, **134**, 431–439.

Whitmont, E. C. The symbolic quest. New York: Putnam's, 1969.

Witkin, H. A. Influencing dream content. In M. Kramer (Ed.), *Dream psychology and the new biology of dreaming*. Springfield, Ill.: C. C. Thomas, 1969, 285–359.

Witkin, H. A., & Lewis, H. B. *Experimental studies of dreaming*. New York: Random, 1967.

INDEX

DREAMS, DREAMS

MYTHS, DREAMS, AND RELIGION   *Joseph Campbell*, ed.

Joseph Campbell compares the functions of mythology and art in "experiencing the mystery dimension of man's being"; Alan Watts lays out our primary Western myths, goading us toward their transformations; Norman O. Brown aphoristically catches Daphne in flight; David Miller presents Orestes, plagued by conflicting Gods, as a modern model; Ira Progoff enters the films of Bergman as waking dreams. Owen Barfield on philosophical double vision, Stanley Hopper on the crisis of imagination. Essays by Rollo May, Richard Underwood, Amos Wilder, John Priest further interlace myth, dream, poetry, philosophy and psychoanalysis, going to the roots of religious feeling in the soul of modern thought. (255 pp.)

THE DREAM OF POLIPHILO   *Linda Fierz-David*

This beautiful book (with 34 illustrations) is back in print after some thirty years. An early Bollingen Series volume, it was written by an inspired founding lecturer at the Jung Institute, Zurich. Fierz-David interprets the *Hypnerotomachia*, published during the Renaissance. The narrative recounts the dream of Poliphilo ("Lover of Polia") who is led by his beloved through a series of fantastic adventures in a legendary and heroic landscape. Polia, who speaks for the sensate spirit of the Renaissance, frees Poliphilo from his introverted obsession with alchemy and the mediaeval restrictions of courtly love. Led back into classical culture, he awakens transformed by the love of his guide, reconnected again to ancient humanism, its psychological depths and erotic wisdom. Foreword by C. G. Jung. (iii, 245 pp.)

ANIMA AS FATE   *Cornelia Brunner*

The first translation into English of a 1963 work by a respected Swiss analyst and longtime associate of C. G. Jung, who contributed the preface. The first part explores the notion of the anima, the contrasexual aspect of a man's psyche, in the works of Rider Haggard, particularly in his novel *She*. This part also provides background and a psychological evaluation of Haggard's adventurous life. The book's second part traces the development of the anima in a series of dreams that a middleaged physician experienced while in analysis over a period of several years. (xv, 277 pp.)

WAKING DREAMS   *Mary Watkins*

The author recovers the immeasurable riches of daydreams, active imagination, and imaginal others, showing with care the relevance of fantasy to the practice of psychotherapy, education, and the drama of individual lives. At once historical, critical, and clinical, this book takes one through both European and American approaches to the image, finally delivering the reader to a close look at his/her own relation to the imaginal world. (viii, 174 pp.)

Spring Publications, Inc.   •   P.O. Box 222069   •   Dallas, TX 75222

Spring Books on Symbols and Dreams

PSYCHE AND DEATH   *Edgar Herzog*
In this two-part study—first presented as lectures at the C. G. Jung Institute in Zürich—Edgar Herzog attends the Death Image; with skill and care he exhumes from fairytale and folklore the macabre variations of this most ancient symbol. In chapters titled "The Horror of Death," "The Death-Demon as Fate," and others Herzog examines the Death Images of archaic humanity, demonstrating that Death originally revealed itself in the guise of an animal: as a Wolf, Horse, Dog, Snake, and Bird. Today Death takes similar forms but appears to human consciousness mainly through dreams instead of via myth and ritual. In Part Two, Herzog focuses on the dreams of patients in psychotherapy and glosses those dreams with remarkable interpretations that link their persons, scenes, and drama to the symbolic images and rites of the ancient past. (Jungian Classics Series #5, 224 pgs.)

ECHO'S SUBTLE BODY   *Patricia Berry*
Collected here are all of Patricia Berry's writings between 1972 and 1982 which together develop a style of psychotherapy based on the primacy of the image in psychical life. The book contains the often referred to but long out-of-print "An Approach to the Dream" and "What's the Matter with Mother," as well as the new papers, "The Dogma of Gender" and "The Shadow of Training/The Training of Shadow." The style poetically concrete, the insights bolstered by clinical example, dream interpretation, and mythical references, each paper revisions an important analytic construct—reduction, dream, defense, *telos* or goal, reflection, shadow—so that it more adequately echoes the poetic basis of mind. (198 pgs.)

CREATION MYTHS   *Marie-Louise von Franz*
The poet Robert Bly once called von Franz's *Feminine in Fairy Tales* one of the five most neglected books of this century. This work, *Patterns of Creativity Mirrored in Creation Myths*, is equally significant. What has happened to creativity in the contemporary world? And, more importantly, how does each individual soul discover the springs and images of its own creativity? These are some of the urgent, crucial questions which von Franz attempts to answer. Full index. (250 pgs.)

COLOR SYMBOLISM
Six essays translated from the important 1972 Eranos Jahrbuch, *Realms of Color*. Adolf Portmann, "Colour Sense and the Meaning of Colour in the View of Biology"; Christopher Rowe, "Concepts of Colour and Colour Symbolism in the Ancient World"; Dominique Zahan, "White, Red and Black: Colour Symbolism in Black Africa"; Ernst Benz, "Color in Christian Visionary Experience"; René Huyghe, "Color and the Expression of Interior Time in Western Art"; Toshihiko Izutsu, "Elimination of Colour in Far Eastern Art and Philosophy." A lasting reference book by eminent scholars. Index. (202 pgs.)

PUER PAPERS   *James Hillman, ed.*
Nine papers on the youth of the spirit and the spirit of youth in poetry and pathology. A pluralistic approach to the puer aeternus, the eternal boy. Includes Hillman on puer and senex, puer wounds and Ulysses' scar, and opportunism. Henry Murray's classic paper on Grope, American Icarus, Tom Moore on Artemis in Puer Psychology, Randolph Severson on Puer Skin Diseases, and the puer figure in Melville (James Baird) and in *Finnegan's Wake* (Tom Cowan). Full index. (246 pgs.)

0882143263 UNDERSTANDING DREAMS

0 JPS

$16.00

MATTOON M A

9010